# Driverless Finance

# Driverless Finance

*Fintech's Impact on Financial Stability*

HILARY J. ALLEN

OXFORD
UNIVERSITY PRESS

**OXFORD**
UNIVERSITY PRESS

Oxford University Press is a department of the University of Oxford. It furthers the University's objective of excellence in research, scholarship, and education by publishing worldwide. Oxford is a registered trade mark of Oxford University Press in the UK and certain other countries.

Published in the United States of America by Oxford University Press
198 Madison Avenue, New York, NY 10016, United States of America.



Library of Congress Cataloging-in-Publication Data
Names: Allen, J. Hilary, author.
Title: Driverless finance : fintech's impact on financial stability / Hilary J. Allen.
Description: New York, NY : Oxford University Press, [2022] |
Includes bibliographical references and index.
Identifiers: LCCN 2021045567 (print) | LCCN 2021045568 (ebook) |
ISBN 9780197626801 (hardback) | ISBN 9780197626825 (epub) |
ISBN 9780197626818 (updf) | ISBN 9780197626832 (digital-online)
Subjects: LCSH: Financial services industry—Law and legislation—United States.
Classification: LCC KF974 .A75 2022 (print) | LCC KF974 (ebook) |
DDC 346.73/082—dc23/eng/20211029
LC record available at https://lccn.loc.gov/2021045567
LC ebook record available at https://lccn.loc.gov/2021045568

DOI: 10.1093/oso/9780197626801.001.0001

*For Bob (my fin), George (my tech), and Linda (my stability)*

# Table of Contents

# Acknowledgments

I would like to thank the village of people who read and commented on my drafts, including Will Allen (who embiggened the manuscript), Dan Awrey, Jon Baker, Andrew Beers, Dick Berner, Sarah Bloom Raskin, Raul Carillo, Shaanan Cohney, Gregg Gelzinis, Erik Gerding, Lewis Grossman, Cathy Hwang, Alex Joel, Aaron Klein, Rosa Lastra, Billy Magnusson, Milan Markovic, Saule Omarova, Frank Partnoy, Elizabeth Pollman, Paolo Saguato, Heidi Schooner, Dan Schwarcz, Art Wilmarth, David Wishnick, Rory Van Loo, Yesha Yadav, and David Zaring, This book benefited from their feedback and conversation—but all errors remain my own. I want to give particular thanks to Pat McCoy, who was not only instrumental in making this book a reality, but has also been a stalwart mentor and supporter.

I also want to thank the many students who participated in discussions about this book, both in my own classes at American University Washington College of Law, and in student seminars at Texas A&M and Boston University. More generally, I want to express my gratitude for a decade's worth of wonderful students who have helped me hone my ability to explain many of the technical concepts in this book.

I also had lots of other kinds of help in writing this book. Abe Cable brilliantly suggested the term "Driverless Finance." Washington College of Law librarians and research assistant William Ryan, Ripple Weistling, and Meagan McCullough lent their master Bluebooking skills. Last but not least, I had wonderful child-care providers who took care of my toddlers while I was writing this book. Without these caregivers (with a special shout out to the incomparable Miss Marie and the amazingly competent Miss Kim), this book could not exist.

# Prologue

**Final Report on the Causes of the 2030 Financial and Economic Crisis in the United States**

**Majority Conclusions of The Financial Crisis Inquiry Commission**

**(as appointed by the 121st Congress)**

**Published October 2031**

Pursuant to our charge from Congress, we have examined the causes of the financial crisis of 2030, the consequences of which still distress the global economy today. In this report we set forth our conclusions.

- **We conclude that the growth of the cryptoasset market was a key cause of the crisis.**

Just over a decade ago, cryptoassets were a fringe asset class, mainly of interest to cypherpunks and kids trading on smartphone apps. Somewhere around 2020, though, the largest banks and other established financial institutions started to dip their toes into the water, cautious but intrigued by the potential of assets that could be created out of thin air by anyone who could write a computer program. Establishment players initially entered into derivative contracts that drew their value from cryptoassets—the fact that a derivative was involved made the investment feel more familiar and seem more legitimate. Over time, though, they dispensed with the derivatives and started investing directly in cryptoassets. And then they started creating cryptoassets themselves.

Although problematic, this development was unsurprising. In the absence of any regulatory restrictions, the appetite for cryptoassets seemed limitless. Whole online communities were devoted to debating the merits of different types of tokens, new crypto-focused hedge funds popped up like mushrooms, and new brokerage apps made it easy for their customers to get loans to buy more and more cryptoassets. The cryptoassets bought using these apps served as collateral for these loans, and from there it was just a hop, skip, and a jump to people using cryptoassets as security for other types of loans as well. Eventually, the biggest banks started accepting cryptoassets as collateral for the loans they made to each other, and once that happened, cryptoassets were firmly embedded in the mainstream financial system.

Many people were thrilled with this brave new world of finance. Now that financial assets didn't have to be tethered to anything in the real economy, it seemed like finance had finally broken the back of the business cycle and made downturns a thing of the past. "This time is different" was a common refrain on Reddit pages, in investor updates from hedge funds, in the conversations that banks had with their regulators, and in the pitches lobbyists made to members of Congress. Only it wasn't different (it never is). The crypotasset market was experiencing a bubble, just like mortgage-backed securities in the 2000s, dot-com stocks in the 1990s, and tulip bulbs in the 1630s.

- **We conclude that the spark that lit the crisis was an artificially intelligent trading agent.**

In 2029, HAL Bank was one of the six largest banks headquartered in the United States, with assets of nearly $5 trillion. HAL Bank and its subsidiaries engaged in a diverse range of financial activities both in the United States and abroad, including new fintech business lines that were pursued by HAL Bank's subsidiary, BotWay. In February 2030, BotWay launched an autonomous agent capable of collecting data from the cryptoasset markets, and then using that data to train itself to trade in those markets. After a few weeks of profitable trading, the autonomous agent started betting against a class of bond-like cryptoassets known as CyberDebt that had been issued by HAL Bank itself. The agent did this by buying up credit default swaps on behalf of BotWay that would pay out if HAL Bank defaulted on its CyberDebt. None of the humans employed by BotWay understood why the agent had adopted this trading strategy, but the volume of credit default swaps that BotWay was buying made the issuers of those credit default swaps nervous, and they started charging more and more for any credit default swap that protected against a HAL Bank default.

The increased cost of credit default swap protection would have been a bad sign for HAL Bank in any circumstances—its lenders, investors, and trading partners would interpret it as a harbinger of bad things to come. What made things worse was that although CyberDebt started out unsecured with no collateral, HAL Bank had agreed with investors from the beginning that a smart contract would monitor its cost of credit default swap protection and automatically post collateral to a wallet for each holder of CyberDebt if the cost of that protection got too high. It got too high, and in an instant, HAL Bank found billions of its dollars locked away.

With all indicators blinking red, HAL Bank's internal risk management systems tried to make sense of what to do. These systems relied on machine learning algorithms to determine how the bank should manage its portfolio of investments. Unfortunately, these algorithms had been trained using market data that was drawn mostly from the time before cryptoassets became a significant feature of the financial markets. They had also been trained to ignore outlier data, and so it was not surprising that the risk management algorithms were flummoxed by these unusual circumstances. It was particularly dangerous that these risk management algorithms were linked to automated trading execution algorithms. As a result, the risk management algorithm's uneven and largely inexplicable interpretation of the events was translated immediately into asset sales.

As HAL Bank started selling—not just cryptoassets, but also stocks, bonds, and foreign currencies, in a way that seemed to lack any particular rhyme or reason—prices of all kinds of financial assets fell through the floor, and all kinds of algorithms at all kinds of financial institutions were thrown into disarray. High frequency trading algorithms hadn't been programmed to deal with this kind of scenario, so they just stopped trading. The algorithms capable of machine learning hadn't been trained to deal with this kind of extremely adverse scenario and were making investment decisions that were unpredictable but highly similar; their correlated behavior magnified the panic. With all the uncertainty in the market, lending between banks started to freeze and HAL Bank in particular was unable to obtain any short-term funding from other banks. Without the bailout that it ultimately received, HAL Bank (together with its affiliates and its creditors) would have been embroiled in a messy insolvency process.

- **We conclude that the damage was exacerbated exponentially by the prevalence of robo-investing services like BetterWealth.**

There are a number of robo-investing services available in the United States, but BetterWealth is the one that captured the public imagination (and market share). Founded by a single mother who wanted to bring investing to the masses, BetterWealth had initially struggled to get venture capital financing in clubby Silicon Valley. But then it was funded by GCVC, one of the first female-led venture capital firms in the country. BetterWealth's low fees and slick interface then captured a huge portion of the retail investing market.

The machine learning algorithms that BetterWealth used to manage investor portfolios had been trained using data drawn only from the last five years, when the financial markets had been perpetually sunny with little volatility. These algorithms didn't know what to make of the market turmoil kicked off by HAL Bank, so most of them just recommended that retail investors sell off their investments and move into cash. Many of BetterWealth's customers had opted into an automated portfolio rebalancing service, which meant that their sales happened almost instantaneously. The impact of the sale of so many of the same assets at the same time was overwhelming—and the trading markets froze.

- **We conclude that the resulting damage to the payments system was the source of some of the most significant damage to the broader economy.**

After the popular press began to speculate that HAL Bank was insolvent (but before its bailout), many of HAL Bank's customers closed their deposit accounts and moved their funds to their MOMCorp e-wallets (most people hadn't focused on the fact that these e-wallets weren't legally considered deposits, and therefore weren't protected by deposit insurance). Concerns about the solvency of banks became contagious, and many customers of other banks followed suit, precipitating runs on deposit accounts at no less than 60 banks. As the world's biggest e-commerce platform, MOMCorp was used to processing millions of transactions a day, but it wasn't set up to process the trillions of transactions a day that occurred once people transferred all of their funds to their MOMCorp e-wallets and started to use those e-wallets to pay their rent, their utility bills, and everything else. MOMCorp's systems started crashing under the weight of too many transactions, and then people started to panic about their e-wallets.

In some instances, MOMCorp had reinvested customer funds in longer-term investments, expecting that people would never want to empty *all* of their e-wallets at the same time and so it was safe to tie up some of those funds. Now, however, there was a run on e-wallets. Seeing these e-wallets emptying at a dramatic rate, MOMCorp's lenders refused to provide it with any more funding, and shareholders who had been comfortable with MOMCorp not turning a profit for years suddenly changed their tune and started dumping their shares. Had MOMCorp been forced to file for bankruptcy, the funds in those e-wallets could have been tied up in bankruptcy proceedings for years. That would have been catastrophic, and so the Treasury Department agreed to make emergency investments in MOMCorp and the Federal Reserve started buying up its debt in order to keep it afloat. Unfortunately, it was impossible to separate MOMCorp's payments business from its core e-commerce platform, or to separate its domestic and its foreign activities, and so MOMCorp's entire sprawling empire had to be bailed out at a cost that dwarfed all previous bailouts.

In the interim, the Federal Reserve took steps to make physical cash available to people, driving truckloads of bills all over the country. The value of that cash had become more volatile, though. Amid the chaos, many people had started using their cryptoasset investments as alternative ways of paying for goods and services, and as the Fed lost more and more control over the supply of money, prices became more unstable. People were never quite sure how much a carton of milk would cost in US dollars, but the volatility of cryptocurrencies was even worse. There was also the problem that every seller had their preferred cryptocurrency (converting your bitcoins into dogecoins into ether had become almost impossible since the cryptoasset exchanges had collapsed during the crisis), and so people were stuck buying from sellers who accepted the type of cryptocurrency they had. Some people ultimately resorted to a grossly inefficient barter system where they had to figure out how many eggs an iPad was worth.

- **We conclude that the government and the Federal Reserve were ill-prepared for the crisis and therefore struggled to contain the fallout.**

Most people who held cryptoassets expected the Federal Reserve to step in and buy them up to keep everything afloat. After all, that had been the playbook during the 2008 financial crisis, when the Fed propped up money market mutual funds, commercial paper, securities repurchase agreements, and corporate bonds. This time, though, there were just too many cryptoassets out there. Because anyone could create cryptoassets out of thin air, everyone had, and the Federal Reserve simply couldn't figure out which of the seemingly infinite number of cryptoassets out there had any intrinsic value. It didn't help that scammers were proliferating, creating new cryptoassets amid the chaos in the hope of scoring some bailout money. In short, there were too many cryptoassets out there for the Federal Reserve to buy, and so it bought almost none.

Even though the trouble had started with cryptoassets that were untethered from the real economy, the real economy didn't escape the fallout of their implosion. Banks had been relying on each other for loans, but now that the cryptoassets securing those loans were not worth the code they were written in, the remaining solvent banks couldn't borrow from each other—and so they pretty much stopped lending to anyone else. Small businesses that relied on marketplace loans from fintech lenders to fund their business expenses were hit particularly hard, because now that cryptoassets had imploded, all other fintech business models were guilty by association. No financial institutions wanted to fund marketplace loans anymore, and when small businesses found that they couldn't roll over their loans, they started laying off employees and defaulting on their credit cards.

Unemployment started to rise, and not just among small business employees. The financial industry itself was decimated, as were the lawyers, accountants, restauranteurs, Uber drivers, and everyone else who relied on it. Silicon Valley took a shellacking too, as so many fintech unicorns became worthless almost overnight. Small-time investors who had been lured into the financial markets by the seemingly endless returns offered by BetterWealth and shiny trading apps lost everything.

Things became much worse as the payments system infrastructure imploded. The Fed had not anticipated the possibility that it might be necessary to limit the number of transactions being conducted on MOMCorp's (or anyone else's) overloaded payments platforms in order to protect the payment processing infrastructure. As a result, when those infrastructure problems became clear, the Fed was paralyzed by the political consequences of choosing who would have their ability to make payments suspended, and so it didn't intervene at all. The Federal Reserve had also fallen behind its international counterparts in developing its own retail payments infrastructure, so it could not provide an alternative means of transacting.

The failure to develop any plan for how to respond to the failure of a tech platform meant that the bailout of MOMCorp was conducted on a very ad hoc basis. Had the government known more about MOMCorp and thought through the possible consequences of its failure, a more targeted rescue might have been possible. Instead, MOMCorp proved to be too big to save without threatening the credibility of the Fed, the Treasury Department, and the dollar. As a result, the bailout of MOMCorp necessitated painful austerity measures to reduce government spending in other areas. Those already living on the margins found themselves homeless. Property crimes and suicides became more common as people struggled to survive, or eventually gave up.

- **We conclude that corporate governance and risk management failures at financial institutions and tech platforms were a key contributor to this crisis.**

While the crisis was in many ways a technological failure, a major reason why the technology failed was that it had been constructed to game the system. Particularly when it came to the machine learning aspects of risk management models, banks and robo-advisory firms chose algorithms and training data that de-emphasized the importance of outlier events in order to minimize capital and margin requirements and thereby maximize profits in the short term. It is therefore unsurprising that those models performed so poorly when outlier events occurred. The drive to maximize short-term profits was also responsible for underinvestments in reliable technological infrastructure, as well as a driver of the unsustainable proliferation of cryptoassets that allocated no investment capital to the real economy, but provided fertile ground for speculation.

We conclude that financial institutions' intentional disregard for the growing risks associated with cryptoassets, trading platforms, and payments infrastructure was exacerbated by the limitations of corporate governance. The boards and senior managers of many financial institutions lacked the technical expertise necessary to oversee their increasingly technology-driven operations, or even to properly assess the offerings of third-party technology vendors. In some instances, this resulted in unquestioning deference to the output of technologically sophisticated models—they assumed that that output was not only accurate, but also legal and responsible.

- **We conclude that failures of financial regulation were key contributors to this crisis.**

We have identified a number of regulatory failures that contributed to the depths of this crisis. The Dodd-Frank legislation passed in the aftermath of the 2008 crisis was designed to promote financial stability in the United

States, and while it did many useful things, it failed to address some very clear threats to financial stability. "Shadow banking" (the provision of financial services by non-banks) remained a particular problem. From the beginning, there were serious concerns about the viability of Dodd-Frank's procedures for liquidating failing non-banks, and then in 2018, the Financial Stability Oversight Council completely abandoned its authority to subject non-bank financial firms to heightened regulation. Dodd-Frank's failure to properly address shadow banking meant that system-threatening risks could build in new tech and fintech firms that weren't being monitored for financial stability concerns.

Other financial laws and regulations in effect in the 2010s and '20s also did not contemplate or fully address the rise of fintech. Operational risk regulation was very light-touch, and was not up to detecting vulnerabilities in the complex technological systems being used by the financial industry; oversight of new artificially intelligent risk management models was also not thorough enough. Ultimately, financial regulators largely delegated responsibility for risk management and oversight of technological infrastructure to the firms themselves, and as we already concluded, the firms were not up to the task of controlling these risks.

Cryptoassets posed particular regulatory challenges. The Securities and Exchange Commission and the Commodity Futures Trading Commission struggled to figure out their approach to regulating cryptoassets; the Basel Committee on Banking Supervision certainly faced challenges when trying to figure out the regulatory capital and liquidity rules that should apply to them. However, because financial regulators were so focused on trying to figure out the intricacies of cryptoassets (and the limits of their jurisdiction over them), they missed their systemic dimensions. A unified approach to cryptoasset regulation, or at least more coordination on their cross-sectoral risks, would have alerted financial regulators to the magnitude of the collective risks building up in the system.

More broadly, regulators failed to hire enough staff with expertise in distributed ledger, smart contract and machine learning technologies. As a result, regulators were severely limited in their ability to detect and respond to new systemic risks. In particular, US regulators lagged their international counterparts in developing the suptech regulatory strategies that could have responded to some of the problems with these new technologies.

- **We conclude this crisis was avoidable.**

BotWay's initial bets against HAL Bank's CyberDebt were the sparks that lit the bonfire of system-wide turmoil, but we conclude that some other financial actor would have lit that bonfire if BotWay hadn't. By February of 2030, the entire financial system had become a powder keg ready to explode. However, we do not conclude that the crisis was inevitable. If caps had been placed on the assets under management for any robo-investing service, and if rules had required that a human stand between the portfolio selection algorithms and the execution of trades, the impact of these algorithms would have been smaller and slower. If laws had been enacted and rules had been promulgated to restrain the growth of cryptoassets—or at the very least, to restrain mainstream financial institutions from investing in cryptoassets—then the real economy would not have buckled under their weight. If the largest tech companies had been prevented from becoming the dominant providers of payment services, then the socially painful austerity measures that followed the bailout of MOMCorp could have been avoided.

# Introduction

Science fiction is full of stories of computers run amok. Dystopian scenarios of financial system failure may make for less exciting reading, but the consequences could be equally terrifying. Imagine if countless financial assets could be created out of whole cloth, with a simple computer program. Then imagine that decisions about whether to buy and sell those assets were made entirely by other computer programs, and that the infrastructure used to trade those assets was automated as well. The detection of a bug in the software of the assets could cause the decision-making software to start a massive sell-off, sending prices haywire and stressing the automated trading infrastructure to the point of overload and malfunction. Chaos and uncertainty would reign, and the non-robots among us who rely on the financial system to make payments and borrow money would be paralyzed.

When regulators, central bankers, and politicians were confronted with a financial crisis in 2008, their emergency interventions mitigated the harm that the financial crisis caused for the global economy. In our dystopian automated financial future, though, it might be impossible to stop the computer programs—even when human beings recognize that the financial system is on the precipice. As the computer HAL might say, "I'm sorry Dave, I'm afraid I can't do that."[1]

This book will show that such a scenario isn't just the stuff of science fiction. It may very well represent our financial future, and future financial crises could cause damage on a scale that makes earlier crises look quaint. As the tech-minded economists Kirilenko and Lo have wryly observed, "whatever can go wrong will go wrong faster and bigger when computers are involved."[2] We are already seeing some dangerous consequences of automation: in the space of five months, two Boeing 737 MAX aircrafts were involved in tragic crashes, killing nearly 350 people. The congressional report into these incidents blamed, among other things, flawed understandings of "software designed to automatically push the airplane's nose down in certain conditions," and criticized expectations that pilots would be able to mitigate any malfunctions of that software system when those pilots were "largely

*Driverless Finance*. Hilary J. Allen, Oxford University Press. © Hilary J. Allen 2022.
DOI: 10.1093/oso/9780197626801.003.0001

unaware that the system existed."[3] Failure to pay attention to the increased automation of finance could have similarly dire consequences—as this book will show, financial crises can also be lethal, and even when they aren't, they create widespread hardship.

## Introducing driverless finance

Unfortunately, most of us are not paying attention to what's happening in our financial system. This isn't new. Finance is so complicated that casual observers are discouraged from trying to figure out what finance actually is or does, and so the financial industry often escapes public scrutiny. We are now in a moment, though, when traditional financial complexity is being overlaid with new kinds of technological complexity, making new fintech innovations doubly hard to understand. Historically, financial regulators and the public at large have tended to wait for something to go horribly wrong before making the effort to figure out how financial innovations work—but waiting that long could have dire consequences. This book is therefore intended to provide a window into new fintech innovations, and their potential impact on financial stability, *before* they combust.

This book refers to the current generation of fintech innovations as "driverless finance," which is obviously a play on the term "driverless car."[4] As this book will explore, fintech innovations are increasingly automating financial decision-making, sometimes using technologies that are surprisingly similar to those used to help cars drive themselves. The term "driverless finance" is therefore descriptive, but it's also useful as a metaphor. When we think about the dangers of driverless cars, we worry about innocent bystanders who could be hit by runaway technology. In a financial crisis, *we* are the bystanders who will be harmed if fintech innovations damage our economy. While fintech innovations are currently being heralded for making financial services more affordable and more accessible, they may turn out to contain the seeds of our next financial crisis.

Deciding how to deal with the rise of fintech will require us to reckon with significant amounts of uncertainty. We already know that financial crises can cause significant widespread harm, and this book will show that we also know a lot already about the new types of risks that fintech innovations are creating. However, we don't know how likely these risks are to come to fruition, and there are probably other risks from fintech that this book hasn't contemplated—I don't have a crystal ball. In addition, while we know that financial crises in developed economies have been reasonably rare events over the last century,[5] we must also reckon with the possibility that crises could become more frequent as a result of the rise of driverless finance. Because it's impossible to predict when a crisis will come, or exactly how fintech innovations will behave during that crisis, the regulatory response to fintech innovation will be significantly influenced by how we perceive driverless finance.

The futurist Roy Amara noted that "we tend to overestimate the effect of a technology in the short run and underestimate the effect in the long run."[6] The benefits of fintech are often immediately obvious because technology tends to be very good at things that humans find very difficult, like processing large amounts of data. However, technology often struggles with the things that we humans find simple to do—like recognizing a face or picking fruit. Often, because we underappreciate the difficulty in these so-called "easy" tasks, too little attention is paid to the inability of technologies to perform them—and so we tend to underestimate the inadequacies of the technology until something unanticipated goes horribly wrong.

While we tend to only appreciate the negative aspects of technology in the long term, we would be better served by retaining a healthy skepticism of new financial innovations: targeting regulation at the beginning of their development process and encouraging simplicity where possible, and maybe even preventing some of the most harmful innovations from ever entering the financial system. As of now, though, the popular narrative about fintech is largely positive. Fintech innovation does have the potential to deliver financial services more quickly and cost effectively, particularly to people who haven't been able to access mainstream financial services before. This book acknowledges these benefits, but it will not spend much time on them for the simple reason that they are already well publicized—in some circumstances, over-hyped. Fintech innovation has many cheerleaders, but far fewer critics. This book does not provide a balanced account of the benefits and costs of fintech and fintech regulation, but it will contribute to a more balanced public debate about fintech's pros and cons by illuminating the risks that fintech poses for financial stability.

## Fintech's critics

When fintech *is* criticized, it is usually because of concerns about consumer predation, privacy violations, or technology destroying jobs. To give a flavor of these types of concerns, in recent years the US House Financial

Services Committee has conducted hearings on things like "Examining Ways to Reduce AI Bias in Financial Services,"[7] "The Impact of AI on Capital Markets and Jobs in the Financial Services Industry,"[8] "The Role of Big Data in Financial Services,"[9] "Evaluating How Financial Data Is Stored, Protected and Maintained by Cloud Providers,"[10] and "Examining the Use of Alternative Data in Underwriting and Credit Scoring to Expand Access to Credit."[11]

A particular concern is that the new technologies being used to make credit approval decisions may perpetuate bias by denying credit to historically underserved minorities. If we think of technology as neutral, free from human prejudices and foibles, then these kinds of concerns about bias may seem misplaced. However, one important lesson from this book is that we should not always accept technological output at face value. Technology could be programmed, by a human, to intentionally discriminate against certain types of people. Or discrimination might happen unintentionally: new types of computer algorithms are being trained to develop their own decision-making rules from data sets provided to them. As a result, the decisions that such algorithms make will only be as good as the training data. If that data reflects past discrimination and bias, then the decisions that the algorithm ultimately makes will also be tainted by that discrimination and bias—garbage in, garbage out, as they say.

Concerns have also been raised about the types of data that consumers using fintech services will generate, and how that information will be treated. New technologies are significantly accelerating the amount of data being created, and the best-case scenario is that these new troves of data will be used to fight financial crime, provide people with more tailored financial services, and improve financial inclusion (for example, by allowing credit applicants who wouldn't qualify under traditional metrics to demonstrate their worthiness using different data sources). However, data regarding a person's financial transactions can be particularly sensitive, and we can easily imagine dystopian scenarios where a personalized record of our entire transaction history could be used against us—by the firms maintaining the data, by governments, or by hackers.

There are also questions about the impact of technology on the availability of jobs for humans. This issue is not specific to fintech—it applies to all kinds of technologies that automate activities that once required human manpower. When it comes to finance, jobs held by consumer service representatives, financial planners, and loan assessors might be particularly vulnerable to automation.

The issue that is receiving far less attention, though, is the potential for fintech innovation to undermine financial stability. This needs to change—when we are evaluating fintech innovations, their impact on financial stability should be a primary concern. While it is true that financial crises do not occur every day, it is unwise to assume that they will remain once-in-a-generation events. Things tend to fail faster, harder, and more frequently when there are complex technologies involved, and so fintech's threats to financial stability should be scrutinized. To be clear, this doesn't mean that consumer protection, privacy, and employment issues should be neglected. However, because the aggregate impact of a financial crisis could dwarf these kinds of everyday harms, we should also pay close attention to the potential for fintech to generate significant new threats to financial stability.

## Terminology

If this is a book about the potential threats that fintech poses for financial stability, we first of all need to understand what fintech and financial stability actually *are*. Neither term has a settled definition. Financial regulators and policymakers regularly refer to "financial stability," but there have been few attempts to define it. "Fintech" is a term that is always evolving, and there is no clear consensus about whether it describes business models, firms, or technologies—nor is there complete agreement about the business models, firms, or technologies that should "count" as fintech. In this introduction, I will develop working definitions of these terms that will be used throughout the book. However, these working definitions are not definitive statements of what constitutes "financial stability" and "fintech": these terms will continue to spawn disagreements over definitions, and to evolve over time.

## What is financial stability?

Since the financial crisis of 2008, references to "financial stability" in legislation and policy documents have proliferated. In the United States, the Dodd-Frank Wall Street Reform and Consumer Protection Act (which was the primary legislative response to the crisis) is described as "An Act to promote the financial stability of the United States. . . ."—but the term "financial stability" is not defined anywhere in the nearly 1,000 pages of that legislation. Nor, to my knowledge, has the term been defined in any of the thousands of pages of rules that have been adopted to implement that legislation.

This is not a uniquely American problem. In the United Kingdom, for example, one of the Bank of England's objectives is "to protect and enhance the stability of the financial system of the United Kingdom,"[12] but the term "financial stability" is not explicitly defined in the relevant legislation. The Financial Stability Board, a body that was formed to promote financial stability at the international level, does not define the term in its Charter document. Article IV of the International Monetary Fund's Articles of Agreement provides that "a principal objective is the continuing development of the orderly underlying conditions that are necessary for financial and economic stability,"[13] but once again, "financial stability" is left undefined. I could go on.

As one report observed, "the less-than-ideal definition of financial stability has not usually been regarded as a fundamental barrier to getting on with the job."[14] However, this "know it when I see it" approach can be problematic. Laws that seek to promote financial stability might be viewed as illegitimate if they don't have a clearly defined goal. Furthermore, when there is no consensus view about what financial stability is, it is difficult to formulate cohesive policy solutions to achieve it. For example, if financial regulators think that we have enough stability so long as we're not currently experiencing a financial crisis, then they might not put in the important and difficult work of making the system more robust to future shocks. Of if the financial industry misunderstands "financial stability regulation" as something that aims to eliminate *all* risk from the financial system, then they will almost certainly oppose financial stability regulation as destructive of financial progress (particularly when the economy is doing well).

Even when policymakers accept the need for financial stability regulation, if they only worry about financial institutions, then their policy measures will focus on those institutions to the neglect of the financial markets that are also vital to the provision of financial services. (This was a key mistake in the lead-up to the 2008 crisis: steps that individual banks took to save themselves—most notably, selling assets at fire sale prices—created problems for whole asset markets, and made the financial system as a whole much weaker).[15] In fact, there is not even much agreement about the types of institutions, let alone markets, that financial stability regulation should be worried about—the last crisis made it clear that it's not just banks that can cause problems, but there's still no consensus about where to draw the line for other institutions. For example, are hedge funds a cause for concern? Should they be subject to financial stability regulation? The influx of new fintech firms is further muddying the waters regarding which institutions should be subject to financial stability regulation, and which should not.

Even when the promotion of robust banks, non-bank financial institutions, *and* markets are all recognized as part and parcel of financial stability, too strong a focus on these institutions and markets can cause people to misunderstand why financial stability is an important regulatory goal in the first place. If the financial system could fail without inflicting harm on anyone other than sophisticated financial players, then there would be much less justification for regulation. The broader economy relies on the financial system to manage risks, however, and to amass and allocate capital. The transactions that fuel economic growth also require payment services that are typically provided by the financial system. For these reasons, financial system failure has significant implications for the people and businesses that make up the broader economy. Financial stability regulation should not lose sight of the fact that the endgame is protecting the economy as a whole, not the profitability of the financial industry.

This book will therefore use a working definition of financial stability that has sustainable economic growth as its ultimate goal. Financial stability regulation should aim to achieve that goal by ensuring that the institutions and markets that make up the financial system are robust enough that they will continue to be able to help people manage risks, invest, borrow, and make payments even if some kind of unexpected shock occurs.

Defining financial stability in this way has some important implications. First, it recognizes that financial stability regulation is required even in good times, when the financial system might not seem on its face to need any government intervention. Of course, that does not mean that financial stability regulation should try to eliminate all risk from the system—risks that won't harm broader economic growth should be welcome. Second, defining financial crises in this way assumes that financial crises are *not* inevitable. Some people—including many who work in the financial industry—see crises as organic parts of the business cycle that cannot be avoided and therefore must simply be endured.[16] This book disagrees with this kind of fatalism—a topic that will be taken up in more detail in Chapter 1. It is probably true that no regulatory regime will ever be completely successful in eliminating financial crises, but notable regulatory failures have contributed to the gravity of past crises. Improving financial regulation can make financial crises less likely and less severe.

Another important implication of defining financial stability in this way is jurisdictional. It suggests that financial stability regulators will be most successful if they have jurisdiction over the entire financial system, and not just some institutions or some markets. The financial system is global, though, and regulatory authority is often national (although there are some international coordination mechanisms). Not only do regulators face geographical boundaries on their authority, but there are often also functional boundaries within a jurisdiction that prevent a single regulator from having oversight over all of the institutions and markets that make up a national financial system. As a result, financial stability regulation will always be incomplete—but again, the opportunity to mitigate the consequences of financial system failure make even incomplete approaches worthwhile.

## What is fintech?

When people talk about fintech, some of them are talking about business models, others are talking about firms, and still others are talking about technologies. The business models that are commonly recognized as "fintech" often don't have much in common, other than that they all rely primarily on technologies that were developed in the last decade or so. These business models include marketplace lending, crowdfunding, mobile payment services, robo-advisory services, and cryptoasset-related business models. Some draw the line at these consumer-oriented business models, but others think that "fintech" also includes business models like high frequency trading by sophisticated hedge funds. All of these business models require some explanation.

*Marketplace lending platforms* accept loan applications online, assess those applications (often using nontraditional data sources, like information drawn from social media profiles), and then match each loan with investors willing to fund it. For regulatory reasons, the loan is first made by a bank and then sold to the ultimate investors (predominantly large institutional investors), who receive a note evidencing their right to repayment. The platform is also responsible for processing repayments and providing administrative services. So far, the marketplace lending business model has focused on unsecured loans rather than mortgages (amounts are typically under $50,000 for small businesses and around $10,000 for individual consumers).[17]

*Crowdfunding* refers to any type of business model that uses a web or smartphone-based platform to facilitate payments of small amounts of money from a large group of people. Crowdfunding can be used for donations (like GoFundMe), or to fundraise in exchange for non-pecuniary rewards (like Kickstarter). Marketplace lending can also be considered a type of crowdfunding, but when people refer to "crowdfunding" in the fintech context, they are usually talking about equity crowdfunding. Equity crowdfunding platforms allow investors to buy stock in start-ups or other early stage small businesses, broadening the funding options for these businesses beyond venture capitalists and angel investors. Equity crowdfunding fans also praise its inclusivity, in terms of expanding investment opportunities for everyday investors. There are certainly investor protection concerns associated with crowdfunding, and securities regulators around the world have adopted regulatory regimes that seek to balance their sometimes conflicting goals of protecting investors and encouraging capital intermediation. However, at least at present, equity crowdfunding platforms seem to pose little threat to financial stability. Because of this book's focus on financial stability, there will be very little discussion of equity crowdfunding in it.

A variety of different *mobile payments* business models have emerged in the last decade. Many of these seek to make payments more efficient for users by providing a type of digital wallet that can withdraw funds from a user's bank account or credit card, store that balance, and then pay amounts from that balance to other consumers and businesses upon receiving initiating instructions from the user's phone. Venmo is a prominent example of this type of mobile payments service, as is AliPay. AliPay (as well as some other mobile payments providers) requires users to scan a QR code (a type of barcode) to send messages to debit and credit the relevant digital wallets, although other providers have different methods of initiating payments. There are also some mobile payments providers that don't use a digital wallet at all. ApplePay, for example, just provides a more efficient way to pay from the user's bank account or credit card.

*Robo-advisory firms* provide advice to consumers on financial products ranging from bank deposit accounts to insurance policies to investment portfolios. The most developed robo-advisory business model involves the provision of robo-investing services, which offer investment advice at a fraction of the cost of what a human financial planner would charge. This business model uses computer algorithms to automate the process of assessing a customer's financial situation and risk tolerance, and of selecting and rebalancing an investment portfolio to reflect that customer's profile. Robo-investing is sometimes billed as being more competent, and less likely to succumb to kickbacks and other conflicts of interests, than a human financial planner. It may not live up to that promise, though.[18]

The idea of a *cryptoasset* was pioneered by the creator(s?) of Bitcoin,[19] and has since been emulated and tweaked by the developers of innumerable other cryptocurrencies, tokens, and other variations on the theme. Cryptocurrencies can be used to pay for goods and services (at least theoretically), whereas tokens are usually created as investments. The rights associated with these tokens are embodied in "smart contracts," which are simply computer programs that are hosted on a distributed ledger along with the tokens (all cryptoassets, including tokens and cryptocurrencies, rely on distributed ledger technology, which we will discuss shortly). Many new intermediaries, including wallet providers and exchanges, have cropped up in order to facilitate cryptoasset transactions.

*High frequency trading* now accounts for the majority of all stock trading in the United States, and is also common in other asset markets, ranging from government bonds to foreign currencies.[20] High frequency trading is characterized by executing an extremely high number of trades, and then exiting from those trades within tiny fractions of a second. Human beings are not capable of executing trades that quickly, and so trading orders are placed by computer algorithms. The profits per trade might seem insignificant, but high frequency trading can be extremely lucrative because of the volume of trades executed. Although some people would disagree that high frequency trading "counts" as fintech because the strategy is not available to consumers, this book takes a more inclusive approach to defining fintech.

The diversity of these fintech business models makes it clear that "fintech" is more of an umbrella term than a coherent phenomenon. When the plural term "fintechs" is used, though, it's usually to describe the types of *firms* that engage in these business models. These fintech firms usually aren't regulated as banks, and they are often relatively small start-ups—although some have grown rapidly over the last decade (fintech firms like SoFi, Betterment, Coinbase, and Stripe, for example, are well on their way to becoming household names). Importantly, though, the term "fintechs" usually isn't used to describe the real tech giants, like Amazon, Facebook, Google, and Apple.

When these firms engage in fintech business models, they are typically referred to as "techfins" rather than "fintechs"—given the size and scope of these techfins, there has already been significant alarm raised about the potential impact of their financial activities on financial stability.

Too much focus on fintech and techfin firms, however, can obscure that banks and other established financial institutions are also adopting the underlying fintech technologies to improve their own delivery of financial services.[21] For example, asset management behemoths like Charles Schwab are already using machine learning technology to allocate investors' funds among different asset classes.[22] And JPMorgan Chase has launched its own digital currency "JPMCoin" in order to improve payments processing.[23] Like the techfins, some of these established financial institutions operate at such a scale that any risks associated with the technologies they use will be amplified. The established financial industry's use of these technologies should not be ignored. This book will therefore use a comprehensive (but admittedly somewhat unwieldy) approach to defining "fintech"—it will use the term to refer to the underlying technologies, as well as the fintech business models and firms discussed above.

The most significant technological innovations underlying fintech business models are cloud computing, distributed ledger technology, and a type of artificial intelligence known as "machine learning." As this book progresses, it will engage with these technologies in much more detail, giving specific examples of how they are being used, how they could be used in the future, and the financial stability risks associated with those uses. However, it's helpful to have a brief introduction to these technologies at the beginning.

*Cloud computing* involves the storage of data on a network of servers, instead of locally, like on the hard drive of a computer or a phone. This frees up the hard drive of individual devices, allowing larger amounts of data to be stored more efficiently. It also provides some protection against technical failures, because data can easily be moved from server to server—if one server fails, data will continue to be available if other servers are able to pick up the slack. The allocation of data across servers will depend upon the type of cloud computing service offered. In some clouds, the allocation of data is automated, in the sense that the network itself is given free rein to decide where to store data at any given time (often shifting it across national borders). In other clouds, technical and contractual arrangements are in place to allocate data only to a restricted group of servers.

*Distributed ledger technology* underlies cryptocurrencies, tokens, some new types of payments processing, and potentially many, many more business models. A distributed ledger is essentially a huge database, hosted by a dispersed group of computers and servers, that displays the current ownership and all previous transactions that have been carried out with the cryptoassets associated with that ledger. As with cloud computing, this dispersal makes the ledger more robust, because the ledger can remain unharmed even if an individual computer or server fails. It is important that the ledger be robust, because not only is it a record of transactions, it is also needed to process them—if a change in ownership isn't reflected in the ledger, then there has been no transfer of the asset and therefore no transaction. Each distributed ledger has its own protocol for determining which transactions will be approved and added to the ledger, with some verification procedures being much more complicated than others.

A *machine learning algorithm* is trained to devise its own decision-making rules from the data sets provided to it; the algorithm can then follow those rules in executing an assigned task. Machine learning algorithms are therefore more autonomous than the computer algorithms that the financial industry has relied on for decades, which must be programmed with more specific instructions before they can perform.[24]

## A note on jurisdiction

These technologies are being deployed around the world, by multinational banks and techfins as well as by start-ups operating in fintech centers like London, Singapore, Hong Kong, Sydney, Silicon Valley, and New York. The technologies do not vary much by jurisdiction, and so many of the technological risks discussed in part II of this book are relevant for policymakers around the world. However, fintech business models (as opposed to the underlying technologies) often *do* vary by jurisdiction, in order to comply with local market expectations and regulatory requirements. In its descriptions of business models, as well as in its prescriptions for policy solutions, this book focuses on the United States, because that is my jurisdiction of expertise. With that said, many of the regulatory solutions that I propose in Chapter 6 could easily be adapted to suit other jurisdictions—particularly those regulatory solutions that are technological in nature. It is my hope that this book will inspire debate among policymakers outside of the United States, as well as within.

After all, as I have already mentioned, the financial system is global, and financial instability that arises in one country can easily spill over into other countries' financial systems. A shared international understanding of financial stability threats is therefore highly desirable, and while the financial stability implications of fintech have been largely ignored, an important exception is the work that the international Financial Stability Board has done on the issue. Since 2017, the Financial Stability Board's FinTech Issues Group has issued a number of important reports on fintech and financial stability: these reports form the foundation of much of the analysis of fintech's risks in part II of this book, and are essential reading for anyone looking to explore this topic further.[25] However, the Financial Stability Board's activities have largely been restricted to identifying and reporting on nascent risks—they have made few recommendations for addressing these risks. Part III of this book begins to fill this breach.

## Overview of the rest of the book

This introduction finishes with a roadmap that will help guide readers through the rest of the book. Part I of the book, which consists of a single Chapter 1, explains why policymakers should take a precautionary approach to fintech innovations. Chapter 1 devotes considerable time to exploring the catastrophic consequences of the financial crisis of 2008, and the financial innovations that helped cause it. It also engages in a thought experiment, imagining how distributed ledgers and smart contracts could have made the last crisis even worse had they existed in the mid-2000s.

The purpose of this historical review and thought experiment is to vividly demonstrate the potential harms associated with new financial technologies: as a society, we tend to support precautionary regulation of pharmaceuticals and self-driving cars because we recognize their potential to threaten human lives, but we're less comfortable with precautionary regulation intended to protect our financial system. To help overcome this reluctance toward precautionary regulation of new financial technologies, Chapter 1 demonstrates that the costs of financial crises are not just economic, but also tear at the fabric of our society.

Part II of this book consists of three chapters, organized around three key functions that the financial system performs for the broader economy: risk management, capital intermediation, and payments processing. The focus of part II is on identifying the ways in which fintech could precipitate or exacerbate a financial crisis by compromising one or more of these functions. Throughout this part, I emphasize the increased speed, complexity, and coordination that come with using new technologies to automate the delivery of financial services. Each chapter uses different case studies of technologies and business models to illustrate these themes. Chapter 2 focuses on how advances in machine learning technology are being applied to manage financial risks: by robo-investing start-ups, by more established banks and asset managers, and by insurance companies. Chapter 3 uses the case studies of marketplace lending, high frequency trading, and cryptoasset markets to explore how technology is changing the ways in which our financial system intermediates capital. It finishes with some observations about how cryptoassets might also hamper the ability of central banks to carry out monetary policy. Chapter 4 uses mobile payments and distributed ledger technologies as case studies to demonstrate how operational problems in the payments system can trigger and transmit financial distress. It also examines the risks associated with increased reliance on third-party technology vendors.

Part III, which also consists of three chapters, engages with the thorny issue of how to respond to the threats identified in part II—as well as other, so far-unidentified threats that may emerge in the future. Chapter 5 sets out the inadequacies of our current financial regulatory system when it comes to fintech. It starts by describing the challenges that technological innovation poses for regulation generally, then looks more specifically at the difficulties inherent in regulating fintech. Some financial regulators have been experimenting with new regulatory approaches in light of fintech's ascendance, but most of the experimentation so far has focused on supporting private sector innovation, rather than mitigating the negative consequences of that innovation. The inadequacies highlighted in Chapter 5 demonstrate the need for the new types of regulatory approaches explored in Chapter 6.

Chapter 6 proposes a variety of precautionary regulatory strategies for addressing the rise of driverless finance, but before doing so, it reckons with the resource and jurisdictional challenges that impede such regulatory responses. Having settled on some (admittedly imperfect) ways of addressing those challenges, it recommends a variety of regulatory responses ranging from licensing regimes for cryptoassets and robo-investing models to so-called "suptech" technological interventions to principles-based oversight regimes for risk management and operational technologies used internally by financial firms.

As ambitious as the proposals in Chapter 6 are, they only address a slice of the questions posed by fintech's new fusion of finance and technology. The rise of fintech is an inflection point that invites engagement with these big picture questions. Chapter 7 therefore considers several big picture questions about the roles that we expect finance and technology to play in our society, and what our expectations of government should be (whether as a regulator or market participant). These questions invite further discussion about the role of expertise and the government's capacity to innovate. Chapter 7 also engages with the slice of the broader debates about competition, privacy, and cybersecurity that relates to financial stability. Chapter 7 doesn't provide concrete policy recommendations—instead, it furthers debate about these issues as the rise of fintech makes them ever more urgent.

# PART I
# THE CASE FOR PRECAUTION

# 1

# The Case for Precaution

When new financial technologies emerge, we don't know exactly how they will work, and we don't know exactly how they will interact with other parts of the financial system. We definitely don't know about the future technologies that will emerge to interact with the technologies we are currently contemplating, and all of this makes the task of financial stability regulation very hard. To make things even more difficult, any technological problems that threaten the stability of our financial system will probably not be everyday occurrences, but will instead happen in the rare and unpredictable circumstances sometimes referred to as "tail events" by economists, and "edge cases" by technologists.

As a result, not only are we wrestling with an uncertain future, we are wrestling with the most uncertain parts of that uncertain future. There is no way to precisely calculate the risks associated with new financial technologies as they emerge. Instead—unavoidably—regulatory approaches to new financial technologies will have to be informed, at least to some degree, by assumptions and value judgments about the likely costs and benefits of these new technologies. This chapter explains why, in the face of the uncertainty associated with new financial technologies, we should take a precautionary approach.

## Dealing with uncertainty

I will elaborate on the meaning of "precaution" soon, but it basically boils down to an admonition to be "better safe than sorry" when the consequences of a new technology could potentially be catastrophic. To understand why such an approach is needed, it helps to first understand the concept of "Knightian uncertainty." In his classic work *Risk, Uncertainty and Profit*, economist Frank Knight distinguished between risk, which is something that will occur with a known probability and therefore lends itself to measurement; and true uncertainty, which cannot be measured at all.[1] The

*Driverless Finance.* Hilary J. Allen, Oxford University Press. © Hilary J. Allen 2022.
DOI: 10.1093/oso/9780197626801.003.0002

term "Knightian uncertainty" therefore describes a world of "unknown unknowns" where we may not even know the types of risks we face, let alone their probability of occurring. Knightian uncertainty is an apt description of our financial future.

We could throw our hands up in the face of this Knightian uncertainty, leaving new financial technologies unregulated and simply letting the free markets shape their development instead. After all, if we can't be certain about the problems that financial technologies will cause, it's possible that regulating those technologies will limit their benefits without solving the right problems. In fact, regulation could even unintentionally make things worse in some respects. However—while these are real concerns—this book makes the case for why regulation is needed, and can succeed. There are regulatory strategies that are well suited to addressing evolving new technologies, even if we can't precisely identify the risks associated with those technologies in advance (Chapters 5 and 6 will discuss regulatory strategies in more detail). And if no regulation is applied to new financial innovations, technology will skew to the benefit of the innovators—quite possibly at the expense of society as a whole.

We can't reasonably expect innovators to promote financial stability on their own, because they lack both the incentives and the ability to do so. First, financial stability is a classic "public good," in the sense that everyone benefits from it, but the public can't be forced to pay for it. Therefore, in the absence of regulation, innovators lack incentives—other than possibly altruism—to worry about the stability of the financial system. Second, financial crises are a systemic problem, and avoiding them typically requires coordinated action by many market participants. Even the most altruistic innovators are not in a position to know about their competitors' actions, or to force them to behave in a particular way, in order to mitigate threats to the financial system.

Promoting financial stability therefore falls to regulators and lawmakers, and the costs of not regulating can be catastrophic. While we cannot predict precisely how financial stability will be impacted by new financial technologies, we can be reasonably certain that new technological innovations will lead to a more complex financial system that processes transactions more quickly than ever before. Part II will explore these vulnerabilities in detail, but for now it's enough to say that the faster and more complex a system is, the more prone it is to frequent and severe failures. It is also highly likely that technological innovations will exacerbate the herd mentality that characterizes financial decision-making (again, this will be explored more fully in part II of this book). When purchases and sales of assets are carried out en masse, there is increased potential for the types of bubbles and panics that have generated financial crises in the past.

In short, even though we can't predict *exactly* how new financial technologies will interact with our existing financial ecosystem, we already have a sense of how these technologies will exacerbate existing fragilities within the system, making financial crises more likely. And the avoidance, or at least mitigation, of financial crises is a matter of paramount social concern. As famed jurist Guido Calabresi once said, "It is precisely the province of good government to make guesses as to what laws are likely to be worth their costs . . . there is no reason to assume that in the absence of conclusive information no government action is better than some action . . . in uncertainty increase the chances of correcting an error."[2] Despite the fact that we are dealing with Knightian uncertainty, we know enough about how our financial system works and how new technologies might impact it to craft regulations that, while not perfect, increase our chances of avoiding or mitigating future crises. Given the potential costs of doing nothing, these regulatory strategies should be pursued.

## The costs of doing nothing

The financial system is not an end in itself. It exists to allow participants in our economy to manage their financial risks, and to make payments for goods and services. The financial system also exists to move money from those who have it and wish to invest it, to those who need it to grow. This is often referred to as the "capital intermediation" function of our financial system, and a particularly important form of capital intermediation is the provision of credit. If, however, the banks and other financial institutions that ordinarily provide credit lose access to their regular funding sources, or if funding remains available but banks and other financial institutions are not confident enough to tie it up by making long-term loans, then credit will be restricted. Individuals and businesses that need credit will contract rather than expand, and employment and economic growth will contract along with them. This dynamic is what caused the financial crisis of 2008 to metastasize into the deepest recession that the United States had experienced since the Great Depression. While that recession—sometimes referred to as "the Great Recession"—was not as deep as the recession caused by the COVID-19 pandemic, no natural disaster was required to set off the Great Recession. It originated entirely in the financial system, and in that sense, it was very much a self-inflicted wound.

The genesis of the crisis of 2008 was a bubble in residential mortgages.[3] Mortgage lenders (both banks and non-banks) were comfortable in the knowledge that they would immediately be able to sell any risky mortgage loans they made, and they were therefore not particularly worried about the borrowers' ability to repay. The buyers of these mortgage loans were special purpose business entities created solely to purchase the mortgages, then issue securities (known as mortgage-backed securities or "MBS") to investors. Each MBS investor was entitled to ongoing payments that were funded indirectly by repayments on the underlying mortgages.

Financial engineering was often used to create tiers of MBS that were marketed to different types of investors: the investors in the top tier of MBS were the first to receive payments, followed by investors in the consecutively lower (and riskier) tiers. Prior to the crisis of 2008, the top tiers of MBS were viewed as essentially riskless, in part because they were given very high ratings by the credit rating agencies, Standard & Poors and Moody's, and in part because of the conventional wisdom that nationally, housing prices would always go up, and so a diversified pool of mortgages would always generate enough repayments to pay the top tier of investors. If investors in the top tier of securities still remained worried that they might not receive their promised payments, they could (and did) purchase credit default swaps and other financial guarantees to effectively insure against any default associated with their MBS investments.

Many in the financial industry genuinely believed that this securitization process had made mortgage lending safer by moving mortgage risk out of the banking system; others simply didn't care because it was profitable in the short-term. Either way, increasing demand for MBS meant increasing demand for the underlying mortgages, fueling a mortgage bubble. Regulators and politicians failed to take steps to address the growing mortgage bubble, and also largely ignored the web of MBS and other financial contracts intertwined with those mortgages. By the mid-2000s, though, mortgage defaults had started to increase across the nation, compromising the value of MBS.

By 2008, these compromised MBS had become highly problematic for many financial institutions, because those institutions had invested heavily in the safest tiers of MBS—and relied on them as collateral for the cheap short-term funding they used to make other investments. As problems with the MBS were exposed, this funding became increasingly expensive (and sometimes unavailable at any cost). Financial institutions were also adversely affected if they had also invested in the riskier tiers of MBS (as many of the largest financial institutions had). As their customary funding dried up and their balance sheets became more precarious, financial institutions cut back on lending and started to sell off their assets at fire sale prices. Many of them reached the brink of insolvency, and were only saved through government intervention. The investment bank Lehman Brothers was not saved—it filed for bankruptcy on September 15, 2008—causing significant panic in the financial markets.

This financial crisis (like many financial crises before it) caused harm to the broader economy by restricting the channels of credit that would usually allow for economic growth.[4] Without access to credit, businesses were unable to expand and hire people; instead they contracted, and with them contracted employment and economic growth. The statistics from the 2008 crisis are stark. In the United States, 3.6 million jobs were lost in 2008 alone.[5] Unemployment peaked at around 10% in October of 2010, and didn't return to pre-crisis levels until 2017. Household net worth shrank by $17 trillion between 2007 and the beginning of 2009 (although a significant amount of this can be attributed to falling home prices, which were largely overinflated in 2007).[6] Even a decade after the crisis, measures of broader economic growth like GDP remained persistently lower than their pre-crisis trend suggested they should be, with one study estimating the impact of the crisis as a "lifetime present-value income loss of about $70,000 for every American."[7] The GAO has estimated the total cost of the crisis to the American people as $13 trillion.[8]

But we should be careful about reducing the experience of the 2008 crisis to dollar amounts and statistical data points. Commenting on unemployment numbers in the wake of that crisis, Janet Yellen noted that "[t]hese are not just statistics. . . . The toll is simply terrible on the mental and physical health of workers, on their marriages, on their children."[9] Growing unemployment is also associated with increases in so-called quality of life crimes, including shoplifting of necessities, loitering, panhandling, and substance abuse (together with substance abuse's corollaries, driving under the influence, domestic violence, and disorderly conduct).[10] The stress associated with the experience of financial crises can also impact the health of those impacted economically—medical studies conducted following the 2008 financial crisis demonstrated increased rates in heart attacks and suicides, and people were less likely to seek preventative medical care in general because of concerns associated with the costs.[11] Even among people who were able to keep their jobs and some sense of financial security during the recession, many experienced a pervading sense of uncertainty and precariousness that may have caused them to delay life events like marriage, home purchases and retirement.

It is also important to note that the impacts of the crisis of 2008 were not distributed uniformly. For example, unemployment was significantly higher among African Americans, Hispanics, and teenagers in the wake of the crisis than it was for the population as a whole.[12] The recovery from the crisis was also uneven: while almost everyone's net worth decreased as a result of the crisis, those with investments in the stock market saw them rebound relatively quickly with the S&P 500 returning to its pre-crisis high by March of 2013. However, recent statistics indicate that only around 50% of American families own any stocks (and that the wealthiest families own around 83% of all stocks).[13] For most middle-class families, their net worth in 2017 remained lower than it had been in 2007.[14] And, again, these disparities were even more pronounced for middle-class African American and Hispanic families, and for young people.[15] The brunt of the 2008 crisis was therefore borne disproportionately by more vulnerable members of society.

This abbreviated survey of the social costs of the 2008 crisis is drawn from the United States. However, financial crises and their economic fallout do not respect national borders. One World Bank report found that some developing countries lost more than a decade of economic development as a result of that crisis.[16] In parts of Europe, the unemployment situation following the 2008 crisis was significantly worse than in the United States. Countries like Portugal and Greece were propelled into new emergencies as crisis-related economic uncertainty limited their ability to borrow money to fund government spending, which in turn undermined confidence in the Euro, the currency that Portugal and Greece share with the other seventeen European countries that comprise the "Eurozone."

A breakup of the Euro was ultimately averted by significant intervention by the European Central Bank—but central banks are not always able to fully contain financial crises. The social costs of the 2008 crisis that are summarized in this chapter were incurred despite Herculean and imaginative crisis response efforts from the Federal Reserve and other governmental bodies. That doesn't mean that those efforts were worthless—the general consensus is that the recession that followed the 2008 crisis would have been orders of magnitude worse if it were not for this intervention. It does, however, demonstrate that emergency action cannot completely address financial crises once they occur.

Not only are emergency responses to financial crises unlikely to be completely successful, they are also likely to be a very bitter pill for most of society to swallow. Many people heard about funds being pumped into the very financial institutions that had caused the 2008 crisis, saw little relief being provided to everyday people suffering as a result of the crisis, and concluded that there was "a pattern of winners and losers that could not be defended on any principle of desert."[17] This sense of economic injustice was exacerbated in countries that chose to, or were forced to, implement austerity measures that cut government spending on social programs in the wake of the crisis; it continues to be driven home by the record-breaking profits being made by the financial industry. By generating a pervasive sense of unfairness, the financial crisis of 2008 created fertile ground within which populist politics could flourish.

The problems associated with intervening in financial crises after they occur serve as strong arguments for precautionary regulation that is designed to proactively minimize the chance that a financial crisis will occur in the first place. While the 2008 financial crisis has sometimes been referred to as the proverbial "hundred-year storm," we shouldn't expect financial crises to remain once-in-a-generation events. Part II will explore the potential for new technologies to make financial crises more frequent and severe than those we have experienced in the past, and this threat provides an even stronger justification for taking a precautionary approach to financial innovation.

## What exactly do we mean by precaution?

When people hear that a "precautionary approach" will be taken, they sometimes assume that any and all steps will be taken to prevent any and all harms, with the practical result that there will be an outright ban on any activity that has not been proven completely safe. But this is a caricature of precautionary regulation (one that is sometimes invoked to defeat precautionary policy proposals). In fact, this "no harm" caricature of precaution couldn't possibly work—policymakers would be paralyzed as they tried to both prevent the harms of an activity and prevent the harms that would come from depriving people of the benefits of that activity. However, a more realistic version of precaution can be enormously helpful in addressing the threats that the "unknown unknowns" of new technologies pose to our financial system.

When it comes to fintech, we should take more stringent action to address the potential risks than we would in the absence of a precautionary approach, and we should take that action earlier.[18] We shouldn't try to eliminate all risks, but we should recognize that there is often a time lag between the benefits and harms of innovation, with the benefits often being obvious at the time of creation but the harms taking some time to manifest. As a result, we should err on the side of caution if the harms associated with new fintech innovations may be irreversible and catastrophic, and place the burden on the innovator to demonstrate why the technology should be allowed to proceed, rather than requiring the regulator to make a case for why regulation is necessary. While the costs associated with precautionary regulation of fintech should be considered, the primary concern is to ensure a stable financial system that can continue to facilitate the capital intermediation, risk management, and payments functions necessary for economic growth.

Adopting a precautionary approach like this would help address some of the structural problems that financial regulators currently face in addressing new technologies. Some of the most difficult challenges that regulators face are informational—how do they find out about new technologies while there is still time to influence their development, and then when they do find out about them, how to they make sense of the complex new technologies involved? One practically useful consequence of placing the burden on innovators to demonstrate why their technology should be permitted is that it requires them to bring the technology to regulators, and to explain it.

Admittedly, the explanation given will be colored by the optimism of the innovators. Regulators will therefore have to consider the information provided to them critically, to try to understand the downsides of the innovation. When the technology is complex, this can be a very challenging thing to ask of financial regulators, who may lack the necessary technical expertise to look critically at the innovation. Regulators may end up deferring to and internalizing the rosy perspective of the regulated industry—at the expense of the public interest. This phenomenon is known as cognitive capture.

To some extent, cognitive capture is unavoidable. Regulators need information to make their decisions, and much of the information about what the industry is doing can only come from the industry itself. However, a precautionary approach can help limit the effects of cognitive capture. Committing to a precautionary approach means giving regulators the resources they need. With the right personnel with the right technical expertise, regulatory agencies will be better equipped to really assess new financial technologies. Of course, even technically sophisticated regulators need to be careful not to be overwhelmed with enthusiasm for new innovations, and capture can also persist if those skilled regulators want to avoid confrontation with the innovators. A precautionary approach can disrupt this "don't rock the boat" mindset, though, instilling a healthy sense of skepticism in regulators because the burden shifting entailed in the precautionary principle is mental as well as structural. Regulators administering precautionary regulation are primed to presume that activities have downsides, particularly downsides that will only manifest in rare circumstances (and when it comes to financial stability, unlikely events with catastrophic ramifications are exactly what we are worried about).

It is particularly important that our regulatory structures instill this precautionary mindset in regulators, because the public at large rarely focuses on matters of financial regulation. While all members of the public have a continuing vested interest in promoting financial stability, it becomes increasingly difficult to marshal their attention as memories of previous crises fade. Even when members of the public remain focused and concerned, it is often challenging for them to coordinate with similarly concerned individuals, or to engage with complex products and rules that they may not be informed about. By default, then, regulators become the primary caretakers of financial stability.

## Precaution in other contexts

Although the United States is often stereotyped as being particularly hostile to precautionary regulation, that is not always the case.[19] In some areas, United States policy is very precautionary—this is perhaps most evident in the range of "better safe than sorry" counterterrorist measures that have been adopted in the United States since September 11, 2001. But a precautionary approach is also evident in how the United States regulates many different types of innovation. The most obvious example is the Food & Drug Administration's approach to regulating drug safety. While there is an ongoing debate about whether the FDA should formally incorporate "the precautionary principle" into its decision-making process, that debate is focused on the merits of the

FDA adopting a very strong form of precaution that requires a demonstration that a drug is largely riskless before it can be approved. For the purposes of this chapter, it is more important to observe that the FDA already deploys a softer, but still stringent, form of precaution in reviewing new drugs. In fact, attempts by the Trump administration to encourage the FDA to take a less precautionary approach to approving a vaccine for COVID-19 were widely considered to have undermined the agency and its reputation.[20]

Since 1962, the FDA has required manufacturers of drug products to demonstrate their safety and efficacy to the FDA's satisfaction before it will license manufacturers to market and sell those drug products to the public. Such an approach is precautionary in many of the senses described in this chapter. For example, the FDA errs on the side of preventing drugs with uncertain but potentially catastrophically unsafe outcomes from entering the marketplace (at significant economic cost to the pharmaceutical industry, and also, sometimes, at significant personal cost to patients who might benefit from those drugs). It shifts the burden to the innovator to demonstrate why the drugs should be permitted, instead of requiring the regulators to make the case for why regulation is necessary. As part of that process, innovators are required to submit their drugs to the FDA, and so the FDA is not required to expend resources trying to figure out which new drugs have been released to the public. The regulation is process driven, in the sense that testing focuses on how a drug achieves its outcome (thus alerting the regulator to potential side effects), instead of the FDA simply ruling on whether the drug does or does not achieve its stated purpose. In order to carry out this process, the FDA has developed significant in-house scientific expertise, and also relies heavily on external experts who are independent from the industry.[21]

As is often the case, it took a crisis to motivate the implementation of this precautionary regulatory approach: the 1962 amendments to the Food, Drug and Cosmetics Act that implemented this drug approval process were enacted in response to the worldwide epidemic of severe birth defects caused by the anti-morning sickness drug thalidomide. The tragic and shocking nature of these birth defects, which were widely reported on, made them very salient for the public. This salience was ultimately enough to galvanize support for the legislative amendments, which had previously faced staunch political opposition—in the end, the pharmaceutical industry committed to supporting the amendments preemptively, fearing an even stricter legislative response if the amendments weren't passed.[22]

The response to the thalidomide tragedy illustrates that society's attitudes toward precautionary regulation are often influenced by how policy issues are framed. Behavioral economist Daniel Kahneman described the importance of framing as follows: "intuitive decisions will be shaped by the factors that determine the accessibility of different features of the situation. Highly accessible features will influence decisions, while features of low accessibility will be largely ignored."[23] Because of this characteristic of human cognition, information or possibilities that we can easily recall or imagine will inform regulatory policymaking to a much greater extent than less visceral or more attenuated outcomes.

Framing regulation as policy intended to prevent bodily harm or death therefore tends to encourage a more precautionary approach, because we can easily call to mind examples of injury and death, and they scare us. Precautionary policies have sometimes been criticized for entrenching people's fears, but fears of irreversible and catastrophic outcomes can be quite rational, and some degree of (rational) fear is often needed to overcome industry opposition to regulation. Fears of harm to human life are certainly inspiring precaution with regard to the development of another new type of innovation: the driverless car.

Although driverless cars are already on the road in several US states, there is typically a licensed driver behind the wheel able to take over if something goes wrong. While these vehicles are already very effective at the basics of driving—typically, better than a human driver—their responses to unusual circumstances remain unpredictable, with potentially devastating consequences. If something does go wrong, it can be hard to figure out why a driverless car behaved in the way that it did, or to prevent it from making the same mistake in the future.

The potential dangers of driverless cars were vividly and tragically illustrated when a driverless car struck and killed a pedestrian in Tempe, Arizona, in March of 2018. Although there was a licensed driver behind the wheel of the car, she was not paying attention and was unable to intervene in time (automated technologies that encourage human users not to pay attention, but then require intervention in the case of an emergency, are particularly dangerous. This is a theme we will return to in part II). There have also been several instances of Tesla's Autopilot mode malfunctioning and killing the drivers involved, but it is the image of an unsuspecting Arizona pedestrian being struck that captured the public imagination, and served as an inflection point in the regulation and development of driverless cars. As a *New York Times* headline stated following the Arizona incident, "Despite High Hopes, Self-Driving Cars are 'Way in the Future.'"[24]

A single pedestrian fatality was enough to diminish expectations about the current viability of driverless cars, with the industry now accepting that these cars are not yet "safe enough," and that much more testing and development will be needed before these vehicles are marketed and sold to the public. In comparison, the possibility of a future financial crisis seems much less salient to the public (at least at present). Society is therefore demanding significant precaution with respect to driverless cars while largely ignoring the much more widespread consequences that financial innovation could have for our economic system. Many innocent bystanders to financial crises have already died—this chapter has already noted the increased number of heart attacks and suicides that resulted from the 2008 crisis, and there were surely many others whose precarious financial position post-crisis led them to forgo preventative medical care that might ultimately have saved their lives. But these deaths were only the most dire of the harms suffered as a result of that financial crisis. It is important not to lose sight of the less visceral, but nonetheless devastating, costs of financial instability. If viewed collectively, the widespread economic, psychological, and political costs of a financial crisis should be more than enough justification for precautionary intervention. And yet, many new financial technologies are being developed without any regulatory oversight.

To help make the case for an urgent precautionary response to new financial technologies, this chapter has reminded readers of the harm caused by the 2008 financial crisis (memories are short, and for many, the 2008 crisis has already receded into the back of their minds). While future threats to the financial system will no doubt be different to the ones that caused problems in 2008, public support for a precautionary approach to new technologies cannot be built without an appreciation of how deep the consequences of financial system failure can be.

## The costs of precautionary regulation

Given the costs of financial crises, if regulation can be even partially successful in preventing or mitigating them, then it is worth pursuing. Of course, regulatory compliance is expensive for the private sector, and there are many who argue that the industry should not have to bear these compliance costs unless they are outweighed by the dollar value of the benefits of the regulation. However, it is very difficult to quantify the benefits of financial stability regulation—what numbers should we use? Methodologies for estimating the cost of the 2008 crisis vary enormously, and the cost of that crisis probably won't be predictive of the cost of a future crisis. Furthermore, because we don't know the probability of a future crisis occurring, we can't assign a value to avoiding that future crisis, even if we agreed on a ballpark figure for its likely cost. And even if we could agree to assign a particular dollar value and probability to a future crisis, how could we demonstrate that existing regulation would be successful in preventing it? After all, if the regulation is successful, we'll never know, as the result will simply be the absence of a crisis that might otherwise have occurred.[25]

Because the benefits of financial stability regulation can be so hard to pin down, and because regulatory compliance costs tend to be readily quantifiable, hard empirical assessments will often conclude that the costs of financial stability regulation are not justified. But the dollar amounts of compliance costs should not be used as the primary metric for determining whether financial stability regulation should be adopted; doing so ultimately uses the profitability of the financial industry as our barometer for whether regulation should be adopted. The financial system exists (or at least, should exist) to facilitate the risk management, capital intermediation, and payments services that the broader economy needs to grow. As such, from a public policy perspective, we should only be concerned about the regulatory costs borne by the financial industry if they interfere with these functions.

Such interference is possible: financial institutions may have to devote funds to regulatory compliance that they would otherwise have used to develop new and useful financial products and services. Although many of the largest financial institutions are profitable enough to pay for both compliance and innovation, the complexity of financial regulation can be particularly forbidding for tech start-ups with no experience in dealing with the highly regulated world of finance. Regulation might chill innovation from these start-ups that could otherwise have resulted in cheaper, more efficient, and more inclusive financial services. Although not all financial innovation is socially beneficial (a theme we will return to shortly), if the innovation in question is socially desirable, then regulatory chilling of that innovation is a valid concern.

Before concluding this discussion of "regulation as a cost," it is important to note that financial regulation also provides benefits to some financial institutions. For banks, these benefits are very clear, and include things like access to cheap deposit funding (subsidized by government deposit insurance schemes) and the availability of loans from the central bank in an emergency. For non-bank providers of financial services, the benefits can be more intangible but still important. Financial products and services are what are known as "credence goods," meaning that it can take time for their value to become apparent and so there is an element of trust involved when a consumer selects such products and services. The existence of a regulatory regime creates respectability that generates consumer confidence, assisting financial institutions in finding a market for their products and services. Non-bank financial institutions may also benefit from implicit assumptions that the government support provided to banks will be extended to them, and indirectly, to their customers, in an emergency. Financial regulation may therefore, at least in some respects, help facilitate innovation in financial products and services—so we should think long and hard about the type of innovation that regulation should seek to promote.

## Innovation isn't always good

At the heart of debates about regulation and innovation, there is often an implicit assumption that innovation is a good thing. But it is important to acknowledge that this is not always the case—at the very least, we should accept that innovation is not always *unqualifiedly* good. During the past decade of breakneck technological progress, with tech companies dominating the news cycle and the stock market, it has sometimes seemed heretical to suggest that innovation is anything other than an improvement to our current state. However, now that journalists, policymakers, and society as a whole are starting to voice concerns about big tech, we have a real opportunity to reckon with the downsides of technological innovation.

"Innovation" is a term that is tricky to define; often, attempts to do so end up in a discussion of whether a particular innovation is "disruptive," in Harvard Business School Professor Clayton Christensen's sense of a "process by which a product or service takes root initially in simple applications at the bottom of a market and then relentlessly moves up market, eventually displacing established competitors."[26] Christensen's perspective on disruptive innovation is informed by economist Joseph Schumpeter's work on innovation as a force of "creative destruction" that propels economic growth,[27] which lends the process of innovation significant luster. However, not all financial innovation is disruptive, and not all financial innovation propels economic growth.

It is more comprehensive and more objective to use a definition of innovation that focuses on the process of change (which may or may not result in an improvement), and also includes incremental innovations that neither disrupt nor destroy. This book will use a definition of financial innovation proposed by law professor Dan Awrey that meets these criteria. Awrey describes financial innovation as "an ongoing process of experimentation whereby institutions, instruments, techniques and markets are (or are perceived to be) created."[28] This definition is broad enough to encompass the many financial innovations to be examined in part II of this book, without presupposing that they will necessarily be beneficial.

Of course, many new financial technologies will have benefits. Much of the positive buzz about new fintech business models focuses on inclusion and efficiency. The FDIC estimated that in 2019, approximately 7.1 million American households had no access to a checking or a savings account.[29] When banks are not available to serve consumer needs, fringe providers fill the void. The financial services provided by these fringe providers (including check cashing services and payday loans), "cost[] more, take[] longer, risk[] more, and do[] less to build their financial futures" than equivalent services provided by mainstream financial institutions.[30] Many new fintech innovations seek to provide lower-cost alternatives to the unbanked population—Richard Cordray, the former director of the CFBP, expressed particular enthusiasm about new forms of prepaid cards and accounts that might make transacting easier and cheaper, and new data-driven methods of credit scoring that might make credit cheaper and more accessible.[31]

Precautionary regulation could possibly chill some of these innovations and benefits, but not everyone is convinced that underserved consumers will benefit from financial inclusion efforts driven by fintech entrepreneurs. If fintech business models try to exploit groups of consumers with little financial sophistication or experience, then fintech's promise to expand access to financial services could be seen as a little sinister. We should therefore be cautious about depending on private sector innovations to address the financial needs of underserved groups. Sometimes, these needs might be better addressed through more targeted public sector investments and programs.[32] Furthermore, the question of whether increased access to financial services is, on balance, beneficial to society needs to be examined in the broader context of financial stability.

New financial technologies that make financial services more accessible could ultimately cause damage to our broader economy (and the experience of the Great Recession suggests that the most vulnerable sectors of the population, the very people that fintech claims to make financial services more accessible for, are likely to bear the brunt of the costs of any resulting recession). While potential threats posed by different fintech business models will be explored in more detail in part II of this book, this chapter's discussion of the 2008 financial crisis has already demonstrated that providing more credit to more people more cheaply can fuel asset bubbles that generate risks to the financial system as a whole.

It would also be wrong to assume that *all* of the financial innovation that is currently being undertaken is intended to make financial services more accessible to underserved populations. Many innovators are designing cheaper capital intermediation, risk management, and payments solutions for customers who already have access to the traditional banking system. Other innovators are working on more efficient solutions to be used internally by financial institutions. If these new services are only marginally more efficient in the short term, and in the long term they end up making our financial system more fragile (for example, by making it more complex), then chilling their development would be good public policy.

Some innovations will not even result in marginal improvements for their users. If innovation is driven entirely by a financial institution's desire to generate fees by repeatedly introducing updated versions of existing products and services, and if the new versions don't achieve anything significantly different to the older versions, they will increase the complexity of the financial system without providing any real improvement to the user. Or, if the innovator is a start-up firm, their innovations may be designed more to attract the interest of venture capital investors than to satisfy genuine needs for their users.

It might seem counterintuitive that there could ever be a market for a product that does not meet genuine market needs, but in fact, there are many ways in which this can happen. Demand can be generated by fads and trends, rather than a reasoned evaluation of the product or service, with users primarily enticed by the story that has been spun by the innovator. Demand can also be manipulated by hiding some of the costs and risks associated with a product or service from customers. In sum, "[w]e cannot say that innovation is 'good' simply because there is a market for it."[33]

Even when a financial innovation is not predatory, manipulative, or otherwise bad, if it benefits the supplier rather than meeting the customer's needs, we have less to fear from a precautionary approach (in terms of its capacity to limit innovation) than some might have anticipated. We also have little to fear from limiting innovation that primarily exists to evade or "arbitrage" regulation (in the sense that a product or service achieves the same economic function as a regulated product or service, but does so in a way that manages to avoid the regulation). Innovations designed to arbitrage existing regulations often spur the creation of more regulations, and then new innovations are created to innovate around the new regulations in an unending cycle of increasing complexity. A precautionary approach can help stop this cat and mouse game by shifting the burden to the innovator to demonstrate that the innovation meets a need beyond exploiting regulatory loopholes.

## Imagine if credit default swaps had been cryptoassets

During the 2008 crisis, it became clear that financial innovation is not always an unmitigated improvement. New products like mortgage-backed securities and credit default swaps (both of which had been designed to arbitrage existing regulations) proved to be much riskier than anticipated. No precautionary regulation had been implemented with regard to these products before the crisis; in fact, the exponential growth of the credit default swap market was facilitated by the distinctly un-precautionary Commodity Futures Modernization Act of 2000, which Congress enacted in order to forbid any regulation of swaps. One way to make the case for precaution with regard to new financial innovations is to consider how these older financial innovations, which caused significant damage last time around, might have caused bigger problems—and caused them more quickly—had they incorporated some of today's new technologies. For example, we could consider the havoc that a credit default swap might have wreaked had it been hosted on a distributed ledger and run by a smart contract.

A credit default swap (or "CDS") is a type of contract that derives its value from an underlying debt instrument, like a mortgage-backed security or some other kind of bond. A CDS in many ways works like an insurance policy, allowing the holder of a debt instrument to buy protection in case a "credit event" occurs (like the bankruptcy of the issuer of that debt instrument). When a CDS is used like this, to manage the risks associated with holding the relevant debt instrument, the protection buyer is using the CDS to "hedge." The person buying a CDS doesn't have to own the underlying debt instrument, though (this stands in contrast to a real insurance policy: the law doesn't allow a person to buy homeowner's insurance for their neighbor's house). This means that a CDS can be used to bet on whether a credit event will occur (in which case, the CDS is being used to "speculate").

CDS were an integral cause of the 2008 crisis, during which they came to be vilified as "weapons of mass destruction."[34] Prior to the crisis, however, CDS were enormously popular, and the explosive growth of the CDS market was intimately linked with the rise of the mortgage-backed securitization market discussed earlier in this chapter. The CDS and MBS markets were connected in a number of different ways. CDS were used by investors in MBS who wanted to manage the risk associated with their investment (using CDS to hedge in this way closely resembled getting an insurance policy that paid out if the issuer of the MBS defaulted). CDS were also used by people who hadn't invested in MBS directly, but wanted to speculate on the movement of the MBS market. Finally, CDS were used as fodder for even more securitizations (debt securities issued by special purpose entities holding portfolios of credit default swaps were referred to as "synthetic CDOs").

A CDS is created when the parties sign a contract, which is typically based on a form devised by the International Swaps and Derivatives Association (as a result, these contracts are colloquially known as ISDAs). It is not difficult to imagine that, in the near future, parties may start to dispense with using paper ISDAs, and instead memorialize their contractual arrangements in the computer programs known as smart contracts (the International Swaps and Derivatives Association is already actively exploring the possibilities for smart contract-based swaps in a series of white papers).[35] Smart contracts are essentially agreements in digital form that are designed to be self-executing and self-enforcing—these agreements establish the rights and obligations associated with tokens that are hosted on a distributed ledger, and execute on the distributed ledger automatically, without any human intervention.[36]

Even structuring traditional paper contracts so that they are hard for the parties to modify can pose threats to financial stability. Rigid MBS contracts, for example, were described as "suicide pacts" that exacerbated the 2008 crisis.[37] Depriving financial contracts of even more of their flexibility by turning them into self-executing computer programs could have made the financial system even more fragile, as we will explore.

Let's go back to the lead-up to the 2008 crisis (a time before distributed ledgers). The insurance giant AIG had issued an estimated $1.8 trillion of CDS that would require it to make payments if the underlying MBS suffered some type of credit event.[38] AIG was not in a position to actually pay out on all of those CDS—at the time, AIG's parent company reported total capital of $95.8 billion—but AIG had assumed that the underlying MBS would never default, and so it would never be required to make any payments.[39] However, as time progressed, and the mortgages backing those MBS began to default in alarming numbers, people started to admit the possibility that MBS themselves might default, which made AIG's position riskier. Worried that AIG might not be able to make payments on its CDS if the MBS failed, the banks and other investors that had bought CDS from AIG turned to provisions in their ISDA contracts that required AIG to provide them with collateral if the risks associated with MBS increased. It was these calls for collateral that ultimately forced a government bailout—to the tune of tens of billions of dollars—to prevent AIG from failing.[40]

AIG's downward spiral would most likely have been hastened, perhaps irretrievably, if the CDS it had issued had been programmed as smart contracts. For example, on several occasions in 2007, the investment bank Goldman Sachs demanded that AIG post collateral in response to downgrades of the MBS referenced in the CDS that AIG had issued to Goldman. Pursuant to the ISDA agreements governing the arrangements between Goldman Sachs and AIG, these collateral calls were authorized if Goldman Sachs believed that the value of the underlying MBS had decreased. However, AIG had dismissed the possibility of such collateral calls—in fact, many senior people at AIG were unaware that the ISDAs authorized these collateral calls at all—and so no one at AIG had developed any way of assessing what the appropriate amount of collateral should be. As a result, Goldman Sachs was largely in a position to dictate how much collateral it was entitled to in a collateral call.

What happened in reality was that when Goldman Sachs made its collateral call, AIG objected, the parties negotiated, and they ultimately agreed that AIG could post much less collateral than Goldman Sachs had initially demanded. Had smart contracts existed at that time, though, and had the parties used them to automate the collateral call process, Goldman Sachs would simply have had to type the dollar amount of desired collateral into a computer (remember that AIG didn't negotiate for any rights with respect to collateral calls). Then the smart contract would have withdrawn that dollar amount from AIG's account on the distributed ledger. There would have been much less scope for flexibility or negotiation in Goldman Sachs's treatment of AIG, and AIG's solvency might have been in jeopardy as early as 2007.

When AIG ultimately did reach the brink of failure in September 2008, again as a result of collateral calls in connection with the many CDS it had issued, AIG's insolvency was averted by the government pledging to provide AIG with the funds necessary to cover those collateral calls. If the CDS had been automated, though, would there have been a way to suspend collateral calls until AIG received its infusion of government funds, or would AIG's accounts have been automatically debited for the collateral, rendering AIG insolvent before government aid could arrive? Parties to a paper contract can agree among themselves not to enforce a contract when it is not in their best interests to do so, but there is much less flexibility in a smart contract. Unless a smart contract were programed in advance to delay execution following the announcement of a government bailout of a counterparty (an unlikely event that would probably not have been contemplated at the time the smart contract was programmed), such news would not prevent default—even though the announcement of the relief succeeded in saving AIG in 2008.

If AIG had become insolvent, then there would have been significant ripple effects through its contracts with other financial institutions (including, notably, Goldman Sachs), jeopardizing their solvency and thus their ability to perform capital intermediation, risk management, and payments functions. Indeed, fear of such a domino effect is what prompted the federal bailout of AIG in the first place. As it was, even solvent financial institutions pulled back from lending, with credit becoming less available and more expensive in the wake of the financial crisis. Cuts to small business lending, which was hit particularly hard by the credit crunch, are illustrative. Bank lending to small businesses dropped from over $710 billion in the second quarter of 2008 to $670 billion in the first quarter of 2010.[41] Had more financial institutions become insolvent, and had a greater sense of panic taken hold among the institutions that survived, one can only imagine how little credit would have been available in 2008 and 2009, and how deep the resulting recession would have been.

This chapter's alternative history is based on an expectation of entirely automated CDS. In the future, it may be technologically possible to create a contract so that some of its terms are programmed into a smart contract, while other terms remain in their more traditional paper format to allow for more flexibility. This is the approach that the International Swaps & Derivatives Association is currently promoting as it explores potential uses of smart contracts in swaps documentation.[42] However, interactions and feedback loops between the automated and non-automated provisions of the contract will create lots of potential for unanticipated outcomes. Parties to this kind of hybrid contract may not always know in advance which types of terms will be non-contentious and therefore suitable for automating, and which are likely to be more complicated in operation and therefore require human intervention to resolve. Inevitably, parties trying to make decisions about which provisions to automate will sometimes get it wrong.

In fact, when it comes to using smart contracts to automate the operation of CDS, we are in the realm of Knightian uncertainty. The precautionary approach we have formulated therefore urges caution—but it does not automatically demand an outright ban on using smart contracts in this context. It does, however, counsel that the use of smart contracts for such purposes should not be developed entirely by private sector bodies like the International Swaps & Derivatives Association. Our starting position for smart contract CDS, as well as for other new financial technologies, should be that regulators be involved in their design process from the beginning, to encourage a product that minimizes anticipated harms to the stability of the financial system.

## Precautionary regulation is process-oriented

The financial system becomes more fragile as it becomes faster, more complex, more interconnected, and more correlated, and so regulators need to be particularly alert to any new innovation that contributes to these forces. If regulators don't focus on the development process, then it is easy to be fooled into thinking that a new product (like a smart contract CDS) that achieves roughly the same result as an existing product (like a paper CDS), should be regulated in the same way as the existing product. However, if the same functional result is achieved through radically different technology, the associated risks may also be radically different. For example, the Dodd-Frank legislation enacted in the wake of the 2008 crisis established a detailed new regulatory framework for swaps, but there is nothing in that legislation that contemplates smart contracts, or addresses their inflexibility. Regulators following a precautionary approach would be encouraged to focus on changes to the *processes* by which CDS (and other financial products) achieve their results.

Regulators will gain a better understanding of the process by which an innovation achieves its result if they are able to observe the development of that innovation from the beginning. Precautionary regulation should therefore ensure that the regulators are aware of, and able to observe, the development process of innovation in the first place. They then need the power to intervene in the development of the product, if necessary, in order to affect the process by which the innovation will ultimately carry out its functions. Chapter 6 will explore how these powers can be conferred on regulators; this chapter focuses on explaining why process-oriented regulation is so important.

One benefit of targeting regulation at the design process is that an innovator will likely be very thorough in checking for glitches if they know that a regulator needs to sign off on their product before it can be marketed and sold. Merely by virtue of knowing that they will struggle to explain an exceedingly complex innovation to a regulator, innovators may be encouraged to eliminate superfluously complex features before seeking regulatory approval. Regulating the process of innovation could therefore have an overall simplifying effect—as former Governor of the Bank of India Y.V. Reddy described:

> A regulator has a job to try to understand innovation and regulate it, but it doesn't mean that the innovator has the right to introduce the innovation in the market . . . if I can't understand [it] I won't permit it until you make me understand, or until you redesign it in a way that we can understand.[43]

Targeting regulation at the design process is also likely to have other simplifying effects. From a technological perspective, it is much easier to make changes to a product as it is developed, rather than trying to superimpose features onto a finished product. Making superimposed features work within an already functional product increases the chances that the components of the products will interact in unanticipated (and potentially problematic) ways. As a result, if regulators conclude that certain safeguards need to be included in a product, or that a particular feature is too problematic and should be excised from the product, it will be simpler and more effective for these changes to be made while the technology is still in beta mode. It will also be less costly for the innovators to make the changes earlier in the development process.

In some instances, problems with a new product may be so overwhelming that safeguards and revisions cannot address the regulators' concerns. In these instances, regulators might be justified in banning the product from the outset. As we have already explored, bans should not be the default option, but they will be appropriate sometimes—particularly if the product is so complex that the innovators cannot explain it in a way that is accessible to regulators. When dealing with this level of complexity, it is quite possible that the product is harboring risks unanticipated by both regulators *and* innovators, and regulators would be justified in preventing the product and its attendant risks from entering the financial system. Importantly, doing so would keep the product from adding to the overall complexity of the financial system—a result that cannot be achieved by waiting to take action until after a product has shown itself to be problematic.

Banning an innovation before it even reaches the market will certainly deprive society of its potential benefits. This loss of benefits may ultimately be a harm that even outweighs the risks associated with the product. However, in an environment of Knightian uncertainty, difficult trade-offs will have to be made on the basis of imperfect information. While regulatory mistakes are inevitable, regulators should err on the side of protecting financial stability, and thus the broader economy, to the best of their ability—even if we cannot prove in advance that they will succeed, or put an exact dollar value on avoiding a crisis. Regulators will be most effective in doing so if they target the design process. Maintaining the current practice of waiting until a problem has occurred before taking regulatory action is not a neutral approach. Instead, it stacks the deck in favor of the innovators who get to profit by generating risks that, if they come to fruition, will be borne primarily by the rest of society.

## Time is of the essence

The financial applications of smart contract and distributed ledger technologies (as well as machine learning and cloud computing technologies) are still in their early stages. This means that there is still time for regulation to have a real impact in guiding the financial applications of these technologies in a way that is more likely to benefit society as a whole. That window of time will close soon, though, and we don't yet have a precautionary regulatory framework in place for financial innovation. Time is of the essence in developing this kind of regulatory framework.

The speed of technological development is not the only reason that regulation needs to be implemented quickly. It also becomes more politically challenging to regulate financial technologies once they become established. As business models based on these technologies become more entrenched, an ecosystem of market participants will evolve that relies on those business models to service their needs—as well as to provide them with income. These market participants will become a vocal constituency against regulation of the relevant technologies, and the public at large (who would be the ultimate beneficiaries of any financial stability regulation) are unlikely to be interested enough to provide countervailing support for regulatory intervention.

When it comes to cryptoassets running on distributed ledgers, we are already on the cusp of such an outcome. In May of 2021, the global value of all outstanding cryptoassets was $2.4 trillion, up from $200 billion just two years before.[44] That period also saw a significant shift in the kinds of investors interested in cryptoassets: one Bitcoin billionaire observed that "[s]omething really cool for us crypto nerds happened in the last six months, like we went from hoping to be an asset class to being an institutional asset class *like that*."[45] With more established financial institutions investing in cryptoassets, it's not surprising that the issue of cryptoasset regulation is becoming politically charged: one newspaper article commented on the "long list of cryptocurrency companies scrambling for influence in Washington as the Biden administration begins setting policy that could shape the course of a potentially revolutionary industry that is rapidly moving into the mainstream."[46]

If that policy bends too far in favor of the industry and too far away from precaution, the financial stability risks of cryptoassets will go largely unregulated—at least until something goes wrong. Once something does go wrong, there may be political support for regulation that targets the specific problem that occurred. However, regulation that is implemented incrementally as problems unfold will spur the industry to innovate around that regulation, inviting more incremental regulation. Layering regulation over cryptoassets over regulation over cryptoassets, unintentionally but inevitably, makes the financial system more fragile by increasing its complexity. It's a far better approach to proactively address concerns about the innovation *now*.

* * *

Although we tend to think of financial crises as economic events, it is important to focus on the social costs that flow from them—after all, these ultimate social costs are the reason why we have financial stability regulation in the first place. If the financial system could fail without harming society as a whole, then financial regulation could rightfully operate on a much more limited scale. Financial system failure does translate into real harm for society, though—and the experience of the 2008 financial crisis suggests that the financial system itself will recover long before the rest of the economy does. We should therefore approach the latest generation of financial innovations, which are likely to exacerbate the already significant levels of complexity, speed, and correlation associated with our financial system, with precaution. In this venture, time is of the essence: the growing public skepticism about the benefits of big tech provides an excellent political opportunity to implement a precautionary approach to new financial technologies, and it should not be wasted.

# PART II
# FINTECH THREATS TO FINANCIAL STABILITY

# 2

# Fintech and Risk Management

There are many different ways that we can think about what the financial system does. It certainly makes a lot of money for the employees and shareholders of financial institutions, but that's not the reason why the financial industry (particularly the banking industry) is given special legal authorizations and government subsidies. Instead, that support is usually justified on the grounds that the financial system performs functions that are extremely useful for economic growth and social stability.[1] This book divides these useful functions into three categories: risk management, capital intermediation, and payments.

Each chapter in this part of the book will expand on one of these functions, discuss how fintech innovation is changing how the function is being performed, and consider whether threats to financial stability might be introduced or enhanced as a result of those changes. It's impossible to do this without getting a little bit into the weeds, both in terms of the finance and the technology, but I have endeavored to make these descriptions as accessible as possible and to combine theoretical discussions with real-world examples. In this chapter, we start with explanations of the financial system's risk management function and machine learning technology before evaluating the likely impact of machine learning innovations on financial risk management. The chapter finishes with three case studies, which look at the robo-investing industry, BlackRock's Aladdin platform, and insurtech.

## What is risk management?

The financial industry offers many different products and services that help people and businesses to manage their risks. Most obviously, insurers offer a range of policies that cover everything from property damage to untimely death, but the financial industry also helps people and businesses to invest money to provide for their financial needs in an uncertain future. Investment comes with its own risks, though, and this chapter focuses on how fintech

*Driverless Finance*. Hilary J. Allen, Oxford University Press. © Hilary J. Allen 2022.
DOI: 10.1093/oso/9780197626801.003.0003

innovations are changing how we manage these investment risks (the end of the chapter will also briefly discuss the insurance industry's use of new technologies).

Some of the most important categories of risk that can impact investments include market risk, credit risk, liquidity risk, operational risk, and systemic risk (all of which can feed into and exacerbate one other).[2] Systemic risk, which can lead to interconnected failures of financial institutions and markets, is the greatest threat to financial stability, but people managing their own financial investments tend to lack both the incentives and the information needed to address systemic risk. Systemic risk management therefore ends up being the regulators' responsibility; when investors and the financial industry talk about "risk management," their focus is usually on market, credit, and liquidity risks. These are risks that we will focus on in this chapter (and Chapter 3). We will look at operational risk in Chapter 4.

Market risk is about managing the many different kinds of changes that can happen in the marketplace and impact the price of an investment. For example, an increase in interest rates tends to negatively affect the value of bond investments. A bond investor can manage that risk, though, by diversifying their investment portfolio to include other types of assets, like stocks. Credit risk (sometimes also referred to as counterparty risk) is the risk that the person you are dealing with will not be able to deliver on their obligations to you. Credit risk can also be managed by diversification strategies—our bond investor with a diversified investment portfolio would suffer a little bit if the issuer of one of their bonds were to go bankrupt, but an investor who had *only* purchased bonds from that issuer (and purchased lots of them) would suffer a lot more. Liquidity risk is the risk that assets cannot be turned into cash when needed—at least, not without taking a significant hit on the price of the asset. Again, diversification can help our investor manage their risk: they can keep some cash in a bank deposit account that will be easily accessible in case of emergency, while investing their other funds in other assets (like their bonds) that might generate a better return, but might be harder to sell for cash during a market crash.

A significant amount of economic research has been done on the best way to put together an investment portfolio, with the aim of maximizing returns while minimizing exposure to financial risks.[3] The key insight of these portfolio management theories is that the ultimate return of the portfolio as a whole is what matters, not how a single asset performs, and diversification within the portfolio is therefore the ultimate risk management strategy.

However, even investment portfolios that were carefully constructed to promote diversification can lose a lot of money if the assets in them unexpectedly turn out to be susceptible to the same kinds of risks. The financial industry has therefore devoted significant resources to constructing models that try to detect unanticipated correlations between assets, and assess the risks faced by an entire investment portfolio.

Some of the most sophisticated portfolio construction tools are used by financial institutions to manage their own investment portfolios, and similar tools are used by financial institutions to manage assets on behalf of investor clients (the asset management industry currently takes care of trillions of dollars of investments).[4] Complex technologies were conscripted into this risk management process long before fintech came into the picture. The computer modeling technique of Value-at-Risk (known as "VaR") gained some notoriety following the financial crisis of 2008 for underestimating the impact of a nationwide housing market failure on investment portfolios,[5] but variations of VaR models remain an important tool in financial risk management. As we think about how to regulate new fintech innovations, we should consider whether these innovations are likely to improve upon traditional VaR models—or whether they are more likely to create new problems for the stability of the financial system. In particular, we need to consider the impact of incorporating machine learning into the risk management process.

## Risk modeling before machine learning

VaR models are widely used to help inform investment decisions, measure compliance with internal risk limitations, and determine if a bank satisfies regulatory capital requirements, among other things. These models generate a number that represents the most an investor should expect to lose on an investment (or an investment portfolio) in a specified period of time. The answer given is provided at a specified confidence level (usually 95% or 99%), meaning that there is always the possibility that the investor could actually lose more—maybe even much more—than the purported "worst case scenario" generated by the VaR model.

VaR is sometimes calculated by looking at the history of returns of a particular investment or portfolio of investments, and determining the probability of losses during that history. For example, if a particular bond lost less than 3% of its value in all but 5% of the days surveyed, a historical VaR model will state with a 95% confidence level that the most value that bond can lose in any given day is 3%. Of course, the past doesn't necessarily predict the future, and so relying entirely on historical performance can lead to underestimation of the risks involved. A more sophisticated way of calculating VaR is to use Monte Carlo simulations to calculate potential losses.

In Monte Carlo simulations, the designer of the model identifies the variables that could change the risks associated with an individual financial asset. These variables will include obvious things, like the prevailing interest rates, but can also include any idiosyncratic variable that the modeler thinks might be relevant, such as political turmoil. The simulation populates each variable with random inputs, modeling the impact of the interactions of the different variables in each scenario (the number of different scenarios used can be in the tens of thousands, which is why significant computer power is needed to run the simulations). Risk managers can then look at all the different possibilities of profit and loss generated by the simulation, and the probability of each possibility occurring, then make judgments about the risks associated with each investment. These calculations are performed for each individual asset, then those assets are considered in the context of their overall portfolios.

While Monte Carlo scenarios are definitely an improvement over models that only look at historical performance of an investment or portfolio, they're by no means a perfect solution to the uncertainty inherent in the financial markets. First of all, if the person who designed the model didn't think of a relevant risk variable, it won't be taken into account in any of the scenarios. Second, the relationship among the variables (for example, interest rates and political risk) is also preprogrammed into the model, and what is programmed may not ultimately be predictive of how those variables will actually interact in the future. In a way, model developers are constrained by their own historical experience of the types of variables that are relevant, and the relationship among those variables, and so they may miss the ways in which different types of asset values may be correlated in the future. The different random inputs that the Monte Carlo simulation uses to populate those variables are also ultimately drawn from historical data.

So long as these types of limitations are not forgotten or neglected, a VaR model incorporating Monte Carlo simulations can provide an important guide to the risks associated with a particular investment portfolio. To help ensure that these kinds of model limitations are recognized, financial regulators around the world have issued guidance relating to model use.[6] The Federal Reserve issued its Supervisory Guidance on Model Risk Management in 2011, and this guidance establishes standards for how regulated financial institutions must construct and test their models. The guidance also documents the regulators' expectations that institutions will limit or control their reliance on a model that exhibits errors or is poorly understood.[7] Although this guidance was formulated before there was significant interest in using machine learning in finance, it continues to be relevant as new technologies like machine learning are incorporated into risk management models.[8]

## Machine learning and risk management

Machine learning is a type of artificial intelligence that has been made possible by technological advances in computing power and the availability of more and more data (and cloud storage for that data). These trends are expected to accelerate exponentially in coming years, and one 2020 survey of senior financial industry employees found that an overwhelming majority of them expect that artificial intelligence will "form an integral part of their business within two years."[9] Broadly speaking, machine learning algorithms scour data, detect patterns and then use those patterns to construct their own decision-making rules. Armed with these decision-making rules, algorithms can figure out how to respond to any new data provided to them. Humans also learn patterns from data, but they are more likely to rely on intuition and narratives to make sense of the relationships between variables, whereas machine learning algorithms rely on probabilities and other statistical methods to deduce connections. Machine learning also differs from human learning in that it is capable of processing far more data, and has the capacity to see relationships between many more variables, than a human could ever manage.

Machine learning is now being incorporated into the financial risk modeling process. While much of the current focus is on using machine learning to test and validate more traditional types of risk management models, it is expected that banks and other financial institutions will increasingly use machine learning technology in their primary risk management models.[10] Financial institutions that have not yet incorporated machine learning into their risk management process may soon find themselves forced by competitive pressures to do so: part of the appeal of machine learning is that it can make the very time-consuming activity of risk management more efficient (and therefore cheaper).[11] But it is also hoped that the technology will be *better* at managing financial risks than previous generations of models.

Models like VaR require humans to define and then program the mathematical relationship between the various risk variables and ultimate losses, and the programmed relationship may not ultimately be predictive of reality. Machine learning algorithms that look for patterns among data, however, might be able to detect relationships between variables that humans have neglected when designing earlier generations of risk management algorithms. If machine learning can be harnessed by financial institutions to create models that are better at predicting the susceptibility of a portfolio to losses, and are able to provide real-time alerts that allow for earlier intervention to address the development of outsized risks, then those institutions may be managed more prudently—which would benefit the financial system as a whole. For these reasons, the Financial Stability Board sees machine learning as a potential force for good.[12]

It's wrong to think of machine learning as a single unified technology, though. Some machine learning algorithms learn in a supervised way, meaning they learn how to answer a question by studying samples of training data in which both the correct answer and the features of that data that help reach that answer have been identified for them. Usually, supervised algorithms learn to predict a numerical value (regression), or to assign something to a specified group (classification). The calculation of possible losses to an investment portfolio is a regression problem: a data scientist could gather data about the historical performance of the investments in the portfolio and provide it to an algorithm, so that the algorithm could learn some lessons about the relationship between the individual investments and the potential magnitude of losses. Classification can also be relevant to risk management—an algorithm might be trained, for example, with data that is labeled with whether a counterparty ultimately defaulted or not in order to develop rules for use in assessing the credit risk of future counterparties.[13]

Unsupervised machine learning algorithms, by contrast, aren't trying to answer a predetermined question. Instead, they are asked to find patterns among data that haven't been previously classified or labeled. For example, one bank has used unsupervised machine learning algorithms to try to figure out relationships between asset prices that traditional risk modeling has missed.[14] With unsupervised algorithms, the task of the model developer is to determine and program how relationships between data (for example, their similarity) will be measured. Unsupervised learning can also be used to compress unwieldy data sets with lots of potentially irrelevant variables, in order to extract the relevant variables for use in other applications—perhaps by a supervised machine learning algorithm learning to calculate possible losses on an investment portfolio.[15] This type of compression is becoming increasingly necessary as machine learning seeks to learn from new kinds of data that aren't already structured in an accessible format.[16]

Within these categories of supervised and unsupervised machine learning algorithms, there are many different types of machine learning algorithms (including neural networks, random forests of decision trees, partial least squares, and support vector machines). Any financial firm that wants to use machine learning in its risk management model therefore faces an upfront choice among algorithms, and that choice will always involve trade-offs. Some algorithms will generate outcomes that will be easier to explain than others—decision trees, for example, tend to be more intuitive to humans than some of the other algorithm types. Some algorithms will be better at avoiding overfitting than others (overfitting will be discussed in more detail, but essentially, it describes a problem where an algorithm becomes so tied to idiosyncrasies in the training data that it can't make accurate predictions with real-world data). Some algorithms are simply better at dealing with certain types of data than others—something that will often only be discovered through trial and error. Some will be easier than others to test, adjust, and fine-tune as things change or errors are detected over time.

This is not an exhaustive list of differences between the different types of approaches, but at least it gives a flavor of the decisions that need to be made in selecting a machine learning algorithm. The question of resources also needs to be considered: Will the financial institution buy a machine learning algorithm off the rack from a third-party vendor, or will it partner with a vendor to develop a bespoke algorithm (or even develop it in-house)? At present, pre-trained algorithms are particularly popular in the financial industry because they are a cheaper option.[17] In addition to decisions about the algorithm itself, many decisions also have to be made about the data that will be used to train the algorithm. The data can be curated in-house or purchased, and again purchased, pre-curated data sets are the cheaper option.[18]

The data collection and selection process requires a lot of judgment calls by the data scientists involved, including the type and number of data points to use in the training data; whether there are errors or outliers to be weeded out from the data set; and how to divide the data set into training and testing data. In the case of supervised learning, the data scientist will also select the features (i.e., the attributes in the data that the algorithm should pay attention to) and label examples within the data as representing a particular outcome. For example, if an algorithm is being trained to assess credit risk, the data scientist will select the type of features in the data that they consider relevant to assessing whether default is likely to occur or not, as well as make determinations about which examples to label as "likely to default."

The initial data collection, feature selection, and labeling are not the end of the data scientist's job—training an algorithm to learn from that data is not a passive process. Interim tests are performed for accuracy, and new data can be added and new features selected during the training process to address any problems that emerge. There are also tweaks that can be made to the algorithm itself. For example, if there are limited data available, the data scientist may err on the side of tweaking the algorithm to ignore idiosyncrasies in the data and focus on constructing higher-level, more generalizable, decision-making rules.

Once its training is complete, a supervised algorithm is exposed to testing data (which has been kept separate from the training set) to see how successfully the algorithm performs when confronted with a new data set where the relevant outcomes have not been labeled. Returning to our credit risk example, the test data set would be used to determine whether the algorithm learned to make estimations of likely defaults that are as accurate as possible, based on the features observed in the testing data. If the data scientist is satisfied that the algorithm has passed the test, it can start to be used in the real world—but machine learning algorithms are not "set and forget." They require ongoing monitoring and fine-tuning to ensure that they continue to work well, at scale, in a complicated world.

With this background on how machine learning works, we're in a position to consider when risk management applications of machine learning technology are likely to improve upon the status quo, and when they're more likely to create pitfalls for the stability of the financial system as whole. Remember that a key flaw in VaR risk modeling is that the data used is often historical in nature and can't properly account for an uncertain future (the potential consequences of low-probability but high-impact tail events are neglected in particular). The last financial crisis also revealed other problems with VaR risk modeling, including that the models were often too complex to understand, and that the models often underappreciated correlations among asset performance during times of stress.[19] Unfortunately, while machine learning can improve upon some of these problems, it will not address others—in some circumstances, it may even make them worse.

## Programming errors and data problems

At every stage of the machine learning process, errors can undermine the accuracy of risk assessments. Looking first at the data collection stage, machine learning is susceptible to what is known as the "garbage in, garbage out" problem: if the data has problems, the decision-making of the trained algorithm will ultimately be flawed too. In the risk management context, there are a variety of data problems that could undermine a machine learning algorithm's ability to assess the risk of potential investment losses. First, there is always a concern that data may just be wrong. For example, an Excel spreadsheet recording the historical performance of a particular asset may be missing a cell, or the wrong amount may have been input. If the algorithm is trained on a sufficiently large data set, a few outlying errors won't have a significant impact on how the algorithm ultimately functions, but there could have been a systemic error—what if an incorrect equation macro had been used to format a cell in an Excel spreadsheet that was used over and over again? Each time that spreadsheet was used, it would have produced an error in that particular cell, but the actual number in that cell would be different in each spreadsheet, and so it would be difficult for a data scientist to detect this kind of error. Putting these kinds of errors aside, though, experience with earlier generations of risk models suggests that from a financial stability perspective, the most dangerous problem is that a model will underestimate the risk of tail events. If machine learning algorithms learn to underestimate tail events, they will suffer the same significant flaw.

Tail events are events that are unlikely to occur, but will have a significant impact if they do occur (they are named after the end or "tail" of the Bell Curve that tapers off, indicating a lower probability of the event occurring). Problems in modern financial markets, from the failure of the Long-Term Capital Management hedge fund in 1998 to the global financial crisis of 2008, can be traced to these types of unlikely events.[20] However, because machine learning algorithms learn by observing probabilities and other statistical relationships, they have an in-built bias against properly appreciating tail events. Machine learning algorithms are better suited to situations where the interactions between variables repeat consistently over time.

Even aggressive attempts to train machine learning algorithms to appreciate tail events will suffer from the limited historical instances of tail events to learn from. While it's generally understood that the more data, the better the machine learning algorithm will perform, there's less consensus on how much data is too little to train an algorithm—the amount needed will depend on the context and will ultimately be a judgment call.[21] In 2017, Rama Cont, the chair of mathematical finance at Imperial College London, said that there were insufficient data available to use machine learning to model most financial risks. He said, "We are not in a big data situation really. The only situation where we are really strong with data is consumer loans, credit cards and so on. We only have one market history, so is the pattern which led to Lehman the same which leads to the fall of bank X the next time?"[22]

The limitations of both the machine learning algorithms themselves and the data they rely on conspire to limit machine learning's ability to assess risks during a tail event. Machine learning algorithms' propensity to misjudge tail events can be exacerbated as software engineers and data scientists work together to manipulate the learning process to avoid what is known as "overfitting." Overfitting refers to a situation where the machine learning algorithm has learned to perfectly understand the features of the test data on which it was trained, but its understanding is so tied to statistical relationships among the training data that it's not very successful in extrapolating lessons that can be used when confronted with unfamiliar data. In other words, the algorithm may have constructed a decision-making matrix that is highly complex (because it explains every single idiosyncrasy of the training data), but it becomes flummoxed when it tries to work in a world that doesn't display those types of idiosyncrasies. Understandably, the people developing machine learning applications seek to avoid overfitting, as it can render their final output useless. However, the various steps that can be taken to avoid overfitting essentially boil down to de-emphasizing low-probability events—which are the very events that we're concerned about when it comes to financial stability.

Data scientists may weed out data that are statistical outliers from the outset (for example, they might decide to exclude information about investment losses in the summer and fall of 2008 because of the atypical crisis environment), or they may decide not to select features within the training data that would encourage a focus on low-probability events. Developers could also tune the model during the training process to penalize it for focusing too much on outliers. These attempts to avoid overfitting might be misinterpreted as a purely technical exercise, but they involve judgments about the importance of low-probability events to the model's output—and those judgments could be colored by a desire to avoid regulation.

Let's say that a large bank wanted to fund more of its investments with borrowed money, which is typically more profitable than funding them with its own cash. Rules limit the amount of borrowed money that banks can use to fund investments, though, and that limitation is expressed as a percentage of "risk-weighted assets" (these rules are known as regulatory capital requirements, and we will return to them in Chapter 5). As a result, a bank with less risky assets needs less of its own money to fund its investments—this creates an incentive for banks to use risk models that downplay the risk associated with their investments. One possible intervention that could be made to downplay risk in a machine learning model is the implementation of an asymmetric cost ratio. This involves tuning the algorithm to penalize some kinds of errors more than others, and it can be used to encourage it to underestimate losses—if the bank's regulatory capital requirements are based partly or wholly on the model's finding, this could be a fruitful avenue for regulatory arbitrage.

Regulation could be implemented that requires developers of machine learning applications for the financial industry to recognize the importance of tail risk in calculating potential financial losses, and constrains their ability to weed or tune out statistical outliers. However, developers will still need data regarding tail events in the first place—and there is, by definition, not much information available about low-probability events. In the absence of real experience with tail events, much of the financial industry's understanding about how investments are likely to perform in unusual circumstances is likely to be informed by conjecture and hypothetical.[23] This type of thinking would be inaccessible to a machine learning algorithm that needs to learn from documented data.

While it will be difficult for a machine learning algorithm to learn from human speculation about future risks, it can learn from other previously untapped sources of data. If these new types of data are better predictors of financial risks, then they should be able to improve risk management overall. However, although there has been significant interest in using new types of data in this context (for example, distilling market sentiment from social media profiles to improve the assessment of market risks),[24] many of the new data types suffer from limitations. First, this data is often unstructured—it's a lot harder for a machine learning algorithm to learn from social media profiles than neat excel spreadsheets that set out historical price information about a particular investment. To get new data types into a form that can be used to train a supervised machine learning algorithm, unsupervised learning can be used to categorize and compress the data, but that will result in an added degree of complexity for the model. Assumptions about the relevance of tail risk will become even more embedded during this process, because the underlying data compression by the unsupervised algorithm is designed to root out and discard statistical outliers from the data pool.[25] Furthermore, even when categorized, these new data types may not be representative.

People often cite IBM's claim, made in 2016, that 90% of all the data in the world was created in the last two years[26]—even if this is an overestimation, there is no doubt that the vast majority of new data have been created since 2009. That time period has been characterized by generally favorable economic conditions that may not have tested financial investments—at least until the start of the COVID-19 pandemic, which could itself be considered an outlier that models try to control for. In short, as Rama Cont warned, there simply may not be enough usable data available to make a machine learning algorithm a good predictor of financial risk. Unfortunately, given the current enthusiasm for applying machine learning to risk management problems, cautions about the insufficiency of data may not be heeded.[27]

## Inscrutable models and automation biases

We have just learned that the machine learning process is not a purely technical exercise. From the selection of the type of machine learning algorithm through the selection and structuring of the training data through tuning and testing the model, decisions by (human) software engineers and data scientists permeate the training process. Each decision that they make is informed by assumptions and judgment calls—particularly about the relative importance of tail events—and will have a significant impact on how the algorithm will ultimately discharge its tasks. For all of its technological sophistication, machine learning therefore remains susceptible to risk modeling failures—yet people might nonetheless be lulled into believing that the sophistication of machine learning will solve all of our risk management problems.

The tendency to defer unquestioningly to the output of computer models (machine learning or otherwise) has been referred to as "automation bias," and it is a mental shortcut that many humans take.[28] Answers generated by computers are perceived as having in-built legitimacy, and so people often accept their accuracy at face value without thinking too hard about how the computer arrived at the answer. As a result, the more "driverless" a risk management model purports to be, the more likely human beings may be to defer to its risk assessment without interrogating its underlying process. This is particularly likely to be true if the model is providing the type of answer that someone wants to hear (like that an investment with a high rate of return is not actually all that risky). And deference to computer models can also have other problematic psychological impacts on humans. For example, humans working alongside a computer model may feel licensed to engage in very risky behavior, if the computer model is expected to be responsible for automating good risk management overall.[29]

Automation biases occur naturally, but they can be exploited intentionally (particularly to deter scrutiny from regulators). Model developers may try to encourage automation biases by selecting the most complex and least explainable forms of machine learning algorithms. After doing so, the developers of a machine learning model could tinker with the data and the algorithm to de-emphasize tail risks, knowing that regulators would be discouraged from questioning the algorithm's automated processes. Financial institutions may even be able to convince regulators that the developers of these extremely complex and sophisticated technologies, rather than the (stereotypically luddite) regulators, should be responsible for determining whether machine learning algorithms' output complies with regulatory requirements.

When model complexity is exploited for the benefit of the model users, that complexity can cause problems for financial stability. What financial stability really needs is some kind of check on automation biases. The Federal Reserve's guidance on the use of models by regulated financial institutions is helpful in this respect, because it sets out standards that require models to be challenged by subject matter experts who were not involved in constructing them.[30] Implementing this kind of safeguard may become increasingly difficult, though, as risk modeling technology moves into areas of data science and computer programming that are outside of the traditional expertise of financial institution employees. When they can't engage with the inner workings of the model, financial experts can only check the model's output to see if it gels with their human experience about how risk should be calculated in a particular context.

Sometimes, this may be enough, as can be seen from an example drawn from the use of machine learning in medicine. A seminal study focused on a machine learning model that had learned that any patient with asthma had a reduced risk of dying from pneumonia. This in fact turned out to be true, but only because asthma was such a dangerous precondition for pneumonia that patients with asthma were treated earlier and better—not because having asthma itself makes pneumonia less harmful.[31] Imagine how dangerous it would have been if doctors had started deferring to the model unquestioningly, and paid *less* attention to asthmatics with pneumonia—fortunately, doctors were able to use their medical knowledge about how lungs work as a check on the machine learning algorithm.

Calculating financial risk is rarely this clear-cut, though, and so financial experts are less likely to be able to detect anomalies in the output of machine learning models. Even if a truly bizarre outcome were identified by a subject matter expert, the technology doesn't currently exist to train a machine learning algorithm not to make the same mistake again in the future. Financial institutions who have invested heavily in developing a machine learning risk management model probably won't want to throw it all away, and so they might try to justify keeping the model by impugning the judgment of their subject matter experts. After all, humans haven't always had a particularly good track record of estimating financial risks (there is an entire academic field of behavioral finance that is devoted to examining why humans make poor decisions about financial risks—particularly tail risks).[32] Indeed, the great promise of machine learning is that it will use new types of data and find patterns that do a better job of explaining the relationships among risk factors than our collective human intuition and experience. These relationships will, by definition, seem counterintuitive.[33] Humans don't see the world in terms of statistical patterns, but instead try to incorporate information into narratives, and so we may reject accurate information about financial risks that is generated by an algorithm if it doesn't fit our preconceived story about how such risks work.

The use of machine learning algorithms therefore puts humans involved in risk management in a very difficult position. The algorithm's conclusions should not be dismissed out of hand just because they are not intuitive, but they also shouldn't be accepted at face value merely because they were generated by a sophisticated machine. It is therefore crucial that financial experts (as well as the boards of financial institutions and financial regulators) be able to interrogate the inner workings of the models, at least to some degree. In recent years, there has been significant interest in finding ways to making machine learning algorithms (which have sometimes been referred to as "black boxes") more "explainable."[34] Supervised algorithms can be restricted to learning about a smaller and therefore more manageable number of features, or a machine learning model can be chosen because it is more intuitive and easier to explain (like random forests of decision trees—although everything is relative, and these models are still complex). Throughout the training process, tuning can also be employed to make a model simpler, and therefore more accessible. The trade-offs for all of these complexity management strategies may be a less predictive model, and missed opportunities for understanding how risks are generated in a genuinely complex environment like the financial system.

There has also been significant interest in finding ways to allow machine learning models to remain complex, but provide accessible explanations after the fact. For example, it is technologically possible to program a machine learning model to provide an explanation of how a particular decision was reached. Interfaces can also be set up to allow users (and regulators) to play with the model by altering variables to see the impact of such changes. Simpler explanatory models have been created to explain more complex underlying models.

If, however, the ultimate goal is not to understand how a particular outcome was reached but instead to understand how the model as a whole works—which is what risk managers and regulators really need in order to understand how all of the many variables are likely to interact in unanticipated circumstances—many of these steps toward "explainability" will provide limited insight. While there may be technological advances in the future that will be genuinely helpful in explaining the internal workings of a machine learning-based risk model,[35] there is always the risk that incremental steps toward "explainability" will counterproductively create a false sense of security that humans actually understand how a model is likely to perform. The Federal Reserve's model guidance recommends that when there is uncertainty about how a model operates, financial institutions should not rely uncritically on the model's output, and should supplement their decision-making with other models or approaches.[36] Given the many obstacles to truly understanding how a machine learning model will make decisions about financial risks, financial institutions should always limit the amount of deference they afford to the model's outputs. Humans must always be kept in the loop in financial decision-making—and the output of machine learning models should always be taken with a grain of salt.

## Increased coordination and correlation

There could be real problems (particularly during tail events) if an algorithm is used to automatically purchase and sell financial assets based on the output of a risk management algorithm. Any individual investor or financial institution that automates their trading like this could lose a lot of money as a result, but this is a book about financial stability, not about how to run a bank or an investment portfolio. Individualized losses, while unfortunate for those involved, are less of a concern from a public policy perspective. However, if poor risk management occurs on such a scale that it could generate negative spillovers for the overall financial system (and ultimately for the broader economy), then financial stability regulators need to be concerned.

Some members of the financial industry have already raised the alarm about systemic risks arising from the mass adoption of artificial intelligence,[37] and regulators should be particularly worried about the aspects of machine learning technology that can coordinate and magnify the impact of risk management errors. Of course, "herd behavior" has always been an issue in finance. Everyday investors become wrapped up in the same exciting stories about why a particular investment will never fail, and then they experience the same panic once those failures seem inevitable.[38] Financial industry professionals tend to follow the crowd when making financial decisions—after all, it's easier to avoid getting fired if you do what everyone else is doing, even if that turns out to be a mistake.[39] The resulting coordinated financial decision-making (otherwise known as herd behavior) is responsible for many of the dynamics that create financial instability—but to be clear, "coordinated" as used here doesn't imply any deliberate or conscious agreement to behave in the same way. I'm talking about the types of collective behavior that can result from many different investors each pursuing their own individual self-interest.

An asset bubble, for example, occurs when multiple investors decide it is in their best interest to keep purchasing a particular type of asset—even when the price is no longer a reasonable approximation of the value of that asset. Investors do this because they believe that so long as the price keeps going up, they can make a profit from selling the asset for more than they purchased it for. Because the price of the asset is a reflection of the collective market opinion about what the price of the asset should be (as manifested in the buying and selling behavior of lots of different investors), if more people are buying the asset, the price will go up, and if more people are selling, the price will go down. As a result, if everyone is buying at the same time, the asset price climbs steeply. The opposite is also true: if investors collectively start to panic and sell at the same time, the price drop will be precipitous. Timing is everything—investors don't want to sell until the price has gone as high as it can go, but once the price starts to drop, investors want to sell as quickly as possible in order to maximize their profit (or, in a worst-case scenario, avoid the losses that will come if the price drops below what an investor initially paid for the asset). That's when the bubble bursts.

Not all asset bubbles make the financial system unstable. When the dotcom bubble burst in the early 2000s, a lot of people lost money, but the financial system as a whole didn't experience a crisis. Bubbles typically become a financial stability problem when lots of investors (especially financial institutions) rely heavily on borrowed money to purchase assets, because then losses incurred on those assets are not just the investor's problem, but potentially a problem for their lenders—and through those lenders, for the broader financial system and economy. Imagine that an investor borrows $10 to buy a $11 bond. If the price of that bond falls to $9, our investor will still have to repay $10, and selling the bond won't raise enough cash to repay the loan. The investor's options are to default on the loan, which will harm their lender, or to find the $1 shortfall somewhere else. One way that the investor can raise that extra $1 is to sell some of their other assets to raise cash to repay the loan.

If we're just talking about one investor, there won't be any systemic consequences from either scenario. However, if you multiply this scenario by a significant number of investors all acting in similar ways, lenders could be seriously compromised by a wave of defaults (particularly if the lenders had also invested directly in the problematic bonds themselves), and wide-scale asset sales could drive down the prices of other kinds of financial assets. If those other financial assets were also purchased with borrowed money, then the cycle will repeat itself with more defaults and panicked asset sales. This is known as a "fire sale externality," and it explains a second channel (in addition to loan defaults) through which individual investment losses can metastasize into a full-blown financial crisis.[40]

The takeaway from all of this is that a crisis is more likely if everyone is behaving in the same way, and as the case studies at the end of this chapter will illustrate, several of the new machine learning business models seem likely to make herd behavior much worse. Not only are machine learning business models likely to reduce the number of decision-makers, machine learning technology is also likely to standardize risk assessment among the remaining decision-makers. The limited data available for training financial risk management algorithms won't just make those algorithms less accurate, it will also make their operation more consistent when applied to similar assets. And herd behavior will become even worse if multiple financial institutions are relying on the exact same prepackaged data set, or the exact same pre-trained algorithm provided by a third-party vendor (only a few financial institutions have the resources and desire to develop machine learning algorithms entirely in-house; if they rely instead on the relatively small group of third-party vendors and experts able to set them up, there will be a lot of consistency in the choice of the type of machine learning algorithm and the training, testing, and tuning strategies used).

If machine learning algorithms consistently underestimate the risks associated with a particular type of asset, making it seem like a great deal for the price, they could contribute to a bubble in that asset class. If those same algorithms subsequently determine that the risks of an asset type have increased to the point where the asset is overpriced, then a significant sell-off will be triggered (it's not an exact precedent, but the 1987 stock market crash has been partially blamed on firms delegating their risk management decisions to computer models that were both homogenous and poorly understood).[41] This bubble-bust dynamic would be particularly acute if the algorithms were not trained to notice the initial stages of disenchantment with an asset and factor those into their risk assessments. Algorithms would then continue to recommend buying as usual, without adjusting for stressed market conditions, until conditions become so fraught as to trigger a panicked sell-off—either because the algorithm changes its risk assessment, or because investors collectively begin to distrust the algorithm and abandon its recommendations.

To help understand the potential impact of a few similarly trained machine learning algorithms making decisions about similar assets on behalf of vast numbers of investors, we can think back to the role that credit ratings played in the financial crisis of 2008.[42] Credit ratings are an assessment of the credit risk that an investor faces with respect to a debt instrument (like a bond) issued by a corporation or government. The market for credit rating agencies is extremely concentrated, with Standard & Poor's, Moody's, and Fitch being the only ones of any significance. In the years leading up to 2008, Standard & Poor's and Moody's in particular developed a lucrative business line in issuing credit ratings for the mortgage-backed securities we met in Chapter 1, as well as other financial products built on them, like CDOs and synthetic CDOs. Investors in trillions of dollars' worth of these securities more or less delegated their credit risk assessment to the two credit rating agencies, and so when each of those agencies started downgrading their ratings *en masse* in 2007 and 2008 (after determining that their methodologies for assessing credit risk had been significantly flawed), those downgrades had widespread ramifications that helped spark the 2008 crisis.[43]

Standard & Poor's and Moody's role in coordinating credit risk assessment in the lead-up to the 2008 crisis suggests that we should be very wary of the financial industry collectively relying on risk assessments coming from a few machine learning algorithms. (As an aside, Standard & Poor's recently made an aggressive move into the machine learning space. In 2018, it purchased the artificial intelligence startup Kensho Technologies for $550 million—at the time, it was the most expensive artificial intelligence acquisition ever.[44] Following this acquisition, we can reasonably expect that machine learning algorithms capable of classification will be used to help assign Standard and Poor's credit ratings. This is an avenue for machine learning to have an even greater impact on financial decision-making.)

To sum up, there will be problems if more and more investment decisions are made in the same way. There will be greater problems if those investments decisions are consistently wrong, and we have already explored a number of reasons to worry about the ability of machine learning models to assess the financial risks associated with tail events. There is also one more limitation on machine learning models' accuracy that becomes clear when we think about the potential scale of these models' impact. If investments are increasingly channeled toward just a few large asset classes (as a result of instructions from the same or similar algorithms), then it will become increasingly likely that a problem with one large asset class will impact how investors feel about the remaining large asset classes.[45] This type of risk cannot be diversified away, leaving investment portfolios more susceptible to a shock to the financial markets. However, algorithms that have learned from historical data will not perceive how the impact of their own recommendations will undermine diversification as a strategy for managing risk within a portfolio of investments.

So far, this chapter has been long on predictions of how risk management applications of machine learning might harm financial stability, and short on details of how machine learning is currently being used in the financial industry. A recent survey of the financial industry's use of artificial intelligence found that fully automated financial decision-making—with human input largely eliminated—is still a ways off.[46] This is good news, because it means that there is still time for precautionary regulation to have a meaningful impact on how the risk management applications of machine learning develop. However, progress is already being made toward this automated financial future, which means that opportunities for regulatory intervention are narrowing. The remainder of this chapter will provide a snapshot of the current state of technology in the form of several case studies: it will look at the use of machine learning in the robo-investing industry and in BlackRock's Aladdin platform, before concluding with a brief look at the increasing interest in insurtech.

## Robo-investing

The term "robo-advising" is used to describe any automated service that provides advice about financial products. Robo-advising is available for banking and insurance products, but it is best known for providing advice about investing in securities like stocks and bonds. Often referred to as "robo-investing," these services can profile a customer to determine their risk tolerance and goals, and based on that assessment, recommend a diversified portfolio of investments. They can also provide advice on rebalancing portfolios when market risks change, or when the customer's circumstances change. Some robo-investing services combine this advice with trade execution services, automating purchases and sales of investments for their customers.[47]

As with many of the fintech businesses discussed in this book, increased efficiency is the key driver of the robo-investing business model. Robo-investing services aim to replicate the advice a client would get from a human financial planner, but they can provide it at a much lower cost because of economies of scale (an algorithm can service many more customers than a single human being ever could). Robo-investing can also be a tool for promoting financial inclusion, because people who only have a small amount to invest and couldn't ordinarily afford a financial planner might be able to afford recommendations from a robo-investing service. Some people are also cautiously optimistic that robo-investing will eliminate some of the conflicts of interest that are rife within a financial planning industry that relies heavily on commissions from the issuers of investment products.

There is a lot of variation in the level of human involvement in the different robo-investing business models available right now. In some models, the customer will continue to interact primarily with a human adviser, but that human adviser will rely upon an algorithm to improve the quality of the services they provide. These business models are not very different from more traditional relationships between financial planners and clients, and perhaps shouldn't be called "robo-investing" at all. At the other extreme, some interfaces are entirely automated, where the algorithm provides all of the advice and services and the customer has no interaction with any human—Wealthfront, for example, is highly automated. Providers like Betterment strike a middle ground by offering an automated interface with the option of receiving additional advice from human finance professionals. The underlying investment decisions remain the primary responsibility of the algorithms, though: it would be cost-prohibitive for low-fee robo-investing models to keep a human permanently in the loop to check any bizarre recommendations generated by their algorithms.

Not all robo-investing services rely on machine learning technology: some business models rely exclusively on more traditional algorithms that are programmed with instructions on how to construct an investment portfolio. However, a recent survey found that of all the financial sectors, the investment management industry is most aggressively embracing artificial intelligence, particularly in terms of relying on new types of data sets (drawn from the news and social media, among other things).[48] Many robo-investing services are increasingly turning to machine learning technologies to collect information about clients' financial circumstances (to determine risk tolerance) and improve portfolio selection and monitoring (to better maximize return).[49] Where machine learning is incorporated into robo-investing services, regulators should be mindful of all of the concerns we have raised about programming errors and incomplete data sets. On a typical day, a robo-adviser's recommendations are likely to be as good if not better than those of a human adviser, but we should be seriously concerned about the underestimation of market and credit risks during tail events.

Some people hear about companies like Betterment and Wealthfront, and dismiss any risks that robo-investing could pose to financial stability. After all, in 2020, Betterment and Wealthfront each had only around $20 billion worth of assets under management.[50] That is a drop in the bucket when compared with asset managers like Vanguard, Charles Schwab, and BlackRock, which respectively reported $6.2 trillion,[51] $4.1 trillion,[52] and $7.4 trillion[53] of assets under management in 2020. But as this book has made clear from the beginning, fintech innovation is not restricted to start-ups. Schwab and Vanguard, for example, have already started their own robo-investing services, which had $40.7 billion and $161 billion worth of assets under management in 2020.[54] If this trajectory continues and machine learning is increasingly adopted by established asset managers, the technology will have a real impact on financial markets.

The economies of scale that make financial advice cheaper for investors also allow algorithms to influence the behavior of far larger groups than would be possible for a single human financial adviser. Robo-investing algorithms start by classifying investors into types based on risk tolerance and investment objectives, and then constructing portfolios for each type. In 2016, a survey by FINRA of US robo-investing platforms found that most of them had between five and eight possible investor profiles.[55] Obviously, such an approach will coordinate investor behavior more than if individualized portfolios were constructed for each client. In the future, machine learning technology will probably allow for greater numbers of investor classifications based on more granular information about the investors, but the number of possible classifications will still be restricted by the number of available data points that can be used to distinguish each investor from one another.

Most robo-investing services start their relationship with the investor with an online questionnaire that is used to assess the investor's financial situation and risk tolerance, and the investor classification is typically based entirely on the investor's responses to the questions posed. Trying to obtain more data points about investors in order to create more investor classifications, or to keep an eye on an investor's classification as their financial circumstances change over time, would require the use of unstructured data like social media postings. Unsupervised algorithms can be used to turn this type of data into a digestible format for other machine learning algorithms to use, but this would be very expensive for the robo-investing service to pursue (and as we've already discussed, using unsupervised algorithms to structure data sets poses its own risks for financial stability).

If each robo-investing platform only has a limited number of investor classifications, and relies on algorithms that behave in similar ways to those used by the other platforms, then investment behavior will become much more monolithic. Competitive pressures from these lower-cost models may also drive human financial advisers out of the market, further expanding the influence of the algorithms. As a result, asset bubbles could become more prevalent, and their busts more abrupt—particularly if robo-investing services are programmed to automatically rebalance portfolios to conform with their investment recommendations. Financial stability regulators should therefore pay close attention to the burgeoning robo-investing industry—both the fintech start-ups, and the more established players.

## BlackRock and Aladdin

For evidence that established financial industry players are aggressively experimenting with machine learning for their risk management operations and services, we need look no further than Aladdin, BlackRock's risk management and portfolio construction platform. Aladdin itself is not new—development started in the early 1990s, and some types of portfolio rebalancing were able to be automated by the mid-1990s. Aladdin has become increasingly sophisticated over time, though, and BlackRock is now aggressively exploring how data science and machine learning might be used to improve its services. Given the size of BlackRock's assets under management, the use of these technologies could have a sizeable impact even if BlackRock were the only firm using Aladdin. However, Aladdin has a much bigger footprint because BlackRock is also a vendor: more than 200 institutions (including big names like HSBC) rely on the analysis that Aladdin provides.[56] BlackRock has said that Aladdin creates and reviews "over 1 million daily risk and exposure reports on portfolios,"[57] and operates in more than 65 countries.[58] One estimate from 2018 found that Aladdin had an impact on the management of $20 trillion worth of assets—roughly 10% of all the assets in the world.[59]

BlackRock has largely avoided financial stability regulation—because it doesn't owe any fixed amounts to its customers, regulators haven't been all that worried that a run could drive it into insolvency. However, the sheer scope of Aladdin's influence has raised some concerns about its potential impact on financial stability. A 2013 article in *The Economist* magazine noted that "it's unprecedented to have a single firm that has such a grip on the way that not only itself, but its rivals, look at the world."[60] Jody Kochansky, the head of the Aladdin Product Group, dismissed those concerns, observing that for each Aladdin client, "it's all their own data, running on separate computers, separate databases. They dial the models based on their views of the markets, their views of risk. Aladdin doesn't dictate to them how to run their business."[61] This defense is not entirely convincing, though. Even if the underlying data is different (and as we've already discussed, there may not be much variation because there is often limited data to draw from when assessing financial risks), if the machine learning algorithm calculating the risks associated with that data has learned the same or similar decision-making rules as the machine learning algorithms used by many other financial firms, that could nevertheless coordinate investment behavior.

In 2018, BlackRock established an AI Labs division, which hired more than 30 data scientists and data engineers in its first year. That same year, Kochansky wrote a blog post stressing the potential for artificial intelligence to improve risk management, noting that opportunities for innovation have exploded in the past few years as a result of "unprecedented access to masses of data and improved computing power—the two ingredients necessary for AI to scale."[62] Aladdin has already significantly coordinated the way that market and credit risks are assessed; as Aladdin increasingly relies on machine learning, the limitations and unpredictability of this technology will certainly apply on a global scale. BlackRock and its clients could possibly fail as a result of mismanaging their own risk exposures, but financial stability can be harmed even if they *don't* fail. If Aladdin perpetuates destructive market activity like widespread fire sales of financial assets, then the broader economy will probably suffer.

## Machine learning and insurance

Insurance is often left out of conversations about both fintech and financial stability, but AIG's failure during the last financial crisis revealed that insurance firms can threaten financial stability, and there is a vibrant insurtech industry thinking of ways to apply machine learning technologies to the delivery of insurance services. This chapter will therefore conclude with a brief consideration of insurtech's financial stability risks—after all, insurance is a crucial risk management service for many businesses and consumers.

Insurance works by taking in policy payments from a pool of insured people or businesses, then paying funds out if an insured event (such as a person's death, in the case of a life insurance policy) befalls one of them.

Insurers calculate the required policy payments based on the risks associated with the individual insured, as well as the risks associated with the entire pool of insureds. Insurers are also required by law to maintain minimum amounts of capital in order to ensure that they are able to pay out upon the occurrence of insured events. The amount of capital required is a function of the risks the insurer faces.

Risk assessment is therefore central to the insurance business model, and machine learning is increasingly being used as part of the policy underwriting and pricing process.[63] The use of machine learning to assist with calculating capital reserves is pretty nascent, but there are academics and start-ups actively exploring potential applications.[64] While the use of machine learning is likely to improve the accuracy of risk assessment most of the time, just as with the asset management industry already discussed, the impact of tail events is likely to be underestimated (in the case of insurance, tail events often take the form of unexpected catastrophes, like extreme weather events or pandemics). This underestimation of risk can have consequences for the insurers themselves, as well as for the broader financial system.

Insurance firms are thought to be a lot less fragile than banks because they are less susceptible to the risk of runs. Unlike depositors, most insureds can't demand payments from their insurer at will—instead, they have to wait for an insured event to occur. However, we shouldn't completely discount the possibility of run risk for insurers, because many life insurance and annuity products do allow investors to cash out early.[65] Even in the absence of run risk, though, an insurer can fail if it underestimates the risk of insured events to such a degree that it doesn't have enough reserves to satisfy all of its payment obligations to its policyholders. If an entire segment of the insurance industry were to rely on one machine learning algorithm (or a few machine learning algorithms that learned from highly similar data sets and therefore operated with very similar decision-making rules), then an underestimated risk could cause many insurers to fail together, ultimately destabilizing an industry on which the broader economy relies. As securitization of life insurance policies and annuities becomes more common,[66] the broader financial system could also be harmed if algorithms used for underwriting and pricing insurance policies underestimate the risks involved in issuing a policy, and then the underpriced policies are securitized and sold to investors.

Insurance firms are also important investors themselves. They do not keep the premium payments they receive under their proverbial mattresses—instead, they invest them in other financial assets, and the amount of money involved is so significant that their investment decisions can have implications for the financial system as a whole. Insurance firms' investment decisions already tend to be reasonably correlated,[67] and reliance on machine learning for managing their portfolios will probably make their investment behavior more uniform. If one or more machine learning models lead the insurance industry to consistently underestimate the risk of an insured event occurring, and if that event does occur, it could result in a coordinated fire sale of investments by the insurers in order to raise cash to make the necessary payments to their insureds. As this chapter has already explained, these asset fire sales can depress asset prices and inspire further asset selloffs, sending the broader financial system into a tailspin.

Insurance firms therefore have the potential to harm the stability of the financial system with poor risk management, even if they remain solvent. However, critiques of insurtech applications of machine learning so far have focused almost exclusively on the potential for consumer harm, neglecting financial stability issues.[68] While insurtech start-ups currently operate on a relatively small scale, incumbent insurers with a much larger footprint are also eyeing insurtech innovations.[69] The incorporation of machine learning into the underwriting and reserving processes of large insurers would dramatically expand the potential for the technology to impact the stability of our financial system.

* * *

Incorporating machine learning into risk management functions could be a boon for efficiency. Banks and asset managers could lower the costs associated with monitoring the risks of investment portfolios, and some of these lowered costs could be passed on to consumers. Insurance firms could similarly improve efficiency in pricing insurance policies. However, gains in efficiency should be regarded skeptically if they come at the price of a less stable financial system. This chapter has demonstrated that the large-scale automation of financial decision-making could exacerbate complexity and coordination within the financial system, compounding the impact of any risk assessment errors made by the technology. There are therefore reasons to be concerned about fintech's future impact on the financial system's risk management function. The next chapter will consider the impact of fintech innovation on a different function of the financial system—capital intermediation.

# 3

# Fintech and Capital Intermediation

There's a lot of buzz about fintech innovations that offer new, quick, and cheap ways of trading financial assets. There's also a lot of buzz about new ways of making loans to people who used to struggle to get credit. All of these activities (and more) can be described as "capital intermediation." "Capital" is a slippery term that can have several different meanings. In the previous chapter, we touched on regulatory capital requirements, which are rules that require banks to fund their investments with a minimum amount of their own (that is, not borrowed) money. Capital means something entirely different when we talk about "capital intermediation," though. Here, capital really just means "funds"—funds that some people have and want to profit from, and funds that other people need and are willing to pay for.

This chapter will consider the ways in which fintech innovations are changing how the financial system gets funds from investors to users. Importantly, despite a lot of hype to the contrary, this chapter will show that fintech is not necessarily "disintermediating" the financial system—intermediaries have been displaced by a few fintech business models, but the chains of intermediaries involved in getting funds from investors to users are becoming longer and more complicated as a result of other fintech business models.

## Capital intermediation basics

The financial system helps intermediate capital by providing ways to aggregate funds from multiple investors, and by helping investors select and then monitor the performance of their investments.[1] These functions are often performed by financial institutions that sit between the people who have the capital, and the people who need the capital. The most familiar financial institution is a bank: for hundreds of years, banks have intermediated capital by taking deposits and then using those deposits to make loans. In recent decades, the banking business model has become more sophisticated, with

*Driverless Finance*. Hilary J. Allen, Oxford University Press. © Hilary J. Allen 2022.
DOI: 10.1093/oso/9780197626801.003.0004

banks increasingly relying on other (non-deposit) types of funding and using those funds to make many different types of investments. At the same time, non-banks have also become increasingly crucial to capital intermediation. Investment funds, ranging from the simplest money market mutual funds all the way up to highly sophisticated hedge funds, are particularly important intermediaries of capital. These funds accept capital from investors and then use that capital to buy portfolios of investments that the funds select, monitor, and rebalance.

Because financial institutions are relied upon so heavily for capital intermediation, financial stability regulation pays a lot of attention to them (banks have received by far the most scrutiny, for reasons that we will explore shortly). Financial stability regulation has paid less attention to the importance of financial *markets* to capital intermediation, though. Unfortunately, as this chapter will explore, markets for stocks, bonds, derivatives, and other financial assets can both generate and transmit shocks that can compromise the whole financial system. As a result, existing financial stability regulation is already lacking when it comes to financial markets, and it will become even more deficient as new technologies make the operations of financial markets speedier, and increasingly complex.

Increased speed and complexity are a feature of many fintech innovations, not a bug. These innovations were designed to increase the efficiency of capital intermediation, allowing those that need capital to obtain it more quickly, more cheaply, and in more customized ways than ever before—these innovations are also allowing investors to profit in new ways. We should judge innovations by their overall impact on society, though, not purely by their appeal to investors and users of funds, or else we will ignore the costs of financial activity that end up being borne by other, unrelated people. Using the marketplace lending, high frequency trading, and cryptoasset business models as examples, this chapter will highlight some threats that fintech poses for capital intermediation—and if capital intermediation breaks down, that can be bad news for everyone who participates in our economy.

We will pay particular attention to cryptoassets in this chapter, because these have the potential to exponentially increase the amount of risk in the financial system—if cryptoassets were to be widely integrated into our financial institutions and markets, they would pose perhaps the greatest threat of all the innovations considered in this book. First, though, we will explore some background on how financial institutions and markets help intermediate capital, and highlight some of the fragilities that existed in those capital intermediation processes well before the rise of fintech. We will then be in a position to consider where fintech innovations could help address these fragilities, and where such innovations are likely to make them worse.

## Banks and bank runs

To help us understand the financial stability risks associated with capital intermediation, we will start with the prototypical financial institutions—banks.[2] In the classic bank business model, banks convert deposits into loans, and by doing so, they provide credit that the economy needs to grow. Banks also help the economy grow by providing payment services that allow people to transact, as well as forming a key part of the "transmission belt" for central banks' monetary policy (monetary policy is a complicated topic, but the short version is that central banks increase or decrease the supply of money to match the needs of the economy, and because such a large part of that supply takes the form of bank deposits, an unstable banking system jeopardizes central banks' ability to adjust the money supply).

Financial stability regulation focuses on banks because of the importance of these functions, and also because of banks' inherent fragility. The classic bank business model involves funding long term loans (for example, thirty-year mortgages) with deposits that can be withdrawn from the bank at will. The economics of this business model make sense for banks because depositors, who can always demand their funds back, are willing to accept a very low interest rate from their bank. Banks can then turn around and charge much more interest on the long-term loans that they extend, profiting from the difference between the interest they charge and the interest they pay. This banking business model is also useful to society, because it allows deposit funds to be deployed for long-term economic growth, rather than just sitting under a mattress. However, this business model means that banks only ever have a fraction of the cash deposited with them available to return to depositors at any given time.

Most of the time this is not a problem, because depositors are usually content to leave most of their money in the bank, ensuring a reasonably reliable source of funding for the bank's loans and other investments. However, if depositors start to doubt their bank, they may rush to withdraw their deposits, believing that if they don't hurry, other depositors will beat them to it and exhaust the supply of available funds. If this happens, the bank really will be short of cash following the unexpected withdrawals, and may need to start selling its assets at a discount in order to keep up with subsequent withdrawal requests. If the value of the bank's total assets after these sales is less than the bank's total liabilities, then it will fail.

This self-fulfilling prophecy is called a bank run, and the associated panic and uncertainty can jump from bank to bank, jeopardizing the entire banking system.[3] Banking panics occurred repeatedly in the United States in the late nineteenth and early twentieth centuries, but they were largely eliminated by the introduction of government-backed deposit insurance in 1933.[4] The knowledge that the government will pay depositors back if their bank can't has inspired such confidence that even during the financial crisis of 2008, there was no widespread banking panic in the United States.

Fast forward to now. Despite technological improvements in recent decades, many of the basics of the banking business remain the same. Some people might worry that the latest generation of mobile banking apps will bring back bank runs, because it's now so easy to transfer funds at a touch of a button,[5] but mobile banking apps don't really change that much. You can't withdraw cash from your phone (you still need to go to a bank branch or an ATM for that), so the best that a mobile banking app can do is an electronic transfer of funds from the bank to some other account. These types of electronic transfers have been available for decades, and while mobile banking apps might make such transfers quicker and easier or allow for transfers of larger amounts, the availability of deposit insurance will probably continue to reassure depositors that their funds are protected—and that such transfers are therefore unnecessary.

## Shadow banking

Even though it doesn't seem likely that mobile banking will revive runs on banks, runs can still impact other types of important financial intermediaries—intermediaries that are not protected by deposit insurance. Regulators have traditionally been less concerned about panics at non-banks, though, because non-banks tend to have features that help insulate them from pressures to sell their assets quickly. If a financial institution (like an investment fund) doesn't owe any fixed amount to its investors, then the institution is contractually permitted to provide investors with less money than they expect, and therefore faces less pressure to quickly liquidate assets for its investors. In business models where the investors *are* entitled to a fixed amount, but can't just demand it whenever they want (as is the case with many insurance policies), then the institution will have time to liquidate assets in an orderly fashion to meet its liabilities. These characteristics make it less likely that a financial institution will suffer insolvency as a result of discounted asset sales.

Unfortunately, although these features go some way toward making certain types of financial institutions less fragile than banks, they do not guarantee financial stability. A non-bank financial institution that loses its regular funding sources during a panic may be able to remain solvent, but its ability to provide capital intermediation services will probably still be compromised (we'll explore this possibility in more detail in our case studies). If the broader economy relies on that institution for capital intermediation services and there are no good substitutes, then financial stability regulators need to worry about panics that could cause that institution to lose access to funding—but if future panics and their impacts are idiosyncratic to new and untested fintech business models, financial stability regulators might not anticipate them. We can, however, look at past examples of non-bank runs, such as the 2008 run on money market mutual funds, for some clues as to how future panics might play out.

Investors in money market mutual funds purchase shares in those funds with the expectation that the shares will always be valued at one dollar. The true value of each share fluctuates, depending on the assets that the fund has invested in, but a special accounting regime allows each share to be consistently valued at one dollar so long as its true value never deviates too far from the dollar price. If the value of a share in the fund drops too far, though, then the fund will have to revalue its shares below one dollar (which is known as "breaking the buck"). In September 2008, a money market mutual fund with exposure to Lehman Brothers broke the buck, and that event caused many investors in other money market mutual funds to panic.

The panicked investors wanted to redeem their money market mutual fund shares as quickly as possible. They feared that if they waited too long, their fund would have already sold its best assets to satisfy other investors' redemption requests, leaving them less likely to receive one dollar per share. Of course, everyone would have been better off if none of the investors redeemed their shares, because then the fund wouldn't have been forced to start liquidating its investments. However, because the investors didn't trust each other to act in the collective best interest, they rushed to sell before the other investors and the runs became a self-fulfilling prophecy.[6]

Before the 2008 crisis hit, money market mutual funds' investments in the commercial paper market were an important source of funding for large corporations, but during the run, these funds stopped buying commercial paper. The Federal Reserve ultimately intervened with temporary guarantees designed to inspire confidence in the funds and slow down redemption requests.[7] In short, even though money market mutual funds have every contractual right to provide their investors with less than a dollar per share, the fear that funds would not live up to investor expectations was enough to cause a panic that prevented money market mutual funds from discharging their typical capital intermediation function, threatening the corporations that relied on commercial paper. Emergency intervention from the central bank was needed to get capital flowing again.

This experience suggests that even if fintechs aren't as vulnerable as banks to run-precipitated insolvency, panics may still compromise their ability to perform their capital intermediation functions. It also demonstrates that speed is an exacerbating factor for any run: the quicker the requests for cash come in, the quicker asset sales must take place, which increases the likelihood that those assets will have to be sold at discounted prices. New technological innovations that speed up the ability of investors to cash out can therefore exacerbate runs, and this dynamic may reach its nadir if asset sales become fully automated.

To highlight just one possibility we are already a little familiar with, many investment portfolios include money market mutual funds as a low-risk place to store cash until a more attractive investment opportunity arises. If a widely used robo-investing service were to invest numerous customers' capital in money market mutual funds, and then abruptly withdraw all of that capital by way of simultaneous automated transactions, the affected funds would have to start liquidating investments rapidly, harming others (like the corporations in the commercial paper market) that depend on those funds' investments.

Since 2008, it has become widely acknowledged that a purely bank-centric approach to financial stability regulation is inadequate.[8] Other types of institutions clearly perform capital intermediation functions that are vital to the economy, and they each have their own fragilities. More than a decade after the crisis of 2008, though, there is still a lot of confusion and uncertainty about how financial stability regulation should treat financial institutions that aren't banks. Non-bank financial institutions that perform similar functions to banks are often referred to as "shadow banks," but trying to determine precisely what does and doesn't count as shadow banking is very controversial—and can be a distraction. If our ultimate goal is broader economic growth, we can ignore this classification issue and simply ask ourselves whether broad-based economic growth depends on a particular type of financial institution. If so, we should ask ourselves what its vulnerabilities are, and how they might be addressed.

One response to the 2008 financial crisis was to intensify regulatory scrutiny of the very biggest financial institutions—the ones considered so important to economic growth that national governments would rather bail them out than let them fail.[9] Stricter regulations were implemented for the largest banks, and new regulatory reforms were also implemented for "too big to fail" non-banks in light of the lessons learned about the threats that they posed for financial stability. This was a good start, but the largest banks and non-bank financial institutions should not be the only focus of financial stability regulation. Smaller institutions can also harm the broader economy, especially if a lot of them behave in similar ways, fill a specialized niche role, or are connected through contracts to other financial firms (particularly those that *are* "too big to fail").[10]

Unfortunately, the focus on the largest financial firms often eclipses consideration of smaller firms, and this is a serious problem when it comes to fintech: most of the firms we call "fintechs" are relatively small, and have even been described as "too small to care."[11] This book has already explored some of the dangers in underestimating fintech as a niche phenomenon, but even putting to one side the fact that fintech innovations are increasingly being adopted by the largest financial institutions, smaller fintechs could still impact financial stability. We should be concerned about the potential breakdowns in capital intermediation that could occur if many small fintechs act in the same way, if there are no substitutes for the services they provide, or if they are contractually connected with large financial institutions. Later in this chapter, we will use marketplace lending platforms as a case study to illustrate how a breakdown in capital intermediation by smaller fintech firms could potentially cause problems for our broader economy. Before we do that, though, we're going to explore how vulnerabilities in the financial markets—not just in financial institutions—can disturb capital intermediation.

## Markets and financial stability

At its most basic, a financial market is any place where buyers and sellers can meet (either physically or electronically) to trade a financial asset (including stocks, bonds, commodities, currencies, derivatives, and cryptoassets). If an asset market becomes so compromised that no trading can be done, then that market can't perform its socially useful function of connecting those who want to invest with those who need funding. If a disruption in an asset market could impact broader economic growth, then that asset market is worthy of financial stability regulators' attention.

Now that most trading is done electronically, a financial asset market could be shut down by a technological glitch (financial stability problems caused by glitches will be discussed in more detail in Chapter 4). Even if a market is still technically able to function, though, it won't be able to intermediate capital if no one is willing to trade. Remember that the financial system helps intermediate capital by allowing investors to choose and monitor their investments—markets produce the information on which most investment decisions are based, and that information often takes the form of a price. If something goes haywire in the markets so that prices no longer seem remotely reasonable, there will not be much information available to judge those assets and buyers and sellers are likely to pull out of the market.[12] If this happens on a large enough scale, the market will not succeed in matching those who want to invest with those who need funding—even if the market can technically still process trades. We call this an absence of liquidity, and in an illiquid market where people struggle to sell their assets, prices will be distorted further as sellers who cannot wait are forced to sell at a steep discount.

Prices can also be distorted in the opposite direction, as we saw with GameStop stock in late January 2021. In the space of a few days, GameStop's stock price rose from $76.79 to $347.51, for no obvious reason other than that there was a lot of hype about the stock on social media. There were plenty of buyers in the market for GameStop stock during this period; here, it was the short sellers who couldn't wait, and were forced to close out of their short positions with steep losses (when you short a stock, you sell stock you don't own yet, and you can lose an unlimited amount if the stock price goes up because you will need to repay the difference between the price at the time you sold and the price at the time you close your trade). It can be hard to sympathize with these short sellers—after all, they're betting that the price of a financial asset will go down, and rooting for failure isn't very appealing. However, short sellers play an important role in making sure prices don't get too distorted. They are the only ones who can push the price of an asset down (other than investors who already own an asset and then decide to sell it). In a market without short sellers, the deck is stacked in favor of optimistic buyers and the price can go up and up and up.

One of the most unnerving things about the GameStop episode was that it suggested that trading is becoming more of a game and that financial assets are becoming increasingly detached from reality—a theme we'll come back to in the context of cryptoassets. Even in a distorted reality, though, asset bubbles can't last forever. At some point, bubbles inevitably burst as existing investors lose faith, and that burst is sometimes an overcorrection that drives prices too far down: once again, sellers who can't afford to wait are forced to sell at a steep discount.

The vicious cycle doesn't always end there. If the price of financial assets is driven down far enough, people may start to worry about the financial condition of institutions that have invested heavily in those assets. If the affected institutions face runs or other pressures to sell assets as a result, they may ultimately choose to sell assets that are different from the impaired ones. These fire sales can put downward pressure on the price of assets in *other* markets, spreading the panic, and potentially requiring still more institutions to sell more assets in different markets.[13] In short, even if financial institutions are able to remain solvent amid fire sales, or are not systemically important (in the sense that their failure wouldn't leave a hole in the financial system's ability to intermediate capital), their sales can still undermine financial stability and broader economic growth by undermining markets for important financial assets.

Despite these potential dangers, financial markets do not always receive the attention that they deserve from financial stability regulators. Key pieces of market infrastructure like exchanges and clearinghouses are reasonably heavily regulated,[14] but most market regulation has a lighter touch. Following Louis Brandeis's admonition that "sunlight is said to be the best of disinfectants; electric light the most efficient policeman,"[15] rules have been adopted that require participants in financial markets—ranging from the institutions that create financial assets in the first place to the intermediaries like brokers and exchanges that have evolved to facilitate the trading process—to release information to other market participants, as well as to regulators. These disclosure rules help capital intermediation because they allow investors to assess and evaluate potential investments. They can also protect investors by exposing fraud and conflicts of interest, and these protections inspire confidence that encourages investors to participate in the markets, further aiding capital intermediation. However, rules requiring public disclosures often do little to help financial stability.

In theory, market participants armed with the disclosed information could use market mechanisms (such as shorting, or refusing to extend loans) to discipline other market participants who are taking on too much risk or otherwise threatening financial stability. In practice, this kind of market discipline has a pretty poor track record of protecting financial stability.[16] Because financial system failure typically results from the *collective* impact of many different actions, it is very difficult to draw a straight line from action A to financial crisis B, and so we shouldn't expect that market participants will always be able to identify those who need to be disciplined (especially because publicly available information does not give a complete picture of all of the players in the market and their interactions). Even when market participants are able to identify destabilizing behavior, they tend to lack the incentives to do anything about it—at least, not until things get really bad, by which time any market discipline will probably take a destabilizing form (like a fire sale or a run).

If we're concerned with financial stability, the most important disclosure rules are the ones that compel market participants to provide information (including confidential information) to their regulators. With this information, regulators can begin to piece together a picture of how the market as a whole is operating; in extreme circumstances, the picture that emerges may warrant intervention (such as deploying circuit breakers or other temporary restrictions on trading activity) to maintain market stability. However, regulators' ability to understand market operations and determine when intervention is necessary will be challenged by the increasing prominence of technologically driven trading strategies, and new technology-based asset classes. To illustrate the new types of threats to stability that financial market regulators will have to contend with, we will soon look at two case studies: high frequency trading, and cryptoassets. Our first case study, however, will focus on a new type of financial *institution*—the marketplace lending platform—and its potential impact on the financial markets.

## Marketplace lending

Fintech often claims to be "disrupting" the existing market for financial services by getting rid of financial intermediaries. If this claim were true, it could potentially resolve some of the fragilities we've already discussed that arise when intermediaries are relied upon to transform capital. However, this "disruptive disintermediation" narrative is overstated.[17] In some business models, fintech innovation involves simply substituting new intermediaries for old ones, or layering new types of intermediaries over more established ones (and the interconnections between the new and the more established intermediaries may create unappreciated channels for transmitting risk through the financial system). The marketplace lending business model demonstrates this dynamic: instead of eliminating intermediaries, this business model keeps banks and institutional investors involved in lending and then simply inserts another institution (the marketplace lending platform) into the middle.

New fintech lending platforms first started to appear after the 2008 financial crisis, when they took the form of social media-like "peer-to-peer" programs that would match nontraditional borrowers with nontraditional lenders who liked the borrowers' pitches. This peer-to-peer business model had the potential to get intermediaries out of lending, but it has largely fallen by the wayside.[18] Instead, the marketplace lending model is now the dominant form of fintech lending, and this business model has intermediaries aplenty.

Marketplace lending platforms like Prosper and LendingClub allow a prospective borrower to request a loan using a secure online application form. Algorithms are used to assess the borrower, and then the platform will solicit potential investors (usually large institutional investors like asset managers or pension plans) to fund the loan.[19] The loan won't be extended by the marketplace lending platform, though, or by the investors—at least not at first. Instead, the loan will be made by a bank, then the bank will sell the loan to the marketplace lending platform, and the platform will then sell notes to the investors that promise payments of principal and interest as the borrowers repay their loans. Increasingly, those notes are being securitized, which means that they are being pooled and then other investors (again, usually large institutional investors) are purchasing notes backed by a pool of the first round of notes. To complicate things further, there is new interest in using machine learning algorithms to select the notes to be securitized.[20]

Because of these added layers of intermediation, problems stemming from the activities of the platform could potentially be transmitted to the more established financial institutions. Admittedly, the marketplace lending model seems unlikely to create any new problems for the banks who originate the marketplace loans: because these banks sell the loans to the lending platforms pretty quickly, bank funds are not tied up long-term, which eliminates most of the bank run risk associated with the marketplace loans. The marketplace lending platforms themselves could be more vulnerable, though, and the impacts of their lending decisions could reverberate for the institutional investors—and for the financial markets more broadly.

Ultimately, the extent to which the activities of marketplace lending platforms could threaten financial stability and the broader economy will depend on how big the marketplace lending industry grows. While marketplace lending accounted for only 1% of the total consumer and small-business loan market in 2017,[21] a survey of institutional investors conducted that same year found that "the potential for future adoption is still vast" and that a majority of the investors "believe that marketplace lending will be a significant player in the financial system in the next 10 years."[22] The fact that marketplace loans performed better than expected during the COVID-19 pandemic may increase their popularity with institutional investors; the fact that these loans pay relatively high interest will also make them popular if central banks keep interest rates low for a prolonged period following the pandemic.[23]

If the marketplace lending industry does grow significantly, then marketplace lending platforms will become an important new class of intermediaries that financial stability regulators will have to pay attention to. Marketplace lending platforms rely entirely on algorithms to assess borrowers, and so regulators will have to adapt to overseeing algorithms rather than human loan officers. Some platforms rely on more traditional algorithms that have been programmed to assess borrowers based on things like employment status, income, and credit score, but machine learning algorithms that incorporate nontraditional, unstructured data (like social media information about the borrower) are increasingly being incorporated into the business model.[24] As Chapter 2 explored, there are reasons to be concerned that these algorithms may miss or underestimate key risk factors when they assess borrowers—especially if those risk factors only become predictive of default during unusual circumstances. The incentives of the marketplace lending platforms may exacerbate these failings: the platform offloads the risk of borrower default as soon as it sells notes to investors, and without any "skin in the game," a platform may not be as careful about its algorithmic risk assessment.[25]

In addition to being somewhat insulated from the consequences of their lending decisions, the platforms are also largely insulated from runs because the investors that ultimately fund the marketplace loans have no contractual right to demand immediate repayment (instead, repayment is subject to the terms of the note issued by the platform to the investor, and depends on repayment by the ultimate borrower). While it's theoretically possible that a platform might step up and guarantee those repayments during a crisis in order to mollify their regular investors, a platform probably wouldn't do this voluntarily if it would threaten its solvency.[26] The more pressing threat than platform insolvency is that institutional investors might walk away from the platform and decide to stop funding *future* loans—then the platform will find itself unable to intermediate capital going forward (and if its business dries up entirely, then the platform may just find itself insolvent). Marketplace lending has already become an important source of funding for small business enterprises, who are increasingly taking out and rolling over marketplace loans to meet their ongoing funding needs.[27] Any investor panic that prevents marketplace lending platforms from continuing to funnel capital to businesses that expect and depend on that capital could be a problem.

Financial panics come about, in part, because of limited information and confounding complexity. In these circumstances, it's often too hard for people to rationally assess the risks associated with a financial product or institution, and so they take mental shortcuts instead—like following a herd of other investors into a panic.[28] Investors in marketplace loans are typically provided with very little data about the borrowers and the loans they invest in, and so they depend on the output of the platform's algorithms to judge possible investments.[29] If those algorithms are inscrutable, then that creates fertile ground for the institutional investors exposed to marketplace loans to start distrusting the algorithms' ability to assess creditworthiness and panic.

Such a panic could originate either among the investors that directly fund the loans, or among the investors who buy securitized marketplace loans. If the securitization investors panic first, fears that secondary securitization market demand for marketplace loans is drying up would probably be enough to scare the first group. If institutional investors find their balance sheets compromised as a result of their marketplace loan-related investments, they may be forced to sell these or other investments at a discount—in a worst-case scenario, this could threaten their own solvency while at the same time igniting a fire sale dynamic that transmits problems to other parts of the financial system.

The marketplace lending business model therefore contains the seeds of systemic problems, notwithstanding the current (relatively) small size of the industry. As this book has consistently stressed, we should not wait until something goes wrong, or until new types of fintech institutions become too big to fail, before we start paying attention to new fragilities. In particular, we should not accept at face value any claims that fintech innovation is making the financial system safer by disintermediating it, because the reality is that some fintech business models *add* new intermediaries to the existing chains of established financial institutions involved in providing a financial service.

Marketplace lending platforms aren't the only new kind of intermediary, of course—the rise of fintech has spawned an ecosystem of new types of hedge funds, brokers, dealers, exchanges, wallets, miners, and other players that serve as intermediaries within evolving financial markets, all of whom could impact how those markets function. These new types of intermediaries, and the technologies they rely upon, are largely unfamiliar to financial stability regulators.

## High frequency trading

Over the last decade, some of the most significant technological changes to how financial markets intermediate capital have been wrought by the rise of high frequency trading.[30] The deployment of high frequency trading in the US stock market has been particularly well documented, but the strategy is also used for trading in other financial markets, including foreign currency, treasury bonds, and cryptoasset markets.[31] Because high frequency trading is not a consumer-facing product or service, some people don't consider it "fintech," but throughout this book I have stressed that we should be looking for financial stability risks in *all* new financial technologies, even if they're being used exclusively by sophisticated financial players. I have also consistently stressed that fintech innovations that increase the speed of financial activity warrant attention from financial stability regulators, and no financial business model prioritizes speed more than high frequency trading.

High frequency trading is usually carried out by specialized hedge funds, which rely on algorithms to execute trades far more quickly than any human could—these funds typically hold their investments for mere fractions of a second before selling them again. Because the trading activity is automated, a huge number of trades can be carried out, which means that the strategy can be highly profitable even if the profits on each individual trade are very small. Each high frequency trading firm has its own approach to identifying and evaluating trading opportunities—many use algorithms to automate this part of the process, in addition to automating the execution of the trades. At present, most high frequency traders prefer simpler algorithms to more sophisticated machine learning approaches, because simpler algorithms work faster and time is of the essence in high frequency trading.[32] However, that could all change with future breakthroughs in machine learning technology, in which case the concerns raised in Chapter 2 about machine learning algorithms bungling their response to tail events would apply to the high frequency trading business model as well.

When a market is behaving normally, the presence of high frequency traders in that market can make it easier to find someone to trade with, lowering the costs of transacting.[33] However, this benefit disappears when markets go haywire and high frequency traders stop trading—and high frequency trading activity may be the reason why markets go haywire in the first place. High frequency trading was implicated in the Flash Crash of 2010, for example, which caused the Dow Jones Industrial Average to plunge 5 to 6% in a matter of minutes.[34] Since then, there have been a number of other flash crashes, including regular "mini flash crashes" where the stock prices of individual companies (such as Walmart and Google) fluctuate wildly before settling back down.[35] There was also a US treasury bond flash crash in October 2014, and an Ethereum flash crash in 2017 (markets for cryptoassets like Ethereum will be discussed in more detail shortly).[36] The list goes on. While no flash crash has caused any significant problems for financial stability so far, that does not mean that a flash crash won't cause systemic problems in the future.

Untangling the causes of flash crashes can be difficult, but these crashes are intimately bound up with high frequency trading. The initial trigger for such a crash could be a technological glitch that caused a high frequency trading algorithm to buy or sell an asset at a bizarre price, or it could be human error like mistyping the prices at which an algorithm should buy or sell (these are colloquially referred to as "fat finger errors"). Where high frequency traders use algorithms to choose trades as well as to execute them, the trigger could be something like the algorithm misreading a satirical newspaper or a fake tweet—something that a human could probably tell was inaccurate, but algorithms may lack the time or the ability to process and disregard.[37] Regardless of the type of trigger, if the trading algorithm responds to that trigger with trades that impact the price of an asset, and if other market participants (both humans and algorithms) react to the new asset price with further trades, what we might have thought of as an idiosyncratic problem with one algorithm could snowball into trading behavior that results in truly bizarre market prices that bear no resemblance to any rational assessment of the assets involved.[38]

Algorithms can make and implement trading decisions far too quickly for any human intervention (by their programmers, users, or regulators), even when something clearly erroneous has occurred. The fact that these algorithms work well on their own most of the time can exacerbate this problem, because it can entrench automation biases, creating a "set and forget" mentality that discourages human intervention. And increased speed doesn't just make transactions faster. It also allows time for *more* transactions to be carried out, which multiplies the number of connections between trading counterparties and increases the number of opportunities for something to go wrong.[39]

Given that speed is the name of the game, the programmers of high frequency trading algorithms are unlikely to voluntarily devote lines of code (which would slow down the algorithm's regular functions) to instructing an algorithm on how to identify and respond to bizarre prices or other unusual circumstances. Instead, when high frequency trading algorithms recognize that something is really wrong, more often than not their preprogrammed instruction is to simply stop trading.[40] While high frequency trading is often praised (or at least defended) for improving liquidity in financial markets, if many high frequency traders simultaneously withdraw from the markets in times of turmoil, then opportunities for other investors to trade will be much more limited (particularly in markets where high frequency traders have already displaced many of the traditional sources of liquidity like market makers). In other words, the liquidity that high frequency traders provide is likely to evaporate just when it is needed most. A vicious cycle can then develop: the pricing issues that caused the turmoil become even more acute because there are fewer trades occurring to correct prices, ensuring even more misaligned prices that further reduce liquidity.

If high frequency traders exit the markets and other investors have limited opportunities to trade, those that need to sell may be forced to do so at a deeply discounted price. Sales may be driven simply by panic, or they may be forced fire sales. Or, rather than selling affected assets at a discount, investors might prefer to sell off other types of assets to raise cash. If enough of this occurs, then prices in other asset markets will be driven down, transmitting the panic to those markets and instigating more fire sales. Problems could also be transmitted from one asset market to another through other channels. For example, many derivatives draw their value from other types of financial assets (stocks for stock options, bonds for credit default swaps, etc.). Problems with pricing in one market can therefore jump quickly to the derivatives markets. In short, a future flash crash could trigger fire sales that ultimately contaminate other asset markets and disrupt capital intermediation, even if the financial institutions that participate in those asset markets are able to survive.

## Cryptoassets

Financial stability regulators need to be thinking about how increased speed will impact the financial markets. As part of that process, financial stability regulators also need to be thinking about cryptoassets, because increased use of cryptoassets can increase the speed of transacting. Before we get into the increased speed associated with cryptoassets, though, I'll provide some more background on what cryptoassets actually are. Cryptoassets are purely digital assets, meaning that they are nothing more than computer files. These files are stored on a database—known as a "distributed ledger"—which records the owner of each cryptoasset (the ledger is described as "distributed" because it is not maintained in any one place—instead, copies of the ledger are hosted on a network of different computers, with each computer being referred to as a "node").[41]

There are lots of different types of cryptoassets, including many different kinds of cryptocurrencies and tokens (and there could be potentially infinite variations in the future). The prototypical cryptoasset, though, is Bitcoin—a cryptocurrency first launched in 2009 by the mysterious figure Satoshi Nakamoto. While Bitcoin was eagerly embraced by those who wanted institutions (governments, as well as banks) out of the money supply, it never really took off as a way of making payments because of the volatility of its purchasing power. However, Bitcoin has enjoyed spectacular popularity despite these deficiencies—the prices that people are willing to pay for bitcoins *as financial assets* has skyrocketed. Inspired by Bitcoin's success as a financial asset, new generations of cryptoassets (usually referred to as "tokens") have been created that were never intended as money or payment mechanisms.

This part of the chapter will consider the potential for different kinds of cryptoassets to impact financial stability. The concerns raised here will only be realized if one or more types of cryptoassets become an important financial asset class, and when I first started writing this book in 2019, that was a big "if." It seemed quite possible then that cryptoassets would never play more than a niche role in our financial system. By early 2021, however, cryptoassets had already become much more mainstream,[42] and it now seems more of a question of when (rather than if) cryptoassets will pose threats for financial stability. At scale, cryptoassets could be the most destructive of all the fintech innovations, and if the essence of a precautionary approach to financial stability is "better safe than sorry," we should focus immediately on the threats they might pose and how to address them.

Many types of financial assets that were once viewed as highly speculative and niche are now included in standard asset portfolios.[43] Part of the reason why I suspect that cryptoassets will become increasingly popular is that financial institutions could make huge profits by converting existing financial products into cryptoasset form, or by creating new types of cryptoassets. Financial innovation is often driven by financial institutions eager to capture the fees associated with launching new financial products (even if the new products don't do a significantly better job of meeting market needs than previous versions). Before the rise of fintech, supplying new types of financial assets was always constrained—if only a little bit—because assets had to have some kind of connection to some kind of real-world economic good or service.[44] Now, cryptoassets can be created out of whole cloth by anyone with computer programming knowledge. In the absence of any limitations on supply, cryptoassets provide enormous opportunities for profit that may prove too seductive for the financial industry to ignore.

What about demand, though—won't it serve as a cap on the amount of cryptoassets that are issued? The short answer is yes. Demand will ultimately force some kind of cap on supply. The longer answer, however, is that that demand may not always be rational, which could allow for huge numbers of cryptoassets to be created and sold. Irrationally high demand for a financial asset is usually described as a "bubble," and while we discussed some of the mechanics of how asset bubbles are formed in Chapter 2, we didn't really get into the psychology involved.

The psychology of bubbles is, in many ways, the flip side of the psychology of runs and other financial panics. Financial panics occur because investors fear the worst, and so even if there is no rational reason for that fear, they want to cash in their investment as early as possible in order to avoid being left with damaged goods. These panicked sales ensure that the worst *does* occur, and so they work as a self-fulfilling prophecy. Asset bubbles, however, occur when investors are very optimistic, and want to buy as much and as early as possible in order to avoid missing out on expected returns, however unjustified those positive expectations might be. In the short term, this increased demand drives the price of the asset up further, validating investors' optimism and attracting new investors.

In his seminal book *Irrational Exuberance*, economist Robert Shiller identified "New Era Economic Thinking" as a key driver of this optimism.[45] Stories about the transformative power of fintech can be both very compelling and very misleading (as we saw recently with Wirecard, a huge digital payments platform that was feted as a German tech champion until it turned out to be a fraud and collapsed into insolvency in 2020).[46] Investors become so wrapped up in these stories that, in their enthusiasm, they start to believe that the mundane economic forces of boom and bust won't apply to their investment (and, as the GameStop episode showed us, these kind of stories can spread more easily in the age of social media). Unfortunately, when investors are dealing with new types of assets, there aren't any established valuation methods that can serve as a reality check on this enthusiasm. This is certainly the case when it comes to cryptoassets. In 2017, Shiller had this to say about Bitcoin:

> It is not just that very few people really comprehend the technology behind Bitcoin. It is that no one can attach objective probabilities to the various possible outcomes of the current Bitcoin enthusiasm. How can we even start estimating the fundamental value of Bitcoin . . .? Any attempt will soon sound silly.[47]

Shiller also spoke of Bitcoin as being part of an "idea epidemic,"[48] which is a useful way of thinking about how enthusiasm for Bitcoin has spawned enthusiasm for many other types of cryptoassets, and the potential for that enthusiasm to grow and become increasingly mainstream.

Initial coin offerings or "ICOs" were all the rage in 2017—this was the first wave of interest in capitalizing on crypto technology to create new kinds of financial assets for investment purposes. In an ICO, tokens are sold to members of the public in order to raise capital (the investors pay with cryptocurrency, but that can be exchanged for cash by the developers of the tokens), and then the developers use that capital to fund their projects.[49] Because these tokens are essentially computer files, developers can create them quickly (and relatively inexpensively), simply by writing a computer program that is compatible with the desired distributed ledger.

Once the token has been added to the ledger, it can then be sold; the distributed ledger is updated to reflect that the purchaser is the owner of the token and all of the rights and obligations associated with it. Many of the rights and obligations associated with the token will be embodied in a computer program known as a "smart contract" that is also hosted on the distributed ledger. Because the execution and enforcement of smart contracts is designed to be automated, smart contracts are often explained by way of analogies to vending machines: once the token is purchased, the smart contract follows its own set of if-then rules in carrying out token-related transactions on the distributed ledger (which might include making payments or posting collateral)—and it is very hard to stop its operation.

The distributed ledger operated by Ethereum is currently the ledger of choice for hosting tokens and smart contracts. The Ethereum ledger is a decentralized, permissionless ledger. This means that there is no central authority in charge of determining who has the right to record transactions on the ledger. But something is needed to protect the ledger from bad actors—the ledger is the definitive word on who owns a token, and so if someone is able to update the ledger to say that a token has been transferred to someone else, the token will effectively have been stolen from the original owner. Or, because a token is nothing more than a computer file, someone could copy their token and send the copies to lots of different people (this is known as the double spending problem). The developers of decentralized permissionless ledgers have therefore figured out processes to protect their ledgers. These processes, which are often referred to as "consensus mechanisms," are designed to prevent any solo actor from altering the ledger. Instead, consensus among the nodes that host the ledger determines the current state of the ledger (and thus determines the validity of the transactions that have resulted in changes to the ledger since the last accepted version).

The two most popular methods for maintaining the integrity of the consensus validation process are proof of work and proof of stake. As I am writing this book, Ethereum still relies primarily on proof of work, although it is already starting its transition to proof of stake.[50] Proof of work is based on cryptography and is very complicated. At the risk of oversimplification, it depends on people known as "miners" attempting through trial and error to guess the answer to a mathematical problem that relates to a block of transactions. Once a miner has an answer, they can submit it to all the nodes that host the ledger, and it's very easy for those nodes to verify if the miner's answer works—if it all checks out, those nodes by consensus will adopt the relevant block of transactions, adding it to the distributed ledger.

Successful miners are rewarded with cryptoassets, but they need to expend significant amounts of computer power to make their repeated guesses. A lot of the expense associated with mining comes from the amount of electricity needed to generate the necessary computing power, and concerns about the environmental impact of this activity (among other things) have generated more interest in proof of stake methods. In proof of stake, the right to validate transactions in a particular cryptoasset comes in part from already owning a significant amount of that type of cryptoasset. Some people have raised concerns that proof of stake will be more vulnerable to attacks than proof of work, but proof of work is not bulletproof either (we will take up issues of cybersecurity in Chapter 7, but for now it suffices to say that hackers will try to exploit any vulnerabilities they can find). In addition to vulnerabilities in the distributed ledger itself, there may also be vulnerabilities in the smart contracts that run on the ledger. Hackers were notoriously able to exploit vulnerabilities in the code of the DAO (a decentralized autonomous organization comprised of smart contracts hosted on the Ethereum distributed ledger) to take roughly $50 million of cryptocurrency from it in June 2016.[51]

Threats to token investors can also come from the token issuers themselves—the ICO market in 2017 and 2018 was rife with fraud.[52] Even when an ICO is not an outright scam, investors can still be harmed in more subtle ways. The rights that a token investor has to influence the development of the project they have invested in are typically more constrained and convoluted than the voting rights that a traditional shareholder has. There are also established methods of valuing established financial assets like shares and bonds that, while not a precise science by any measure, ultimately tie back to the fundamentals of the issuer's business. Methods for valuing tokens, however, are still in their infancy and still highly speculative, which creates significant uncertainty for investors. Given all of these problems, it is perhaps not surprising that following a surge of ICOs in 2017 and 2018, interest in the

ICO market plummeted in 2019.[53] However, while interest in ICOs may have waned, cryptoassets continue to evolve.

In the spring of 2021, enthusiasm for cryptoassets erupted into a kind of NFT mania, with a non-fungible token authenticating a digital artwork by Beeple selling at Christie's for $69.3 million worth of Ether cryptocurrency.[54] NFTs authenticate ownership of a particular digital asset, and in a very meta moment, *New York Times* columnist Kevin Roose wrote a column that did a great job of explaining how NFTs work before turning that column into an NFT and then selling it. To be more specific, Roose created and then sold a token on the Ethereum blockchain that he described as "a unique digital collectible that corresponds to an image of this column in PNG format."[55] It sold for $560,000 worth of Ether (most of the proceeds were donated to charity)—but the *New York Times* retained copyright in the column, and anyone can still read the column on the *Times*'s website. So when you buy an NFT, you're not getting anything other than a recording on a distributed ledger that you own the token that is the digital signature. For some collectors, that is important (offering a similar thrill to owning an autographed copy of a book); for others, NFTs' appeal stems from their interest in new technology as well as a desire to profit from it—another example of Shiller's "New Era Economic Thinking."

This NFT mania certainly seems like a bubble, but even if that bubble bursts (just as the ICO bubble did), it is making the idea of investing in cryptoassets more mainstream. It's also making the idea of investing in cryptoassets more fun, making investing seem more and more like a game—albeit one with real money at stake. This kind of attitude could increase demand for exciting new types of cryptoassets to play with. Even if some investors continue to view the cryptoassets themselves as too speculative to invest in directly, demand for those assets can still be sustained if investors (including financial institutions) are happy to incur indirect exposure to those assets—and there are already popular mutual funds that invest in, and swap contracts that derive their value from, cryptoassets.[56]

Eventually, demand for cryptoassets could also be driven by financial institutions looking for new types of financial assets that they can use as collateral for cheap short-term loans. Many of the new types of assets that were created in the lead up to the 2008 financial crisis were used as collateral for a type of transaction called repo, which the largest financial institutions are particularly reliant on and which functions like an overnight loan from one bank to another that is renewed every day.[57] The new types of repo collateral that were developed before the 2008 crisis often had a very tenuous link to real assets (for example, synthetic CDOs were backed by derivatives that referenced securities that were ultimately backed by mortgages on real houses), which made it relatively easy to manufacture lots of them—but very hard to value them. The more assets that were created, the more financial institutions could borrow, and the resulting increased amounts of leverage in the financial system made it much more fragile. In the future, it is conceivable that institutional demand for new types of collateral could spur an explosion of new cryptoasset types where there is no need to even tenuously link the asset to anything that really exists (and we could even see a crypto equivalent of synthetic CDOs where one cryptoasset depends on the functioning of other cryptoassets for its value).

At the most basic level, an unconstrained supply of cryptoassets and cryptoasset-related assets means that there will be exponentially *more* assets in the financial system than there are now—what economist James Tobin described as "nth degree speculation" could become a reality.[58] Exponential growth of cryptoassets would mean more opportunities for asset bubbles to grow, and more assets to be dumped during fire sales. More cryptoassets also mean more trading transactions which mean more contractual relationships between counterparties that can transmit shocks through the financial system. The interconnections that are already growing between cryptoassets and more traditional financial institutions and markets (particularly as cryptoassets become the subject of derivative contracts) suggest that vulnerabilities in any large-scale cryptoasset markets that develop would have many avenues for infecting the broader financial system.

## Runs, fire sales, and cryptoassets

As we've just discussed, the more financial assets there are out there, the more kindling there is available for a run or fire sale in the financial markets. What could spark this type of panic? It's impossible to predict, but there are some potential contenders. While many proponents of cryptoassets tout their ability to disintermediate financial transactions (and it is true that transactions on decentralized ledgers can theoretically be carried out without the involvement of any central intermediary), a market ecosystem of wallets, exchanges, and other intermediaries is already evolving in order to make it easier to invest in and trade cryptoassets. It remains to be seen whether these intermediaries will adopt business models that are vulnerable to runs, but we've already seen that a problem with an intermediary can spark market panic: the value of Bitcoin dropped 36% after the 2014 announcement that a hacker had stolen $450 million of Bitcoin from the Mt Gox exchange.[59]

A panic could also arise as a correction to a bubble in cryptoassets: if enthusiasm starts to wane and demand and prices fall, investors who had truly believed that their new type of investment was impervious to traditional market forces could become disillusioned and start selling en masse (more opportunistic investors would of course also start to sell as the price dropped). Or, in the case of an asset hosted on a decentralized permissionless ledger, a civil war among the people responsible for the distributed ledger's code could create panic (again, Bitcoin has already experienced such a civil war, which resulted in a split into two different distributed ledgers—the classic Bitcoin, and Bitcoin cash—in 2017. There was no panic on that occasion, though—surprisingly, the split didn't even hurt the value of bitcoins).[60]

As with bank runs, concerns about an individual cryptoasset can morph into a (perhaps initially unfounded, but potentially self-fulfilling) panic that the broader market for cryptoassets is in trouble. If the holders of a cryptocurrency like Ether, for example, start to doubt their ability to reliably make payments with that cryptocurrency at a rate that matches their expectations, demand for that cryptocurrency would decrease as they exchanged their cryptocurrency for more readily accepted sovereign currencies. The lack of demand for the cryptocurrency would drive down its value, causing more holders to try and exchange their cryptocurrency holdings for sovereign currencies, potentially rendering the cryptocurrency worthless. This type of panic would resemble a foreign exchange crisis, which shares many similarities with the bank run dynamic we have already explored—people fear that if they don't exchange for a more stable currency first, others will get ahead of them and get a better deal, and so they rush to exchange, even though doing so creates a self-fulfilling prophecy that drives down the value of the first currency for everyone.[61]

Or cryptoassets could spark an *actual* bank run. A terrifying worst-case scenario, from a financial stability perspective, would involve the largest financial institutions using cryptoassets as collateral when they borrow from other financial institutions. As we saw in our discussion of bank runs, there is a mismatch between a financial institution's long-term assets and its short-term funding. Deposits are the most familiar source of short-term funding, but banks have other sources as well—the largest banks are particularly reliant on repo. If cryptoassets were to become acceptable collateral for repo transactions but then subsequently suffer some kind of panic, banks would lose access to their short-term funding (just as they did during 2008, when the synthetic CDOs and related assets that had served as repo collateral were increasingly compromised).[62] Without the short-term funding they are used to relying on, the largest banks would need to engage in fire sales, infecting the rest of the financial system.

Fire sales that originate in a cryptoasset market would play out in much the same way as a fire sale of any other type of financial asset. If a type of cryptoasset were to become compromised by panicked sales and therefore hard to value, financial institutions with exposure to them might need to sell them, or other assets, putting downward pressure on the price of whatever they sell. If this were to happen on a large enough scale, other financial institutions would be pressured to sell assets as prices fell, creating a vicious cycle.

Mandating disclosure has never done a very good job of preventing these kinds of destructive dynamics—as we have already explored, participants in the financial markets typically fail to monitor or rein in undesirable behavior until things have become so bad that their response actually starts a panicked run or fire sale. Notwithstanding disclosure's limitations, though, financial panics are often made worse if there isn't much information available about the assets involved, or if that information exists but is impossible to understand. This is a real risk with cryptoassets. Investors are used to reviewing balance sheets and written disclosures to assess investments, not computer code. While it's possible for written disclosures to describe how smart contracts will govern a cryptoasset, one study of ICOs found that the written disclosure documents that were provided to investors were often inconsistent with how the code of the relevant smart contracts actually functioned.[63] If financial assets are increasingly governed by smart contracts, rather than paper contracts that set out the rights and obligations of investors and issuers, investors without programming ability will not be able to understand what they have purchased, and panics may get worse.

## Problems with self-execution

Financial panics can befall cryptoassets, just as they can befall any other type of financial asset. However, transactions involving cryptoassets have two attributes that are likely to make runs and fire sales particularly bad: smart contracts' speed of execution, and their lack of flexibility. Legal systems dealing with *paper* financial contracts have developed the ability to relax and suspend contractual obligations in the face of a significant unanticipated event, whether through the use of bankruptcy courts, encouraging a contractual party not to enforce their rights, or even by enacting legislation that declares certain contractual terms illegal.[64] Transactions relating to cryptoassets, however, are carried out by smart contracts that will execute their preprogrammed instructions without waiting for any further input from a court or even the parties themselves. Because this increases the speed and certainty of execution, using a smart contract can eliminate many worries about whether a counterparty will perform their contractual obligations, reducing transaction costs. However, financial stability regulators need to consider the risks that could arise from speeding up the execution of financial transactions in this way.

As I write this book, Ethereum is the most popular platform for smart contracts, and so Solidity—the computer programming language developed to program smart contracts for the Ethereum blockchain—is the most popular language for smart contracts.[65] Solidity has been purposely slimmed down to make it easier for computer programmers to create smart contracts, and so before a smart contract can actually operate, the Solidity program that has been written by a human programmer is broken up by a computer into smaller instructions that are then translated by computer into another computer language called bytecode. This computer-driven translation process certainly allows for unexpected interpretations of the Solidity program that could lead a smart contract to function in ways unanticipated by the human programmer, but even a perfect translation of a Solidity program should concern us because of its inflexibility.

A smart contract programmed with Solidity is made up of preprogrammed rules that execute in connection with the data presented to them. The rules are referred to as functions, and the placeholders for data inputs are referred to as variables. A function might be to make a payment to the owner of the asset (as noted on the distributed ledger), and the amount of the payment might depend on variables like the payment date and the applicable interest rate. If the applicable interest rate can change over time, the smart contract would also need to look to an external source to find out what the current rate was before it could discharge this function. In smart contract speak, that external source is called an "oracle," and the parties must trust the oracle enough to automatically incorporate its findings into the execution of the smart contract's functions.

Although some people claim that smart contracts are "immutable"—meaning that their execution is set is stone—there *are* steps that can be taken to better equip the smart contract to adapt to unexpected events. Conditions known as modifiers can be placed on the execution of functions, for example, preventing them from being carried out in certain circumstances. Programming a smart contract to consult an external oracle can also incorporate flexibility into smart contracts, because the oracle can be easily updated after the smart contract becomes operational. Yet another option is to incorporate a set of functions into the contract by reference—the primary smart contract doesn't change, but it is programmed to look to another smart contract to flesh out its functioning, and that other contract can be substituted as circumstances change.

This is not an exhaustive list—other ways of making smart contracts more flexible have been developed, and more will surely be developed in the future. However, taking any of these approaches does increase transaction costs. The Ethereum ledger (on which most smart contracts are currently hosted) charges a "gas cost" for any computing done, and including modifiers or consulting an oracle or other smart contract would increase the amount of computing power (and thus the gas cost) necessary to execute a smart contract.[66] The owners of cryptoassets will probably be willing to bear these charges up to a certain point, but eventually, these ongoing operational costs will discourage measures that cater for very unusual events.

Of course, because the future is inherently uncertain, no contract (paper or smart) will ever be able to cater for every possible eventuality that a financial asset might be confronted with. With paper contracts, though, the parties have opportunities to amend their contracts or agree not to enforce them. Courts can also intervene to fill in the blanks in paper contracts: law professor Katharina Pistor has observed that "the elasticity of law has proved time and again critical for avoiding a complete financial meltdown."[67] In a financial system dominated by smart contracts, though, these kinds of interventions may come too late to prevent runs, fire sales, and other destabilizing harm—Chapter 1 illustrated this problem by considering how automating the execution of credit default swaps could have hastened AIG's demise in 2007 or 2008. These problems arise because, even if the parties agree among themselves not to enforce a smart contract or a court issues an injunction preventing them from carrying out a smart contract, the parties can't effect this on their own. The execution of a smart contract can only be paused, changed, or undone with the consent of whoever controls the relevant distributed ledger, and where the ledger is decentralized and permissionless (like the Ethereum ledger) there is no single individual who can coordinate the process—even if the parties to the smart contract (as well as the public interest) all support it.

Instead, any pause, change or reversal of a smart contract will require the consensus of all the nodes in the distributed ledger supporting the smart contract, which will take time. To give some context, after the DAO was hacked, it took over a month for the nodes of the Ethereum distributed ledger to coordinate their response.[68] It seems highly unlikely that this kind of consensus could ever be achieved *before* the smart contract executes; undoing the transaction will probably be the only alternative. Undoing a transaction requires either a change in the ledger's underlying software, or what is known as a "hard fork," where the ledger is split in two with one version of the ledger not recognizing the problematic transaction. Identifying, contacting, and convincing a majority of the nodes of a decentralized ledger to accept either of these approaches would not be a quick process, and the run or fire sale we are trying to prevent could be over—and the damage done—long before the transaction were reversed.

While this chapter has focused on the Solidity programming language and the Ethereum ledger, we shouldn't assume that future generations of cryptoassets will continue to rely on them—particularly if established financial institutions and the tech giants create their own proprietary distributed ledgers for trading cryptoassets. If this happens, many of the concerns we've explored about coordinating changes to a distributed ledger and Ethereum gas charges will disappear, and there will be more scope for flexibility in smart contracts. It's important to remember, though, that without consensus mechanisms and gas charges to act as roadblocks, cryptoasset transactions could be processed even faster than they are now. Cryptoassets issued by large banks and techfins could also threaten financial stability in other ways—several potential issues are suggested by Facebook's plans for Diem, and JPMorgan's JPMCoin.

## Facebook's Diem

Perhaps no techfin's venture into finance has generated more controversy than Diem, the cryptocurrency proposed by the Diem Association. More specifically, Diem is intended to be a type of cryptocurrency known as a "stablecoin," meaning that its value is tied to some underlying asset to keep it from being too volatile[69] (if a purse on Etsy were to cost 9 Diem one day, 33 the next, and 17 the day after, then the Diem would not be a very appealing method of payment). The Diem Association (which was known as the Libra Association until it was rebranded in December 2020) is a not-for-profit organization that was pioneered by Facebook. Part of the controversy over Diem stems from increasing popular distrust of Facebook: many people wonder if Facebook is pursuing Diem just to generate more data about users and their purchasing habits, which Facebook can then monetize.[70] But there are financial stability implications as well.

In June 2019, the Association issued a white paper proposing "a simple global currency and financial infrastructure that empowers billions of people."[71] The proposal faced immediate and significant backlash, and the Association responded with a revised white paper in April of 2020.[72] These white papers set out the Association's intention for Diem to be traded on a permissioned distributed ledger, with each member of the Association charged with maintaining one of the validation nodes for the ledger. The 2019 proposal to issue one single type of "multi-currency coin" was scaled down to assuage concerns about it taking over the global money supply, and as of April 2020, the plan was to also offer Diem denominated in US dollars, euros, and the sovereign currencies of several other prominent economies. The Association still plans to offer multi-currency Diem, though, to facilitate cross-border transactions and for use in countries for which no currency-specific Diem will be created.

The Association intends to back each Diem with a reserve of sovereign currencies, cash equivalents, and short-term government securities, so that the value of a Diem will be less volatile than the value of something like a bitcoin (it's anticipated that at least 80% of the reserve will be made up of short-term securities, with cash and cash equivalents expected to make up only 20% of the reserve).[73] The reserve will be managed by a subsidiary of the Association that was originally called Libra Networks, and is intended to inspire confidence that Diem can be readily converted to sovereign currencies. The appeal of the reserve to Diem users is obvious, but it also opens Diem up to run-like dynamics—particularly the multi-currency Diem, which will be backed by a reserve of cash and securities that is denominated in a number of different currencies and as a result is likely to be more volatile than the reserves maintained for single currency Diem.

The value of any Diem will fluctuate depending on the composition and valuation of the underlying reserve, but the Association has claimed that a Diem will have an intrinsic value.[74] Much like a money market mutual fund's promise of a fixed one dollar share price, this claim could create unwarranted confidence in Diem's enduring value—at least until something happens to shatter that confidence. Panicked Diem holders would then exchange their Diem for the sovereign currency of their choice, and if this were done at sufficient scale, the entity formerly known as Libra Networks would have to start selling off some of the assets in the reserve in order to raise enough cash to satisfy the exchange requests. Remaining Diem holders who feared that the value of their Diem could plummet against sovereign currencies as the reserve is depleted would be incentivized to exchange their Diem for sovereign currencies as early as possible, creating a vicious cycle. In many ways, this type of run would look a lot like the runs on money market mutual funds that we discussed earlier in this chapter.

The Association has acknowledged the possibility of what it describes as "the unlikely case that the [Diem] network is unable to convert the very short-term government securities in the Reserve into cash fast enough to satisfy all requests to burn [Diem Coins] without incurring fire-sale losses."[75] To address this possibility, the Association has floated the ideas of penalizing or preventing Diem holders from converting their Diem to sovereign currencies during a run. The prospect of these types of measures could be counterproductive, though, encouraging Diem holders to convert if they have even an inkling that a stressed situation is approaching in order to avoid any penalties or lock-ups—and then those conversions could bring about a run in a self-fulfilling prophecy.

Given Diem's proposed scale, a run on multi-currency Diem could potentially play havoc with exchange rates globally. If there were a run on *any* of the different Diem (multi-currency or currency-specific), the rebranded Libra Networks entity would be forced to engage in fire sales that would drive down the prices of short-term government securities, impacting other investors in those securities. The specter of these types of systemic consequences might generate pressure on national authorities to bail out Diem, forcing national taxpayers to ultimately foot Facebook's bill. For the multi-currency Diem, working out the terms of national intervention would be a messy process, with the panic only worsening as the details were hashed out among countries.

## Cryptoassets and monetary policy

Diem therefore raises significant financial stability concerns. It also has the potential to interfere with monetary policy. So far, we have focused on capital intermediation by private actors, but government authorities don't just oversee financial markets; they are also active participants within them. In fact, governments create financial assets (usually in the form of government bonds), and central banks (like the Federal Reserve) are also important traders within the financial markets. These central banks carry out monetary policy functions by buying financial assets from and selling financial assets to private sector entities, and these monetary policy functions are vital for matching the supply of money to the needs of the economy. The rise of cryptoassets has the potential to disrupt these functions.

Although monetary policy may seem arcane, we should all be concerned if private sector institutions—which have no mandate to serve the public interest—usurp control over the money supply from central banks. Former Federal Reserve Chairman William McChesney Martin famously said that the central bank's job is "to take away the punch bowl just as the party gets going":[76] by adjusting the money supply to raise interest rates, a central bank can try to promote financial stability by tamping down on incipient asset bubbles, for example. This question of whether monetary policy tools should be used to promote financial stability is admittedly a very controversial one among central bankers, but we certainly don't need a proliferation of cryptoassets to deprive central banks of their ability to make such a decision if and when needed. In other words, even if a central bank decides not to take the punch bowl away, it wouldn't be wise to let the private sector spike the punch with cryptoassets.

Even the less controversial central bank function of managing inflation could be undermined if central banks lose control of the money supply. When there is a lot of money available in the economy, it is cheaper to borrow, and cheaper money increases purchasing power which drives up inflation. The opposite is also true: when there is less money available, inflation is reduced. If money increasingly takes the form of cryptoassets issued by private entities, then that could displace the use of sovereign currencies and limit the ability of central banks to match the money supply to the economic situation.[77]

Facebook received significant political pushback after the first Libra White Paper was published, partly because of fears about what the stablecoin would do to central banks' influence on national money supplies around the world. As we've already discussed, Diem responded by proposing to offer several single-currency Diems, including US dollar, euro, Pound Sterling and Singapore dollar-denominated Diem—but the Association still plans to offer multi-currency Diem in addition to the single-currency Diem, and the existence of these single-currency Diems does nothing to protect the monetary policy of, say, Australia. It's not even clear that introducing a US dollar Diem would fully address concerns about Diem's impact on monetary policy in the United States. To illustrate how a privately issued stablecoin pegged to the US dollar might impact national monetary policy, we can look to JPMorgan, another private sector behemoth, which has already launched a prototype cryptoasset known as JPMCoin for use by the bank's institutional clients.[78]

JPMorgan bills JPMCoin purely as a payments technology, but JPMorgan could also profit from the seignorage associated with creating JPMCoins ("seignorage" is the profit that represents the difference between the face value of money, and the cost of producing and distributing that money). A bank like JPMorgan can already profit from seignorage when it creates money by extending US dollar loans to borrowers, but regulations (most importantly reserve and capital requirements) impose limits on the ability of private banks to extend loans in US dollars, and so they cap the amount of seignorage profit a US bank can make. In addition, banks have no right to create US dollars for their own spending—that right belongs solely to the Federal Reserve. JPMorgan could create JPMCoins for its own spending, though. At least at present, JPMCoins are not subject to reserve and capital requirements, and so JPMorgan could also theoretically make unlimited loans in JPMCoins. If significant volumes of transactions were consummated in JPMCoins, the Federal Reserve will have lost some of its control of the money supply.

* * *

The institutions and markets that make up the financial system play a vital economic role by connecting those with capital to invest with those who need capital to grow. Many aspects of this capital intermediation process are inherently fragile, though; the capital intermediation process is susceptible to bubbles, runs, fire sales. and other dynamics that can transmit panic from institution to institution, market to market. Although bubbles, runs. and fire sales arise from very human tendencies toward overconfidence and panic (and in that sense are nothing new), they can be exacerbated by the increased speed and technological complexity associated with fintech innovations. Fintech therefore has the potential to disrupt the ability of the broader financial system to intermediate capital, even if it doesn't live up to the hype of disrupting the business models of established financial intermediaries.

# 4
# Fintech and Payments

The last two chapters focused on the role that the financial system plays in intermediating capital and managing financial risks. Another function of the financial system that is just as important—but much less sexy—is that it provides the infrastructure needed to process payments. This infrastructure function is a bit like plumbing; few people pay much attention to how it works, but without it, the transactions that are the lifeblood of our economy would be backed up. Imagine if, all of a sudden, large swathes of the population were prevented from buying food, or paying rent. Even those people who could still make payments would be harmed if others couldn't pay *them*—and all of this could quickly add up to serious economic harm.

When financial regulators worry about this kind of scenario, they're usually focused on how the *failure of a financial institution* might prevent its customers from making payments. Less attention is paid to the *technology* that is relied upon to process payments. The plumbing of our financial system is becoming more technologically complex, though, and this is creating conditions in which that plumbing could fail harder and faster than it has in the past. A small technological glitch could generate unexpected reactions from other parts of the financial system, halting economic transactions in a way that could potentially compound into a financial crisis—but when it comes to managing the fallout from these kinds of technological failures, financial regulation leaves much to be desired.

As mobile payments, distributed ledger, and other technologies are integrated into payments processing, things will only become more technologically complex. The operational risks posed by these new technologies aren't necessarily worse than the ones we already face with legacy payments processing technologies, but they are different, and they underline the inadequacies of our existing regulatory approaches to potential technological failures. Financial stability regulators need to reassess their approach to these kinds of operational risks; at the same time, they also need to appreciate that the new fintech payments providers are susceptible to runs that could undercut financial stability in different ways.

*Driverless Finance*. Hilary J. Allen, Oxford University Press. © Hilary J. Allen 2022.
DOI: 10.1093/oso/9780197626801.003.0005

## How payments are processed

Before we start looking at fintech innovations in payments processing, it helps to have some background on the more standard methods of payments processing. These days, most transactions don't involve handing over cash—instead, they are accounting transactions.[1] Whether a payment is made with a check, debit card, or credit card (or a new payments technology for that matter), the person making the payment (the payer) will have a debit recorded in their account, and the person receiving the payment (the payee) will have their account credited with the same amount. However, before these accounting transactions can be finalized (a process known as "settlement"), someone needs to receive the initial request to begin the transaction, determine whether the request is valid, and determine whether funds are available to complete the transaction.

In countries with well-developed banking sectors, banks and bank accounts are often relied upon to process payments for their customers. This process is reasonably straightforward when both the payer and the payee have accounts with the same bank—then the bank will have the power to make changes to both the payer's and the payee's accounts. However, it is more common for a payer and payee to bank with different institutions. In that case, the "wholesale" or "interbank" payment system comes into play—in addition to the debit made to the payer's account and the credit made to the payee's account, a transfer will need to be made between the payer's bank and the payee's bank.[2]

When banks have accounts with a central bank, a debit can be made to the payer's bank's account with the central bank and a credit can be made to the payee's bank's account with the central bank (if a bank doesn't have an account with a central bank, it will need to work with a bank that does). Payments between banks can either be settled immediately (in "real time"), or settlement can be deferred to allow for more payment instructions from both banks to be collected. When settlement is deferred, all of the debits and credits between two banks can be netted out, and a single payment can be made to settle all of those debits and credits at the end of a specified period of time. Sometimes, banks rely on clearinghouses to make this payment processing more efficient: clearinghouses can sort through, aggregate, and net out the payment instructions received from participating banks, and then provide banks with the details of the changes they need to make to their customers' accounts.

We can make this discussion a little more concrete by looking at how banks, central banks, and clearinghouses help process payments in the United States.[3] Many banks in the United States have what are known as "master accounts" with the Federal Reserve (banks' customers are not permitted to hold accounts with the Fed—an issue we will return to later). Payments are settled by making transfers between these master accounts. For smaller retail payments, banks typically rely on the Automated Clearing House ("ACH") network to transfer funds between their Fed accounts, and these can take days to settle. To settle larger payments more quickly, banks can use the FedWire service provided by the Federal Reserve, or the private sector alternative Clearing House Interbank Payments System ("CHIPS"). FedWire settles in real time, while CHIPS tries to match and net out offsetting payments. Payments made through CHIPS settle as soon they can be matched, and any that remain unmatched are settled at the end of the day.[4]

## Payments failures

That's how payments processing is supposed to work, but how could it go wrong? The risk that payments processing won't be completed as expected is sometimes referred to as "settlement risk,"[5] and settlement risk has credit, liquidity, and operational risk components. We met the concepts of credit risk (otherwise known as counterparty risk) and liquidity risk in Chapter 2: in the context of payments processing, credit risk is the risk that someone involved in the chain of payments processing won't be able to transfer the necessary funds *period*, while liquidity risk refers to the risk that they won't be able to transfer funds precisely when they're supposed to, even though they might be able to do it later. Operational risk has been defined broadly as "the risk of loss resulting from inadequate or failed internal processes, people and systems or from external events,"[6] and in the payments processing context, this could cover everything from an employee stealing funds to a technological problem preventing a bank from sending payments instructions.

Settlement risk is therefore a composite concept, but it can be easier to understand if we break it up into its components. An obvious credit risk, for example, is that an institution involved in processing payments will become insolvent. Customers who hold funds in an account with an insolvent institution won't be able to access those funds, preventing them from carrying out basic transactions like paying rent or buying groceries. For reasons that we will discuss shortly, customers don't have to worry all that much about this kind of credit risk if their funds are held in a deposit account at a failing bank, but credit risk could be a much bigger problem if they keep their funds with another type of financial institution.

Regardless of whether customers keep their funds with a bank or with a different type of financial institution, customers' ability to transact could be cut off by operational problems like technological failures that prevent financial institutions from sending or receiving payments instructions. For example, in October 2015, a "botched transition to MasterCard's processing system . . . caused a cascade of technical problems for RushCard, creating disruptions that stretched on for days," and the consequences of these technical problems snowballed for many RushCard customers, who found themselves unable to pay for rent, groceries, utilities, and medications.[7]

The problems with RushCard didn't impact the economy as a whole, but a similar outage at a widely used payments service could cause big problems. In recent years, there have been noticeable economic consequences for Kenya when the hugely popular M-Pesa mobile wallet suffers outages—even when those outages only last about two hours.[8] The Kenyan Treasury Department has therefore recognized that Kenya's tax revenues would be impacted if M-Pesa were compromised by operational risks for a longer period of time, and has designated the possibility of a "technological disaster" as a "plausible fiscal risk."[9]

While we have just looked at them separately, credit and operational problems could very well intertwine with each other, and with liquidity problems.[10] For example, if a financial institution were to experience a significant and well-publicized failure of its payments processing technology, that could damage confidence in the institution. Customers of the institution who were still able to withdraw their funds might rush to do so, and even customers of unaffected institutions might panic upon hearing the news and rush to withdraw their funds. This could create liquidity problems for those institutions, which could turn into solvency problems if they were forced to liquidate assets at a discount to satisfy those withdrawal requests. This scenario can also be turned on its head: a financial institution experiencing a run could see its technological infrastructure fail, unable to support the increased load of withdrawal requests. This would only worsen confidence in that institution (and potentially, in other unrelated payments providers as well).

Regardless of what triggers it, a widespread failure of the payments system (particularly one that occurs at a time when a lot of payments are made, like at the end of the month) could potentially have much more immediate consequences than the financial crisis of 2008. The 2008 crisis started to impact the broader economy once everyday people and businesses needed to borrow money from financial institutions and were unable to do so;[11] Kenya's experience with M-Pesa shows us that economic harm from lost transactions can start to accumulate within hours.

To address credit problems in the United States, an alternative to bankruptcy has been adopted for failing banks that prioritizes allowing the customers of those banks to keep making payments—but this type of regulation doesn't apply to financial institutions that aren't banks (it also doesn't address technological outages). Also, there could still be credit problems behind the scenes with the payments made *between* banks, and if interbank payments were to come to a halt, then that could shut down even solvent banks' ability to process day-to-day payments for their customers.

When interbank payments don't settle in real time, banks essentially become each other's creditors until settlement is complete: for example, after netting all of Bank A's and Bank B's payments to one another, Bank A might owe Bank B millions of dollars, and so Bank B will suffer losses (maybe even becoming insolvent itself) if Bank A becomes insolvent before it can make that final payment and settle up. Even if Bank A is still solvent, if Bank A is experiencing liquidity problems and doesn't have enough funds on hand when it comes time to make that final payment, that may translate into liquidity problems for Bank B as it waits for Bank A's payment. If Bank B has to start selling off assets at a discount to raise cash in the interim, that liquidity problem could end up turning into a solvency problem for Bank B.

After the terrorist attacks of September 11, 2001, the Federal Reserve feared these kinds of problems in the interbank payments system.[12] Because of telecommunications outages, tragic loss of life, and other operational difficulties resulting from those attacks, some banks couldn't send the payments they owed to other banks (Bank of New York faced particular challenges, reporting at one point that it was overdue in making $100 billion of payments).[13] There might have been concerns about the solvency of the banks that were owed significant amounts of money, but the Fed lent freely to those banks in its capacity as lender of last resort. This intervention seems to have been successful in preserving the confidence of both the customers and the bank counterparties of the affected banks: there were no runs, and the processing of retail payments ultimately remained largely undisturbed in the wake of September 11. If there had already been concerns about the financial health of the affected banks, though, or if FedWire or CHIPS had been compromised, the outcome might have been very different (fortunately FedWire and CHIPS experienced few operational difficulties in the aftermath of the attacks).

In a recent attempt to model the impact that a cyberattack could have on interbank payments processing, researchers noted the disastrous consequences that would flow if the operations of a clearinghouse like CHIPS were to be compromised (either through a direct attack, or because it could not receive payments from banks who were attacked). They found that if CHIPS were prevented from performing its usual netting function, banks would have to make a "massive" number of extra payments over Fedwire, tying up funds in payments transactions that might be needed elsewhere.[14]

This same "cyberattack pre-mortem" also considered what would happen if some banks could still send payments using Fedwire (and have their accounts with the Fed debited immediately), but some of the recipients of those payments couldn't actually access those funds or make payments themselves because they had been compromised by a cyberattack. The report speculated that in these circumstances, questions about the solvency of the banks who were owed payments could inspire runs. Any support that the Federal Reserve could provide in the aftermath of such an attack might not be enough to support banks that were already in a precarious financial condition—and the Fed would not be able to fix the underlying technological problems.

## Payments regulation

Given the importance of payments processing to the economy, the risks involved, and the limitations on emergency intervention after a problem occurs, there is clearly a role for regulation to play in making the payments system more robust to start with. Most of the existing regulation is focused on banks: banks' key role in payments processing is part of the reason why they are regulated so heavily in the first place.[15] Measures like capital regulation, deposit insurance, and emergency lending from central banks are all intended to make banks less likely to fail in the first place, and as we've already mentioned, alternatives to bankruptcy have been designed that prioritize allowing a bank's customers to keep transacting even if that bank does fail.

There is also regulation that is targeted at technological problems and other operational risks that might prevent a bank from providing reliable payment processing services. For example, most regulators around the world expect the banks they oversee to comply with the Principles for the Sound Management of Operational Risk developed by the Basel Committee on Banking Supervision (which require banks to monitor, identify, and mitigate operational risks), and will be phasing in compliance with the Basel Committee's new Principles for Operational Resilience (which require, among other things, the development of a business continuity plan).[16]

In addition to bank regulation, clearinghouses and other institutions responsible for clearing and settling payments (like CHIPS) are usually regulated by their central banks in accordance with the Principles for Financial Market Infrastructures (known as the "PFMIs") developed jointly by the Bank for International Settlements and the International Organization of Securities Commissions.[17] Several of these principles relate to the management of credit and liquidity risks:[18] clearinghouses have adopted their own rules that comply with these principles, including rules about which institutions can use the clearinghouse, and rules about when those institutions can rely on credit to fund their payments and when they need to have their own funds available. Fears about large-scale operational difficulties shutting down a clearinghouse are largely dealt with by Principle 17, which requires infrastructure providers to identify and mitigate their operational risks, and to adopt a business continuity plan that details how the institution will restore service after a disruption.[19]

We've just explored the status quo for payments risks and payments regulation, at least in the domestic context (processing payments when the payer and the payee live in different countries is much more complicated and time consuming, involving a network of correspondent bank relationships and time differences that can create greater settlement risks). The payments landscape has started to shift recently, though. A number of fintech start-ups have sought to capitalize on inefficiencies in the existing system by providing speedier and cheaper payments processing—and banks are starting to respond to competition from these start-ups by adopting fintech technologies that streamline their own payments services.

Fintech innovations that were designed to make payments processing more efficient could also reduce credit risks by reducing settlement time (if the payment settles immediately, there's less time for your counterparty to become insolvent and default on you). They could also provide substitutes for our existing payments processing infrastructure that would be very helpful if parts of the existing infrastructure were to experience technical difficulties. At the same time, these innovations are potentially introducing new types of credit, liquidity, and operational risks into our payments system that—in a worst-case scenario—could paralyze people's ability to transact. If fintech payments platforms become the dominant way people transact (as they have in Kenya and China, for example), a paralyzed platform would mean a paralyzed economy, and so financial stability regulators need to contemplate and prepare for these new risks.

Broadly speaking, the rise of fintech highlights two problems with our current approach to payments regulation. First, if fintech innovations are designed to bypass banks, central banks, and clearinghouses, they will also bypass a lot of the regulations and other support structures that have been developed over the years to manage credit and liquidity risks in the payments system. In particular, because fintech firms don't have access to deposit insurance or the alternatives to bankruptcy that have been adopted for failed banks, they are vulnerable to runs. Second, the new payments processing technologies that are being adopted, by new fintech providers but also by more established banks and other financial institutions, show up the limits of existing operational risk regulation.

## Operational risks in complex systems

Even when you take away the added complications of new fintech innovations, the potential systemic consequences of operational risks aren't very well understood. As the technology used by the financial industry becomes more complex, we can reasonably expect that technological failures will become more common,[20] and we should be very concerned about the impact that these operational failures could have on the stability of the financial system. Financial regulation mostly treats operational risk as something that a financial institution should manage on its own, though, as a matter of internal governance and risk management.

If we go back to the Principles for the Sound Management of Operational Risk we discussed earlier, Principle 4 provides that "[t]he board of directors should approve and periodically review a risk appetite and tolerance statement for operational risk that articulates the nature, types, and levels of operational risk *that the bank is willing to assume*" [emphasis added].[21] But what about the risks that a financial institution might create for others? Similarly, Principle 6 from the newly adopted Principles for Operational Resilience expects banks to "develop and implement response and recovery plans to manage incidents that could disrupt the delivery of critical operations in line with the bank's risk appetite and tolerance for disruption,"[22] but what about the *system's* tolerance for disruption? If the costs of operational failure fall on others, institutions may not invest enough in the robustness of their own infrastructure; they may also underinvest if they expect the central bank to come to their rescue with loans if an operational failure occurs.[23]

Even when a financial institution is willing to invest heavily in their own infrastructure, they might not fully grasp the potential spillovers of their operational decisions (particularly the decisions they make in their business continuity plans about how to resume services when their normal infrastructure is disabled). An institution probably wouldn't know how its competitors would be affected by its operational decisions, and even if it did, no financial institution can compel its competitors to resolve collective problems. Financial regulators, however, have broader oversight and access to confidential information (including business continuity plans) through their supervisory functions. They can also use their supervision and enforcement powers to compel action from regulated institutions.

There is a compelling case to be made for regulators taking a more involved approach to regulating operational risk, but thinking through the systemic consequences of technological failures will still be a difficult task for those regulators. It can be particularly challenging to think about potential technological malfunctions and their spillover effects when we have so little experience with the latest technologies and how they could go wrong. Fortunately, the discipline of complexity science (which studies complex systems and the unpredictable interactions among their components) can supply us with a new way to think about the transmission of operational risks in the payments system.

The overarching payments system, which is made up of banks, fintechs, clearinghouses, central banks, businesses, and consumers (among others) and governed by layers of laws and rules, is a very complex system.[24] It's complex not only because it has many diverse components, but also because the interactions among those components are complicated and often unexpected—because of these interactions, the payments system is much more than the sum of its parts. These interactions can improve the efficiency of the payments system, but experience with other complex systems tells us that it will also prime the system for what are known as "cascade failures," where the system's reaction to even a relatively minor problem in one of its components can spur other problems and reactions, crescendoing into a significant, unanticipated failure of the entire system.[25]

The "relatively minor problem" that starts a cascade failure could be as simple as a technological glitch. Here, I'm using the word "glitch" as a shorthand for all the ways in which software might perform in a way unanticipated by its programmers—a software bug might result in breakdowns of internal or external communications systems, for example, or cause a situation where crucial data cannot be retrieved or has been scrambled. Financial stability regulators are paying attention to how cyberattacks could cause these kinds of problems,[26] but they have paid less attention to how they could occur even without the involvement of a bad actor.

Experience with cascade failures in other complex systems teaches us that we shouldn't assume that the consequences of a glitch will always be minor or contained: glitches have a way of metastasizing within complex systems. For example, the electrical transmission system, which comprises (among other things) generating plants, transmission lines, substations, distribution lines, and consumers, is generally recognized as a complex system. Cascade failures within the electrical transmission system, transmitted by interconnections among system components and magnified through the transmission process, are often the cause of large electrical blackouts. An attack on a component could certainly spark the cascade, but components could also fail because they are worn out, poorly maintained or operated, damaged by fire or weather conditions, or have design flaws. When a component fails (for whatever reason), power flows are redistributed from the failed components to other parts of the system, changing the way the system operates. These new and unanticipated power flows can overload the remaining components of the system, causing more of them to fail and further overloading the remaining components in a vicious cycle.[27]

Interactions of outages and other operational problems in the payments system could trigger and transmit future crises in a way that looks more like a rolling power blackout than a bank run. Unfortunately, parts of our current system of regulation may end up encouraging these kinds of systemic interactions.[28] Take Principle 6 of the Principles for Operational Resilience, which requires banks to "develop and implement response and recovery plans to manage incidents that could disrupt the delivery of critical operations."[29] Principle 6 might encourage a bank experiencing operational problems to resume services as quickly as possible—perhaps before its technology is fully repaired, notwithstanding that using damaged systems could leave the bank more vulnerable to a bigger operational failure. If that bigger failure were to occur and the remaining payments providers picked up the slack in processing payments, they could be overloaded to the extent that *their* stressed systems start to break down, further overloading whoever is left.

Complexity science tells us, somewhat counterintuitively, that steps like Principle 6 that are taken in an attempt to make a system more robust may actually make the system as a whole more susceptible to cascade failures. This is because there is not one single type of robustness—there are in fact five types, and if too much emphasis is put on the wrong types of robustness, the system as a whole will become more fragile.[30]

The five dimensions of robustness are reliability, efficiency, modularity, scalability, and evolvability. Too much emphasis on the efficiency of the system, or on its reliability (which refers to the robustness of the system's individual components), is likely to make the system more fragile. It's not all that surprising that fragility can arise from increased efficiency: a system that is more efficient in moving one thing around (money, for example) is probably going to be more efficient at transmitting glitches as well. The fragility that can come from too much emphasis on reliability is a little less obvious, though. Incremental steps (like Principle 6) that are taken to make individual components of a system more reliable in the face of known problems reduce the risk of those known problems, but by ensuring that those components will continue to function even if there is a problem, and by increasing the complexity of the system as a whole, those incremental steps can combine to ensure that problems are transmitted to the broader system.

If we are trying to create a more robust system overall, increased focus needs to be placed on the system's modularity, scalability, and evolvability. All of these relate to the system's ability to continue functioning well in unanticipated circumstances. The modularity of a system refers to its ability to cope with changes to the organization of the system's components: the components of a modular system can work in parallel or reconfigure when there is a problem in order to avoid crashing the system. Scalability refers to the ability of the system to cope with changes to its own size and complexity (this is particularly important in a payments system, which can experience large fluctuations in the volume of transactions being processed at any given time).[31] Evolvability means the ability to cope with changes to the system that are made over time: a system that is robust in this respect can withstand many unanticipated changes in usage.

Increased focus on modularity, scalability, and evolvability does not mean that a system's reliability and efficiency aren't important. It would be pointless if cascade failures were eliminated by making the components of a system too clunky or broken down to work even in normal times. However, we may have to accept something less than perfectly efficient performance from the system if we want to avoid cascade failures. Chapter 6 will explore some practical applications of this complexity science framework, developing a new type of "macro-operational regulation" designed to increase understanding of operational problems, develop emergency responses, and build in redundancies. This chapter will use the complexity science framework to tease out some of the underappreciated operational risks associated with mobile payments platforms and the payments applications of distributed ledger technologies.

## Mobile payments

"Mobile payments" is an umbrella term that covers a lot of different services that allow people to make payments from their phones. Some, like ApplePay, don't allow users to store any money with them.[32] These types of services use technology to provide new ways of accessing existing bank accounts (the Zelle platform, developed in-house by banks to offer their customers a more convenient way of transferring funds between deposit accounts, performs a similar function). Other mobile payment services, though, provide users with a digital wallet that they can use to store money as well as carry out transactions. Funds might be transferred into and out of these digital wallets from bank accounts (as with Venmo and Alipay), or wallets can be funded in other ways. For example, funds are uploaded to M-Pesa by delivering cash to an M-Pesa kiosk—the updated balance is then recorded on the user's SIM card, and transactions can be accomplished by way of text messages.

So far, most of the concerns that have been raised about the financial stability implications of mobile payments relate to runs on mobile wallets—for example, could Venmo be prone to something like a bank run? People with a Venmo account might believe that their digital wallet is the same thing as a bank account, but Venmo balances are not protected by deposit insurance, and Venmo can't take advantage of the specialized insolvency procedures that ensure that if a bank fails, depositors' funds remain available to them. Instead, Venmo would have to go into regular bankruptcy and customers could find their funds mixed up with Venmo's other assets, completely inaccessible to them until the bankruptcy is resolved (which can take years). If Venmo got some bad press alerting its customers to these potential outcomes, those customers might rapidly withdraw their funds—this would compromise Venmo's ability to continue processing payments, and merchants and service providers who relied on Venmo to receive payments would struggle to pay their own creditors and employees, who would in turn experience their own economic difficulties as a result.[33]

At its current size, a problem with Venmo is unlikely to have much of an impact on the broader economy (Venmo processed only $37 billion of payments in the second quarter of 2020, compared with Visa's processing of $2.14 trillion in the same period).[34] However, as mobile payments services become more popular, and as customers start to become more comfortable storing large amounts of money in their digital wallets, these kinds of problems could have systemic-sized implications. For a sense of their potential scale, we can look to China, where USD$41.51 trillion of mobile payments transactions were processed in 2018 (and that number is growing exponentially).[35] Because many users of the Chinese mobile payments services AliPay and WeChat Pay store funds in their mobile wallets, rather than simply using their mobile wallets as conduits for payments from bank accounts,[36] the system is primed for economically damaging runs. Recognizing the potential for problems, the Chinese government recently overhauled regulation of mobile payments in China. AliPay and WeChat Pay are now required to keep all funds deposited in digital wallets in special reserve accounts with the Chinese central bank.[37] If mobile wallets end up being adopted widely in other countries, then runs on mobile wallets will be a major concern for their financial regulators to grapple with as well.

Services like Zelle and ApplePay that make payments from bank accounts rather than mobile wallets don't pose these same kinds of run risks. They do, however—like all mobile payments services—pose new operational risks that have largely escaped scrutiny. A quick google search yields lots of results discussing glitches, outages, and other problems with services like Zelle, as well as services like Venmo. Sometimes the service simply isn't available when it's needed due to some kind of software bug; sometimes transactions are lost or frozen (it doesn't help that fintech platforms tend to have few people you can call if something goes wrong).[38] Other times, glitches allow users to incur a negative balance—one *Wall Street Journal* article discussed the debt collection efforts that Venmo was taking to recover these negative balances, reporting that "[t]he money shows up in the recipient's Venmo account almost right away, though it can take a day or two for the funds to actually be removed from the sender's bank account. If there are glitches in the interim, users can end up owing money to Venmo."[39]

Of course, traditional online banking suffers from technical outages and glitches too (even if it is more protected from runs). Notwithstanding their problems, could mobile payments providers make the payments system as a whole more robust by providing an alternative way of making payments when banks are down? The answer is maybe: it's theoretically possible, but relationships between mobile payments providers and banks might prevent them from working independently. To use our complexity science vocabulary, while the modularity of the overall payments system would be improved by adding new providers who can serve as substitutes if banks fail, if the new providers rely on infrastructure supplied by the banks, then all the payments providers could be incapacitated together. Linkages with the bank-based payments system can also undercut any improvement that mobile payments technologies might make to the scalability or evolvability of the overall payments system—in other words, ties to legacy banking infrastructure could limit the ability of new payments providers to grow and change over time.

All of this suggests that mobile payments providers would make our payments system more robust if they operated their own proprietary infrastructure—a new set of rails—that minimizes linkages with the banks. However, Venmo, and others like it, ultimately rely on the existing bank payments infrastructure to process payments. This reliance is partly driven by regulation. In the United States, only banks can have direct access to the Federal Reserve master accounts that are used to settle payments, and so a non-bank like Venmo could not access that settlement infrastructure on its own.[40] A payments start-up could theoretically set up its own settlement infrastructure that didn't depend on any account with a central bank, but that infrastructure would only be attractive to early adopters if they could make payments to a critical mass of people, and it would be hard for a start-up to attract the critical mass it needed to get off the ground.

Venmo solved this problem by tapping into the existing banking infrastructure: because it can be used to pay anyone with a bank account, Venmo was able to take advantage of the network effects of the bank-based payments system (something has "network effects" if it becomes more valuable as more people use it). AliPay, however, was able to capitalize on the Chinese e-commerce giant Alibaba's huge network of customers to launch its own proprietary technological infrastructure.[41] Something like AliPay could serve as an alternative way to make payments if the bank-based system were to become compromised (so long as users kept funds in their digital wallets and didn't need to access their bank accounts to fund them). This kind of redundancy would be particularly valuable if the unthinkable were to happen and infrastructure like Fedwire and CHIPS were to fail, paralyzing the entire bank-based system. However, AliPay's relationship with the Alibaba platform entails its own "too big to fail" risks: we will discuss the new types of systemic risk that can arise when tech giants start providing financial services in Chapter 7.

## Distributed ledgers and payments

Although many cryptoassets nominally described as payments technologies are used more for speculation than to pay for everyday goods and services, their underlying distributed ledger technology could theoretically be used to develop new payments rails, and distributed ledgers have some attributes that could contribute to a more robust payments system overall. Transactions on a distributed ledger can settle as soon as the validator nodes reach consensus on the appropriate debits and credits to the ledger—this can happen in real time (or something close to it—sometimes issues like Bitcoin's block size restrictions can slow things down, as we will discuss shortly). Speedy settlement can eliminate a lot of the credit risk that comes with waiting for settlement to occur.[42] Distributed ledgers also have redundancy built into their core technologies, which can address some operational risks (because a ledger is hosted by many different nodes, if one or a few of those nodes fails, the distributed ledger can continue to function. Similarly, if a usual validator node is unable to verify a transaction, others can perform that function for it).[43]

Still, quicker payments processing may allow runs to happen more quickly (leaving less opportunity for emergency intervention), and without clearinghouses or any other body performing a netting function, liquidity risks may be more of an issue. There are also questions about whether distributed ledger technology can scale up to process large volumes of payments without encountering operational problems. As we noted already, private parties often lack the incentives to invest heavily in preventing their own operational failures, because if some of the costs of failure are borne by the broader payments system (and if you expect some kind of government intervention to help you if something goes wrong), why spend all that money? In Chapter 3, we discussed Facebook's controversial plans for a Diem currency that would run on its own distributed ledger—we also discussed some problems with Diem's reliability (in terms of its susceptibility to runs). What we haven't discussed yet are the operational risks associated with Diem.

Because Diem aspires to operate on a proprietary distributed ledger that can be used for both domestic and cross-border payments, it could provide alternative payments infrastructure that improves the modularity of the global payments system. However, Diem would benefit from significant network effects (because of the number of Facebook users around the world), and so it is also possible that Diem could outcompete other payments systems to become the dominant global infrastructure. This kind of dominance would result in fewer alternatives for payments processing if Diem were to fail—and so the Diem Association (and maybe even Facebook) would become "too big to fail."

Even if it doesn't outcompete all the alternatives, the software running Diem's ledger is intended to be open source, which means that users can create "application programming interfaces" ("APIs") that allow the software programs used by the Diem ledger to communicate directly with software used in other payment systems.[44] These APIs can increase efficiency, but complexity science tells us that "shortcuts" like APIs that would directly link Diem with alternative payments processors could make the system less modular and increase the risk of all those payments processors becoming compromised together.[45]

The lack of clarity about how the Diem Association plans to manage Diem's distributed ledger also raises operational risk concerns—it is hard to tell how scalable and evolvable the ledger will be without more information about how the Association operates, and in what circumstances it will make changes to the software that runs the ledger. For example, without the benefit of a clearinghouse to provide netting services that reduce the number of transactions that need to be processed, the ledger could become overwhelmed at peak times. If this were to become a recurrent problem, should some kind of netting procedure be introduced? When deciding whether to make these kinds of changes, will the members of the Association have any obligation to act in the best interests of Diem holders, or will they be permitted to act based on the financial interests of their own shareholders?[46]

These remain open questions, but we do know that Diem is supposed to operate on a permissioned ledger (the initial Libra white paper released in 2019 discussed plans to eventually transition to a permissionless ledger, but the second white paper released in 2020 announced that this plan had been abandoned because of concerns about whether a ledger controlled by an amorphous group could be relied upon to comply with any applicable regulations).[47] A permissioned ledger will certainly be more manageable, but there's no guarantee that an operator of a different stablecoin won't adopt a decentralized permissionless ledger in the future (or frankly, that the Diem Association won't change its mind). It's therefore worth thinking about how scalability and evolvability could become more complicated with a decentralized permissionless ledger.

As we discussed in Chapter 3, there is no central authority that controls the software that runs a decentralized permissionless ledger, and so management of that software can be unwieldy. Even when there is broad agreement that changes to a ledger's software are needed, the lack of centralized control can increase the time and effort needed to make those changes to the distributed ledger's operations. Things are even more complicated when there is no such agreement: the "civil wars" that have occurred over the Bitcoin distributed ledger illustrate the types of problems that can arise.

Remember from Chapter 3 that a consensus mechanism is used to determine which transactions should be added to Bitcoin's distributed ledger. But transactions are not added one by one—instead, they are consolidated into groups of transactions known as "blocks," and once validated by consensus, the entire block is added to the ledger (this is why Bitcoin's distributed ledger is often referred to as the "blockchain"). As Bitcoin became more popular, limitations on the size of these blocks were slowing down the processing of transactions during busy times—in other words, they were limiting Bitcoin's scalability and evolvability. Some members of the Bitcoin community wanted to maintain the existing block size, whereas others wanted to increase the block size to allow for quicker transaction processing. The factions could not come to an agreement, and so in August of 2017, Bitcoin had a "hard fork," meaning that two branches of the ledger were created with each branch using a different software protocol from that time on.[48]

Hard forks are one solution to problems of scalability and evolvability, but they are not a great one. Forking ledgers into successively smaller payments systems with smaller numbers of users can accommodate changes in volume and usage, but it reduces the number of people you can pay—reducing the network effects, and therefore the usefulness, of the payments systems. As we've already established, though, many of these kinds of scalability and evolvability problems can be avoided if the ledger is run by a centralized authority—then there is an identifiable person or group that can coordinate changes to the ledger.

This is the case with JPMCoin, the prototype virtual currency being trialed by JPMorgan as a way of making more efficient payments between JPMorgan's institutional clients. JPMCoin runs on its own proprietary centralized permissioned ledger, and so JPMorgan has the power to approve transactions, and make changes to the software operating the ledger.[49] This means that in some ways, JPMCoin can scale and evolve better than payments systems that rely on distributed ledgers with more convoluted governance structures. JPMCoin is restricted in other ways, though.

It's hard for a new technology to adapt if it's tied to the foundation of a legacy technology—glitches tend to increase when new technologies interface with legacy software systems.[50] But this is exactly the challenge that banks face when adopting new technologies like a distributed ledger. Many established banks depend on legacy systems that were developed in the 1960s and '70s, often using a computer programming language called COBOL that is now largely obsolete.[51] In addition, many banks have grown through merging with or acquiring other banks, with each merging or acquired bank bringing its own IT infrastructure—Deutsche Bank, for example, relied on 45 different operating systems as of 2015.[52] This means that when banks adopt new technologies, it's hard to fully understand the context in which those technologies will operate, and unintended consequences are likely to arise.

In sum, distributed ledgers are susceptible to their own brand of technological glitches. The operators of any payments platforms relying on a distributed ledger should be required to invest in making their infrastructure more robust, but it may be difficult for financial regulators unfamiliar with these new technologies to figure out whether the operators of these platforms are actually doing the hard work of managing their operational risks. Given these difficulties, it's worth asking whether governments and central banks, which have better incentives than the private sector to invest in robust payments infrastructure, should consider providing new payments alternatives themselves.

## Public payments alternatives

Several proposals have been made recently for more accessible, government-provided payment services. Some of these proposals are decidedly low-tech: at the simpler end, there have been calls for post offices to provide payments and other banking services to their customers.[53] There have also been proposals for businesses and individuals to be allowed to open accounts with their central bank—just like banks can.[54] Other proposals are more technologically complicated. The Federal Reserve, for example, is developing a "new instant payment service" called FedNow to "enable financial institutions of every size, and in every community across the U.S., to provide safe and efficient instant payment services in real time, around the clock, every day of the year."[55] And central banks around the world are considering central bank digital currencies ("CBDCs") that would run on a distributed ledger.[56]

These different proposals have different goals. Some of them are focused on addressing economic inequality. For example, postal banking and central bank accounts are intended to make payments processing cheaper and more accessible for individuals who do not have bank accounts and therefore rely on expensive alternatives like check cashing.[57] FedNow's ambitions to make payments faster can help individuals who do have bank accounts, but end up paying overdraft and other similar fees when bills come due while they wait for their paychecks to clear.[58] CBDCs, on the other hand, are less about providing more inclusive financial services and more about ensuring that sovereign currencies can continue to compete against stablecoins that run on private distributed ledgers (like Diem).[59]

In addition to their intended goals, many of these proposals also have potential implications for financial stability. Generally speaking, government involvement in the payments system is likely to help address operational threats to financial stability. Most of the proposals mentioned here involve the central bank, and central banks have stronger incentives than the private sector to invest in the resilience of their infrastructure (after all, central banks are the ones who have to step in with support when other payments providers have problems).[60] Although regulation and supervision can be used to nudge the private sector toward investing more heavily in managing their own operational risks, it's much easier for a central bank to manage the risks associated with infrastructure when it operates the infrastructure itself.[61] Glitches will inevitably develop in any technologically sophisticated system, including one developed by a central bank (this is one argument in favor of some of the lower-tech proposals), but the overall redundancy provided by a publicly provided payments processing alternative can improve the modularity of the overall payments system, making the system as a whole more robust to operational failures (so long as the public service doesn't outcompete all the alternatives).

In addition to operational risks, we also need to consider more traditional concerns about run risk. At the end of 2020, the Bank for International Settlements released a report on efforts by central banks to develop CBDCs.[62] This report expressed concerns that CBDCs could have financial stability implications, particularly in terms of encouraging runs from bank deposits to the CBDC (there could be similar types of runs if individuals were allowed to open accounts directly with the central bank).[63] While we could theoretically embrace this kind of outcome (with a central bank taking the funds that run to it, and investing them for the benefit of society as a whole),[64] most proposals proceed on the basis that banks need to be cushioned from the impact of any shift to a CBDC.[65]This could be done, for example, if a central bank were to lend the funds deposited with it to private sector banks, who could then lend those funds on to consumers and businesses the way they used to make loans funded by deposits.[66]

It's interesting that central banks are exploring CBDCs despite the financial stability risks they have identified. The Bank for International Settlements' report on CBDCs suggests that this is a defensive move, with CBDCs designed to help central banks maintain control over a money supply that could otherwise migrate to stablecoins like Diem.[67] Given the fragilities that inevitably come from increased technological complexity, though, if CBDCs are nothing more than a defensive response designed to outcompete the Diems of the world, central banks might be better off focusing their efforts on determining whether those Diems should be permitted in the first place (an issue we will explore in Chapter 6).

## Other financial infrastructure

Payments systems are not the only plumbing that the financial system provides. Infrastructure is also needed to connect buyers and sellers who want to trade financial assets, and then to process their trades. That post-trade processing involves clearing and settlement systems, and the same distributed ledger technology that is being harnessed for payments processing is also being eyed as way to settle other types of financial transactions. A shift from legacy systems to distributed ledger-based systems for settling trades would raise similar, but not identical, issues to the ones we've just explored in the context of payment infrastructure. The precise contours of these issues will vary depending on what is being traded: in this chapter, we will look at the processing of stock trades in the United States, but much of this discussion would apply to other types of post-trade processing infrastructure as well.[68]

People who want to buy or sell stocks typically submit an order through their brokers, then those brokers can use a stock exchange to find a willing counterparty to the trade. Once a buy order and a sell order have been matched, the trade processing plumbing kicks in. An entity called the National Securities Clearing Corporation (the "NSCC") verifies the information it has received about the trade, then it steps into the middle of that trade, becoming the legal buyer from the seller and the legal seller to the buyer (this means that the buyer and seller no longer face any credit risk with respect to each other, but all of that credit risk is concentrated in the NSCC). Once this clearing process is complete, the trade can then be settled by updating the records of the Depository Trust Company (the "DTC") to reflect the new ownership of the stocks (like CHIPS, the NSCC and the DTC are financial market infrastructures that are regulated in accordance with the PFMIs).

The DTC's records are not updated in real time, though—trades often take days to settle. In the interim, transactions in the same stock are netted out, reducing the number of changes that are actually made on the DTC's books, as well as the number of payments that need to be made from the relevant brokers to the NSCC (and from the NSCC to the brokers). Brokers used to have up to three days to settle trades in most publicly traded stocks (which was often referred to as T + 3 settlement), but that was reduced to T + 2 settlement in 2017.[69] Still, T + 2 is a far cry from immediate or even same-day settlement.

During that prolonged settlement period, the clearinghouse bears the risk that the parties might default, and the parties bear the risk that the clearinghouse might default.[70] The possibility of clearinghouse failure poses settlement risk for each of its counterparties (which adds up to a massive systemic risk), but the long settlement period also affords the parties some flexibility in terms of *when* they need to have assets or cash in hand to settle up. This addresses some of the liquidity aspects of settlement risk (so do the netting procedures that happen during that settlement period, which reduce the amount of assets/cash needed for settlement). The long settlement period also opens up opportunities for some very creative use of the stock that is the subject of the as-yet-unsettled trade: for example, a broker can sell stock that it doesn't own yet, with the intention of obtaining it before it's time to settle up. This is entirely legal (although there may be penalties if the broker doesn't obtain the stock in time for settlement), and means that a stock can effectively have multiple owners at the same time. If the same stock is used as collateral for multiple loans, this can multiply the amount of leverage in the financial system, which can be ominous from a financial stability perspective.[71]

And then there are the operational risks inherent in the stock trading infrastructure that could impair settlement. We can look back to the stock market crash of 1987 for a sense of how big an impact operational failures could have on the stock market. During that crash, "[t]he sheer volume of trade clogged the system and caused malfunctions of communications and information processing systems," and the most significant of those malfunctions was a programming glitch that shut down Fedwire for 2 ½ hours on October 20, 1987.[72] As we foreshadowed in our discussion of payments, these technical problems quickly metastasized into questions about the solvency of affected traders and brokerage firms.[73]

The emergency response to the 1987 crash was a familiar one: the Fed used its lender of last resort function to provide liquidity to the stock market. These liquidity injections can help allay concerns about the solvency of any link in the clearing and settlement chain, but they are not a direct response to technological problems. In 1990, Ben Bernanke took the view that "[t]he technological problems of communications and information availability that plagued the system, while serious, did not in and of themselves threaten to bring down the markets. . . . It was the financial problems—the possibility of insolvency by major players—that were potentially the more serious."[74] In 2021, though, the technological problems might be the more pressing issue. Which begs the question: Could distributed ledger technology help address these operational risks? Could it also help address the credit risks concentrated in clearinghouses?

A distributed ledger could theoretically be adopted to cut out intermediaries like the exchanges, the NSCC, and the DTC, creating what is essentially a one-stop shop for trading, clearing, and settling stocks that settles much more quickly than the current T + 2.[75] Anyone constructing this kind of ledger would have to decide upfront whether the ledger would be used to trade tokens that are digital representations of stock certificates held elsewhere, or whether they would trade stocks that are "native" to the distributed ledger, like bitcoins running on the Bitcoin ledger. If a stock were native to the ledger, smart contracts could be used for things like making dividend payments to stockholders.[76]

As with payments, a shift to using distributed ledgers for processing stock trades would involve a mix of operational pros and cons. It would cut out the clearinghouses that have been reasonably successful in managing the risk of counterparty default, but in doing so, it would eliminate the massive systemic risks associated with the clearinghouse itself failing. The credit risk associated with counterparty default would be limited by real-time settlement, but real-time settlement adds back in some liquidity risks because there is much less margin for error. What if the seller doesn't yet have possession of the stocks in question at the precise moment of settlement, or what if the buyer doesn't have the funds needed for payment at that precise moment? By requiring that sellers be in possession of the stock they are selling at the time of the trade, real-time settlement prevents stock from being used as collateral for multiple loans, reducing one kind of leverage in the system[77]—but faster settlement also means opportunities for more trades and therefore more opportunities for something to go wrong (and as we've already discussed, depending on how the ledger is managed, undoing problematic transactions may be very difficult operationally).

In fact, all of the operational risks that apply to using distributed ledgers for payments processing will apply to using distributed ledgers to process trades, and there will be extra complications when different infrastructures are involved in the trade settlement process (yet again we see that linking legacy and new technologies creates fertile ground for problems to develop). If stocks aren't native to the ledger and so people are trading tokens instead, how do we ensure that the physical custody of the underlying stock certificates matches the ownership of tokens indicated on the distributed ledger?

New kinds of operational risks are particularly likely to arise when people are trading traditional financial products on legacy settlement infrastructures, but the value of those products depend on underlying cryptoassets traded on a distributed ledger (for example, ETFs that derive their value from an underlying cryptoasset). With legacy systems taking days to settle and underlying cryptoassets settling in real time, "[t]iming mismatches and settlement failures are bound to happen" and the prices of the asset being traded and the underlying cryptoasset could diverge significantly.[78] Because the legacy system controls final settlement here, games can continue to be played with the settlement asset that allow the underlying cryptoasset to have multiple owners at any given time, magnifying the consequences of any failure of that crypotasset.

In sum, just as with payments, we're in a place where technological innovations will make some aspects of trade processing operationally safer for the financial system, and others worse. We can say definitively, though, that more attention needs to be paid to the operational risk issues involved.

## A note on vendors

Before finishing part II of this book, we should talk about the increasing importance of third-party technology vendors.[79] Third-party vendors aren't new to finance, but reliance on them is becoming more prevalent with the rise of fintech. Vendors are critical to many of the activities that we discussed in Chapters 2, 3, and this Chapter 4; for example, financial institutions are already buying machine learning technology to help manage their risks, and they may also become interested in buying preprogrammed smart contracts and distributed ledgers to run their new financial products. It's particularly appropriate that we're covering the risks of third-party vendors in this Chapter 4, though, because of this chapter's focus on operational risks.

As with the regulatory treatment of operational risks in general, it's largely left to individual financial institutions to manage the risks associated with their reliance on vendors (including any risks to financial stability).[80] By now, we're familiar with the limitations of this kind of approach. Financial institutions may not have the technical expertise needed to assess their technology vendors in the first place, and even if they do, they may not want to make the costly investments in vendor assessment that could be needed to protect the broader financial system. Some financial institutions have approached regulators about allowing private standard-setting organizations to certify vendors and their technologies, but while this could help address the technical expertise issue, private standard-setting organizations still won't have much incentive to assess technologies for systemic problems (also, this kind of process could very well result in more concentrated reliance on a few certified vendors—we'll turn to the problems with vendor concentration shortly).[81]

Regulators that oversee multiple financial institutions will have a better idea of how the use of technology vendors will affect the broader system. It is therefore helpful that, in some jurisdictions, regulators are authorized to engage in direct supervision of vendors—but that's not always the case. Even when they have this power, regulators will not be able to supervise vendors located outside of their jurisdiction, and they may not be able to oversee the vendors that the vendors rely on (and of course, regulators also face challenges in developing the technological expertise needed to oversee these vendors).

Given these limitations of regulatory oversight (and the inevitability of technological failures even when there's good oversight), financial stability will benefit if financial institutions don't all rely on the same vendor. There are often only a few vendors out there to choose from, though, and a lot of concern has been expressed about the concentration of the cloud computing industry in particular, where a few large cloud providers dominate the entire global market.[82]

Rather than housing voluminous amounts of data on-site, many financial institutions are exploring cloud computing services that allow that data to be stored off-site. That data may include, for example, information about customers and balances that is needed to process transactions, in which case an outage at a cloud provider could shut down transaction processing for multiple institutions, potentially triggering the types of runs and cascading operational failures we have already discussed in this chapter. (This is yet another instance where focusing too much on the reliability of an individual component of the financial system could make the financial system as a whole more vulnerable: while the protections used by individual financial institutions in their own local data centers are usually not as robust as the protections used by cloud providers,[83] a local outage would be much less harmful than an outage at one of the few cloud providers. Our financial system might actually be more robust with lots of comparatively weak data centers).

Fortunately, most financial institutions still store most of their "mission critical" data (like the customer account details used to process payments) on-site. Financial institutions' comfort with using cloud storage for more core functions appears to be increasing, though, and systemic vulnerabilities are increasing with it.[84] These developments underline the importance of creating redundancy in the financial system as a matter of urgency, whether that happens through requiring financial institutions to maintain their own local data centers, engage overlapping services from multiple cloud vendors, or participate in initiatives like Sheltered Harbor, which develops standards for "secure data vaulting of critical customer account information and a resiliency plan to provide customers timely access to their data and funds in a worst-case scenario."[85]

* * *

This chapter is the end of our discussion of the threats that fintech poses for financial stability. While this part of the book couldn't hope to be a completely comprehensive list of these threats, it does show that many fintech business models and technologies are increasing the speed, complexity, and coordination of financial activity in a way that could undermine the stability of our financial system. The next part of the book will draw on this chapter's diagnosis of threats to the payments system, as well as the diagnoses from Chapters 2 and 3, as a foundation for designing financial stability regulation that responds to the rise of fintech innovation (and is also better at dealing with operational risk in general).

# PART III

# REGULATING FINTECH AND FINANCIAL STABILITY

# 5

# Fintech and Financial Stability Regulation

## Status Quo

In part II, we explored many of the new financial stability risks that are evolving with the rise of driverless finance. Diagnosing risks is often easier than addressing them, though. Part III of this book tackles the thorny practicalities of designing financial stability regulation for the fintech era. This chapter explores the challenges that regulators face when dealing with any new innovation, then considers in more detail the approaches that regulators have pursued with regard to fintech so far. Unfortunately, the new regulatory approaches they have pursued for fintech don't really address financial stability risks, and so Chapter 6 will suggest some innovative regulatory approaches that respond directly to the risks identified earlier in the book. Of course, new financial stability risks aren't the only issues arising from fintech's new fusion of finance and technology. Chapter 7 takes a step back and looks at some of the bigger debates about finance and technology, and considers how those debates intersect with the financial stability issues that we have focused on in this book.

### What is regulation?

Before considering the challenges that fintech poses for regulation, it helps to have a baseline understanding of what we mean by the word "regulation." As with so many of the terms used in this book, "regulation" is slippery to define.[1] Regulation certainly includes laws passed by national and state legislatures, but many unelected government agencies also have the power to adopt rules that have the force of law. Private sector organizations are also free to adopt and enforce rules against their own members, and there are even situations when members of the public are authorized to enforce laws against private firms. Also, while "regulation" is usually used to describe laws and rules that impose duties and prohibit activities, it can be used to describe

*Driverless Finance.* Hilary J. Allen, Oxford University Press. © Hilary J. Allen 2022.
DOI: 10.1093/oso/9780197626801.003.0006

laws and rules that enable activities as well. The concept of "regulation" is therefore very broad—but this book will only look at a slice of regulatory activities. The focus in part III of this book will be on financial regulatory agencies, and their regulatory functions of rule-making, supervision, and enforcement (although we will also consider new laws that may be needed to give financial regulatory agencies the authority to engage in rule-making, supervision, and enforcement with respect to new fintech innovations).

Regulatory agencies engage in rule-making in order to flesh out the laws made by national and state legislatures. These agency-made rules can ban or require activities, or allow activities subject to certain conditions. Rules can target products and services directly, for example, by prohibiting certain features of a financial product, or they can take more indirect approaches, like requiring that certain information be disclosed about that product (consumers and investors are then in a better position to make their own decisions about whether they want the product or not).

Agencies' formal rule-making processes follow established procedures that are time-consuming, but are intended to allow the general public to influence and exercise some oversight over what is essentially lawmaking by unelected bureaucrats. For example, before a US administrative agency can finalize a rule, it must first publish a "notice of proposed rulemaking," give the public the opportunity to comment on that proposal, and consider all of the relevant public comments.[2] In addition to formal rules, regulatory agencies also issue less formal guidance that is much quicker to implement, but because it is not protected by these kinds of democratic safeguards, it doesn't have the full force of law (still, regulated institutions ignore this informal guidance at their peril). Some regulatory agencies seek to straddle the divide between more formal and less formal regulation by adopting principles-based regulations, where high-level objectives are adopted through formal rule-making procedures, and informal guidance supplies much of the detail on how to satisfy these objectives—regulated entities are then afforded greater flexibility in determining how they will comply with the high-level objectives.[3]

In addition to making rules, regulatory agencies also supervise compliance with those rules (and their informal guidance), as well as other laws over which they have jurisdiction. Supervision can take the form of requiring reports from a regulated institution or engaging in on-site examinations, and then regulators use that information to assess an institution's compliance. If an agency concludes that the rules are not being followed, enforcement can range from informal "arm-twisting" measures to more formal sanctions like fines. Criminal penalties can even be administered in conjunction with law enforcement authorities. In sum, regulatory agencies have a cocktail of regulatory options at their disposal. The ideal blend of regulatory approaches will vary, depending on what is being regulated—and calibrating the right blend can be particularly challenging when dealing with new innovations.

## Why regulating innovation is hard

Chapter 1 took apart and rejected the conventional wisdom that "innovation always equals improvement." Of course, innovation often *does* improve upon existing products and services, but even when it is an improvement, it might have unintended side effects that warrant scrutiny. Regulators therefore have to remain alert to the new ways in which products and services are being provided. Unfortunately, there are some perennial challenges that make it hard to design and enforce rules around innovation. These challenges are by no means unique to regulating financial innovation—different kinds of regulators overseeing all kinds of new technologies must also grapple with these difficulties.[4]

Most obviously, regulators tend to have far fewer resources than the private sector entities they oversee. This can make it very hard for regulators to keep an eye on what the private sector is doing. Even when regulators are aware of new innovations, they may struggle to understand them—and they may fear failure and embarrassment if they end up adopting rules that betray a misunderstanding of the innovation or have unintended consequences. While Silicon Valley innovators can get away with living by mantras like "fail fast" or "move fast and break things,"[5] regulators face significant scrutiny from the industries they oversee, and those industries won't always be particularly forgiving of regulatory failures. Regulators may therefore be tempted not to act at first, preferring a "wait and see" approach that will better allow them to avoid unintended consequences. However, taking such a "wait and see" approach will often hurt the general public: one UK regulator observed that when private sector technology is developing at an exponential pace, regulators who wait and see are essentially "accelerating backwards."[6]

Even when regulators are willing to rein in problems associated with innovative products and services, they may sometimes lack the authorization or jurisdiction to take formal action. New innovations rarely fit well into regulatory structures that were designed long before the innovations were even dreamt of (the bulk of automobile regulations, for example, were adopted in a time where all drivers were expected to be human, which makes autonomous vehicles a regulatory challenge).[7] While laws and regulations can be updated to give regulators jurisdiction over new innovations, private sector innovation happens much more quickly than laws can be passed or rules adopted. Furthermore, because it takes so long to put laws and rules in place, it will be hard to change them, even if it becomes clear that they are a poor fit as the innovation becomes better understood or evolves.

Regulators should therefore consider compromise measures that they can take, which are more nimble than formal laws or rules but exert more control than a pure "wait and see" approach. For example, they can use tools like agency speeches, testimony, press releases, warning letters, no action letters, interpretative guidance, and private meetings to provide some clarity on the application of existing regulation to new activities.[8] This type of informal regulation can be implemented quickly, and can also be easily refined and improved as more is learned and as circumstances change. Admittedly, too much regulatory flexibility can sometimes cause problems—both for regulators who may struggle to enforce guidance that does not have the force of law, and for the innovators themselves. The trade-off for flexibility is a lack of certainty about the rules that apply, and markets for some innovations may not be able to develop without a clear regulatory signal to users and investors that an innovation is permitted. Regulatory uncertainty can also create an environment where innovators face uncertainty about enforcement—in a murky regulatory environment, innovators might be discouraged from pursuing new projects for fear that regulation will be imposed after the fact. These trade-offs between flexibility and certainty are unavoidable, but the regulatory approach used does not have to remain static over time.

When dealing with a new innovative technology, regulators can start by issuing informal guidance and then make more formal rules as the innovation matures. To be clear, regulators should not feel they have to wait until they understand an innovation perfectly before taking more concrete action (frankly, it is questionable whether innovators even understand their own creations perfectly). Once regulators feel they have enough information to take a more definitive stance on regulating an innovation, they have several options. Regulators can adopt rules that block a new innovation entirely or take the opposite approach and remove all regulatory impediments to the innovation. They are more likely, though, to take an approach that is somewhere in the middle, allowing an activity while imposing some conditions on it.

Once laws and regulations are put in place, innovators will adjust their behavior accordingly. Some innovators may move their operations to other jurisdictions where the activity is either not regulated or regulated differently (this is relatively easy for technology and finance firms to do, because neither require a lot of physical infrastructure).[9] Other innovators may try to avoid regulation by designing products and services that achieve the same outcomes as regulated activities, but rely on underlying processes that were not anticipated by the regulatory regime. These are all forms of "regulatory arbitrage," and they allow innovators to comply with the letter of the law, even as they violate its spirit. Regulatory arbitrage is a persistent challenge for regulators seeking to address new innovations: if regulators try to respond to arbitrage with new rules that clarify the application of the law to a particular activity, then they can expect that innovators will try to arbitrage *those* clarifying rules with new innovations.

## Why regulating financial innovation is particularly hard

Regulatory arbitrage is a concern for many different kinds of regulators, as are constraints on resources and imperfect understandings of rapidly developing innovations. Financial regulators also face more specific challenges, including the preexisting complexity of the financial system in which the new innovations will operate. This complexity ensures that the challenges that regulators face in understanding new innovations are compounded by their difficulties in understanding innovations' likely interactions with existing components of the financial system. Financial regulators must also recognize that their own actions as regulators, as well as the arbitrage that those actions will probably inspire, will further contribute to the complexity of the financial system—and that that complexity may ultimately undermine their regulatory objectives.[10] Fear of unintended consequences in such a complex environment can become a particularly strong constraint on financial regulation.

Financial regulators' jobs become even harder if they are trying to satisfy multiple mandates. Mandates for financial regulatory agencies are established by law, typically by national or state legislatures, and they often include more than one objective. These objectives might include the protection of financial stability, the protection of consumers and/or investors, the promotion of market efficiency, and the promotion of market competition.[11] Any regulatory agency that is supposed to do more than one of these things must consider the possibility that regulations they adopt to advance one of their objectives could potentially undermine their other objectives.

Most financial regulatory agencies don't have express statutory mandates to promote innovation, but private sector innovation can improve efficiency and competition in the markets for financial services—and efficiency and competition mandates *are* common. Consumer and investor protection mandates are also common for financial regulators. Ideally, by making a market for financial services more efficient and competitive, consumers and investors will also benefit—but benefit and protection are not always the same thing. There is a long history of financial innovations that were designed to be superficially appealing but ultimately harmed consumers and investors: many of these financial products and services had hidden features that consumers and investors would reject if they truly understood them.[12] Disclosure regulations have often been adopted to make problematic features more visible, and sometimes—when a financial product or service has had a particularly egregious impact on consumers or investors—regulators have simply banned the product or service.[13] These types of protective regulation can put a damper on financial innovation-generated efficiencies and competition, and regulators with conflicting mandates will have to determine which to prioritize. The financial stability objective can also conflict with attempts to promote efficiency and competition through innovation: part II of this book demonstrated at length that many efficient fintech innovations have the potential to undermine financial stability.

When their regulatory objectives conflict, financial regulatory agencies will need to figure out which objective to prioritize. Chapter 1 has already made the case that financial stability should be the priority goal in any financial regulatory regime. Consumer and investor protection should also be a priority, because vulnerable consumers and investors are typically unable to organize to protect themselves. Unfortunately, though, many of the new fintech-specific regulatory approaches that have been developed over the last five years have focused on promoting efficiency and competition instead. The innovation hubs, specialized charters, and regulatory sandboxes that are discussed below were all designed to facilitate and promote fintech innovation by the private sector, with other regulatory priorities often falling by the wayside.[14]

## Innovation support from regulators

For better or worse, many financial regulators around the world have embraced the goal of facilitating private sector fintech innovation. These regulators recognize that financial regulation is so pervasive that it is almost impossible for fintech innovators to avoid entirely, and that it can be very expensive for innovators to modify products and services late in the game. Understanding the regulatory landscape upfront can therefore save an innovator significant amounts of time and money, because the product or service can be designed with the regulatory requirements in mind. In addition, venture capital firms often won't invest in fintech businesses that don't pass regulatory muster, and so a start-up may need to understand regulatory requirements in order to attract funding. Furthermore, consumers and investors often trust financial products and services more when they know they are regulated—blessing from the regulator can therefore be a significant boon to marketing the new product or service.

For these and other reasons, it makes business sense for fintech innovators to comply with regulation from the outset. However, tech startups with no experience in finance have to invest daunting amounts of time and money in figuring out which regulations apply to them, and which licenses and authorizations their lines of business require—and they have to make these investments before they can even test the market for their products and services. Established financial institutions have an advantage over fintech startups in their familiarity with financial regulation, but uncertainty about how new technologies will be regulated could ultimately discourage their innovation as well.

To help lower these barriers to private sector innovation, financial regulators around the world have experimented with new ways of regulating fintech. Some regulators have relied on existing regulatory powers that allow them to waive the application of their rules. Another strategy is for regulators to issue "no action" or "no enforcement" letters that leave the regulatory requirements in place, but give innovators comfort that their activities will not be challenged as a breach of those requirements. Less formally, regulators can simply provide guidance to innovators to help them understand the regulatory requirements that apply to their product and service, and any changes that may need to make to the product or service in order to comply with those requirements.[15] Recently, many financial regulators providing this type of guidance have started to brand themselves as "innovation hubs."

The first fintech innovation hub was launched by the UK's Financial Conduct Authority ("FCA") in 2014.[16] The FCA's "Innovate" program provides support and services to UK innovators in a number of ways—perhaps most famously through its regulatory sandbox (which will be discussed below), but also by providing feedback to firms during their innovation process. Many other jurisdictions have followed the United Kingdom's lead by creating innovation hubs of their own, and the term "innovation hub" has come to describe any program that provides fintech innovators with access to a regulator in order to request advice and guidance (and perhaps also a waiver or no action letter).[17] Regulators with innovation hubs are trialing different types of outreach—some hold open house sessions in different geographic locations, others invite innovators onto their premises for designated office hours. Regardless of the specifics, a significant investment of resources is required to run an innovation hub properly. Usually, though, no legal changes are needed before an innovation hub can start up.

Some regulators have considered or adopted more formal structures for accommodating fintech innovation. In the United States, for example, the Office of the Comptroller of the Currency adopted a policy authorizing what has come to be known as the "fintech charter."[18] This is a new type of license available to non-bank firms that want to opt into a new federal regulatory regime created with fintech in mind. However, this fintech charter has struggled to gain popularity for several reasons. First, the OCC's authority to create this special purpose charter has been challenged in a number of lawsuits, creating lingering questions about the charter's legality.[19] Second, this fintech charter still imposes significant amounts of regulation, and the time and costs associated with complying with this type of regulation may prove too much for many start-ups.[20] A far more popular regulatory experiment is the fintech regulatory sandbox, which *reduces* the amount of regulation that innovators must comply with.

## Regulatory sandboxes

In 2016, the UK's FCA pioneered the idea of a "regulatory sandbox" in order to help address the regulatory barriers to fintech innovation.[21] Borrowing from the world of software development, where "sandboxing" is used to test software in an isolated environment, the FCA envisioned its regulatory sandbox as "a 'safe space' in which businesses can test innovative products, services, business models, and delivery mechanisms while ensuring that consumers are appropriately protected."[22]Participants in the sandbox are given restricted authorizations that allow them to test products and services with real customers for a period of six months, without having to fully comply with all of the financial regulations that would ordinarily apply. Sandbox participants can therefore save time and money they would otherwise have to have devoted to regulatory compliance, and they also receive personalized guidance on how to optimize their innovation for regulatory compliance in the future. Innovators don't have to participate in the sandbox, of course—it is up to an individual firm to apply to the FCA to be included in its testing groups (which are referred to as "cohorts"). Applications for each cohort are assessed by the FCA on a case-by-case basis to determine whether the product or service is suitable for sandbox testing. More than a hundred businesses have now passed through the FCA's sandbox, trialing a wide variety of different technologies, with distributed ledger technology applications and digital identity verification seeming to be particularly common.[23]

The sandbox concept has proven very popular, and over the last five years, regulators from around the world have adopted variations on the theme, allowing innovators to conduct a limited test of fintech products and services in a lenient regulatory environment. The form of each regulatory sandbox differs depending on the jurisdiction, but most sandboxes reproduce two important attributes of the FCA's sandbox. First, the regulations that would otherwise apply are loosened in some way during the trial period. Second, the regulator usually provides guidance to the innovator on how to design a product or service that will ultimately comply with the relevant regulations, once the trial period is over.[24] Fintech sandboxes can now be found in countries as diverse as Malaysia and Mauritius, Saudi Arabia and Switzerland.[25] There has even been interest in starting up international sandboxes that would allow for concurrent testing of innovative financial products and services in multiple countries: a network of financial regulators known as the Global Financial Innovation Network ("GFIN") is currently working on this kind of cross-border testing.[26]

The appetite for these cross-border trials reflects the fundamental mismatch between the potentially international market for fintech products and services, and the more local nature of the regulatory sandboxes that are currently available. There is a similar mismatch even within the United States, where most regulatory sandboxes have been created at the state level and therefore do not provide innovators with access to the full domestic market for fintech products and services.[27] These state-level sandboxes are less than ideal for the innovators, and they are also a concern from a financial stability perspective. State and local governments and agencies are not ideal candidates to engage in financial stability regulation, because financial stability is the type of public good that cannot be contained within borders. There is little incentive for a small geographical area to spend money on regulation that will largely benefit others—instead, we could very well see states moving in the other direction and *lowering* their regulatory standards, so that they can attract new businesses to their jurisdiction and benefit from any resulting taxes, fees, and employment. This "race to the bottom" dynamic can manifest at the international level as well, with individual nation-states using sandboxes to lower their regulatory standards in order to improve their competitiveness.

To the extent that a regulatory sandbox rolls back financial stability regulations for firms conducting sandbox trials, it can be viewed as a type of deregulation that has the potential to harm the public. There are a number of design features that could be incorporated into a regulatory sandbox to better protect financial stability, though.[28] First, any law, regulation, or policy adopting a regulatory sandbox could specify that the protection of financial stability is an overriding constraint on the operation of the regulatory sandbox. This might mean that firms will be excluded from the sandbox if their innovation has the potential to have a systemic impact (which is particularly likely if the innovator is a techfin or huge bank), or is simply too complex to understand. Or, if a sandbox waives existing financial stability rules for participating firms, these rules could be replaced with more flexible requirements that require firms to consider how their new innovation might impact financial stability and take mitigating steps. For example, vendors designing innovations to be used by other financial firms should be discouraged from trialing their product with any customer that is a large, systemically important financial institution, because that would magnify the impact of any errors during the trial period. Finally, the trial of a financial product or service should be terminated if it becomes clear at any point that the innovation threatens financial stability in any way.

There are also ways in which sandboxes can be harnessed to improve financial stability. To be clear, a sandbox's benefits for financial stability will only ever be indirect and incidental—the innovators themselves have few incentives and limited ability to improve financial stability with their innovation. Still, sandboxes can be used to educate regulators about new technologies that they may have to grapple with in the future, and they can provide opportunities for regulators to intervene early in product development. Ideally, regulatory sandboxes would be designed to maximize the amount of information they produce about new technologies and the number of opportunities they provide for regulators to influence those technologies. In reality, though, the prospects for sandboxes actually generating information and facilitating intervention are mixed.

While financial regulators have been sharing information with one another for decades at both the domestic and the international levels, that information has often been about regulatory best practices.[29] When they have shared any commercially sensitive information, it has generally been done in the context of supervising the financial condition of financial institutions that operate in multiple jurisdictions.[30] In a sandbox, though, the regulator is learning sensitive information about the development of proprietary technology not just so they can regulate it, but also so that they can help it succeed. Information that regulators learn about new technologies would ideally be shared with other financial regulatory agencies (including those in other jurisdictions) to help develop a common understanding of emerging fintech risks and crowdsource ways to respond, but some regulators may want to keep information about technological innovations to themselves, fearing that if it's shared, the information could be used to assist firms that compete with participants in their own sandboxes. If this happens, each regulatory agency will only learn about a limited slice of the fintech innovation that is occurring, and have an incomplete picture of emerging threats to financial stability.

If regulatory sandboxes do not live up to their promise of educating the regulatory community about new technologies, could they still offer opportunities for regulators to shape individual technologies being trialed in their own sandbox? It's hard to figure out whether this is actually happening, because there is very limited data available about how sandboxes are actually working in practice. What we do know is that regulators around the world have often been surprised at how resource-intensive regulatory sandboxes are.[31] If regulators have underestimated the man hours and expertise needed to run a regulatory sandbox, they are probably not in a position to guide the development of fintech innovation in socially beneficial ways. Anecdotally, it seems that many regulators started their regulatory sandbox as a branding exercise, a seemingly low-cost way to communicate to the world that their jurisdiction was "open for fintech business," without fully thinking through what they would like to achieve with their sandbox.[32] It would not be surprising, then, if these regulators failed to think through the impact their sandboxes could have on core missions like financial stability.[33]

## Critique of innovator-focused regulation

Even where significant thought and resources have been devoted to a regulatory sandbox, the question remains whether facilitating private sector innovation is the best use of those public resources. The hope is that private sector innovation will generate benefits for the general public—typically, cheaper and more efficient financial services, especially for previously underserved consumers. However, subsidizing private sector innovation is a very indirect way of expanding access to financial products and services, and it is quite possible that the resources currently being devoted to innovation hubs and regulatory sandboxes will primarily benefit individual innovators, rather than the public at large. Instead of taking the indirect approach of facilitating private sector innovation in the hope that the public's unmet needs will be addressed, governments could consider addressing them directly (for example, by authorizing post offices or central banks to offer financial products and services, as we discussed in Chapter 4).

Because there are very limited data currently available about regulatory sandboxes and other new schemes for promoting fintech innovation, it is impossible to say for sure whether these regulatory strategies are succeeding even on their own terms of improving efficiency and competition. If we broaden our frame of reference to consider whether these regulatory strategies are satisfying the core financial regulatory goal of financial stability, the value proposition for expending resources on these types of programs becomes even less clear. Importantly, because fintech firms are under no obligation to participate in these programs, any incidental benefits of regulator education and opportunities to influence technological development will be skewed toward firms who opt into regulatory engagement, providing regulators with an incomplete picture of the innovations out there. Where the regulators' resources are scare (as they usually are), might investing those resources in financial stability regulation not be a better use than promoting a small slice of private sector innovation? If waivers, no action letters, and regulatory sandboxes are being used to roll back financial stability-related rules that would otherwise apply to providers of financial products and services, is that really good policy?

Unfortunately, with so much positive buzz around fintech innovation, these questions are rarely asked. There is almost no discussion of the financial stability implications of regulatory programs that support private sector fintech innovation, and at first blush, this might seem reasonable. After all, when fintech innovations are being trialed with a small group of retail consumers, those trials are unlikely to have much of a systemic impact. However, the scaled-up versions of these innovations might be much more problematic once launched into the wild, and even in trials, an innovation can cause issues if the customers trialing it are themselves large financial institutions.

In addition to the safeguards for regulatory sandboxes that have already been suggested, some type of forced reckoning is needed for *all* of the innovation-supporting regulatory programs. After seven years or so, regulatory sandboxes, innovation hubs, and similar programs should automatically be terminated (a process known as sunsetting), unless good evidence can be brought forward to justify the continuing investment of resources in these programs.[34] Adoption of these programs was motivated by excitement around financial innovation, but after seven years there should be sufficient data to make a more reasoned decision about whether these programs are at the very least satisfying the relevant agency's regulatory goals of competition or efficiency.

The financial stability impact of these innovation-supporting regulatory programs will probably still be difficult to assess after seven years, but a precautionary approach would suggest that many of the resources that are currently being invested in things like regulatory sandboxes and innovation hubs would be better invested in helping financial regulators maintain the stability of a system that is being rapidly changed by new technologies. As a first step, resources need to be allocated to understanding how fintech is actively undermining the existing regulatory protections that have been developed to protect the financial system. Then, resources should be devoted to experimenting with new fintech regulation approaches that apply to everyone—not just the innovators who seek out the regulators through a sandbox or innovation hub.

## Overview of financial stability regulation

Remember that financial stability regulation exists to ensure that the financial system can keep performing the risk management, capital intermediation, and payments function on which the broader economy relies. There are a lot of different ways to approach this goal. Many of the most familiar forms of financial stability regulation were designed to prevent bank runs, both because of banks' central role in providing these socially useful functions and because of their inherent fragility. When a customer deposits funds with a bank, that customer is actually making a loan to the bank, and so when a customer withdraws their funds from the bank, they are effectively demanding immediate repayment of that loan. If too many depositors seek to get their money back at the same time, then a bank will need to sell its assets to satisfy the immediate pressure for cash. If it is forced to sell those assets too cheaply, the value of the bank's overall assets may be pushed lower than the amount of its outstanding liabilities and the bank will fail—leaving it unable to discharge its socially useful functions. Even if the bank survives, it will be operating with significantly less funding than usual, which may end up restricting its lending activities. Furthermore, the bank's asset sales could drive down the market prices of those assets, harming other financial institutions that had invested in them and potentially compromising those institutions' ability to help manage risk, intermediate capital, and facilitate payments.

Deposit insurance, which was pioneered in the United States during the Great Depression, is one regulatory response to these problems. While many at the time were worried that deposit insurance would create perverse incentives for bank risk-taking, the public demand for an end to banking panics prevailed, and the Federal Deposit Insurance Corporation was created in 1933.[35] The specifics of deposit insurance programs have evolved as time has passed (and as different countries have implemented their own versions), but the fundamentals remain largely the same. Depositors know that if an insured bank is unable to return their funds to them, the government will do it instead (subject to any caps specified in the regulations—in the United States, for example, deposit insurance will only cover up to $250,000 in a bank account).[36] With the confidence that deposit insurance inspires, depositors are usually content to leave their money in the bank (rather than under their mattress) which in turn gives banks confidence that they can rely on deposit funding.

Special resolution mechanisms for banks have also been implemented to inspire the confidence of depositors: if a failed bank were required to declare bankruptcy (like an ordinary corporation), then that would tie up customers' deposits in a protracted court procedure. The desire to avoid such an outcome could encourage depositors in a teetering bank to pull out their funds as quickly as possible, ultimately dooming the bank to failure. Having a special process for resolving failed banks that pays depositors immediately can dampen these incentives.[37] Central banks like the Federal Reserve can also make emergency loans to banks that are temporarily unable to borrow elsewhere. This is known as the "lender of last resort" function, and it has been used by central banks for hundreds of years to avoid circumstances where healthy banks would otherwise be forced to sell their assets on the cheap to satisfy an immediate need for cash, which could ultimately lead to their insolvency—as well as pushing down the market price for those assets.[38]

Although safety nets like deposit insurance, special resolution regimes, and lenders of last resort are very effective in preventing bank runs, they can perversely encourage banks to make more risky investments by insulating them from some of the consequences of taking on too much risk (this was the concern that motivated opponents of deposit insurance in the 1930s). Other types of regulation have therefore been implemented to help ensure that banks are run prudently on an ongoing basis. For example, regulators devote a lot of time and effort to supervising the quality of bank management. There are also prudential rules requiring banks to maintain minimum levels of funding that can absorb losses, and minimum levels of assets that can be turned into cash quickly (in technocratic speak, regulatory capital and liquidity requirements).[39] The main idea behind regulatory capital requirements is that if a bank has funded its investments with at least some money that it doesn't need to pay back, its liabilities are less likely to grow bigger than its assets even if some of those assets start to lose value (in other words, the bank is less likely to become insolvent). The main idea behind liquidity regulations like reserve requirements and liquidity ratios is to ensure that a bank has some cash on hand to address its immediate obligations. Like deposit insurance, these liquidity rules will reduce the likelihood that an institution will need to raise cash by selling assets at a discount during a panic. These types of regulation are by no means perfect—they have been criticized as an inadequate response to the amount of risk and uncertainty in the financial system.[40] But the protections that they do provide were designed specifically with banks in mind.

There are also other types of financial institutions and markets that are crucial to the risk management, capital intermediation, and payments functions of the financial system. Since the last crisis, there is now widespread agreement that financial stability regulation needs to extend beyond banks to so-called shadow banking—but less agreement on how to go about it.[41] It is also now conceded that regulators can't just look at individual financial institutions in isolation—the steps that an institution takes to ensure its own compliance with regulatory capital and other requirements may come at the expense of the stability of the system as a whole.

The need for financial stability regulators to pay attention to the systemic implications of individual banks' and shadow banks' actions has come to be known as the "macroprudential" approach. In the years since 2008, regulators around the world have adopted concrete macroprudential measures like increased regulatory capital requirements for the largest banks (whose actions have the biggest systemic footprint), as well as the adoption of new regulatory capital "buffers" to help insulate all banks from the need to raise new capital during a crisis.[42] Mechanisms have also been adopted, with varying degrees of success, to extend regulatory capital requirements to the very largest shadow banks.[43]

Macroprudential regulation is not just about regulatory capital, though. It requires collaboration among regulators overseeing different parts of the financial system, and a curiosity about "how different developments fit together and where the unseen risks might be hidden."[44] Other developments in macroprudential regulation over the last decade include the creation of new regulatory institutions with systemic oversight capabilities (like the Financial Stability Oversight Council in the United States, the Financial Policy Committee in the United Kingdom, and the European Systemic Risk Board). New approaches to collecting and analyzing data have also been pioneered: in particular, there has been a lot of emphasis on using hypothetical scenarios of systemic failure to assess how resilient financial institutions are likely to be during times of stress.[45]

## How fintech might undermine financial stability regulation

While these are all welcome developments, macroprudential regulation remains very much a work in progress. The question of how to address shadow banking has proved stubbornly difficult—questions about how to regulate non-bank financial institutions will only become more difficult as fintech and techfin firms become more integral to the provision of financial services. Under existing regulatory regimes, deposit insurance and special resolution mechanisms won't be available to these firms unless they obtain bank charters (an expensive and time-consuming process that many fintech firms are eschewing).[46] To the extent that fintech firms *do* obtain bank charters, their business models may be unfamiliar to bank regulators, complicating supervision and enforcement.

Macroprudential regulation should also look at markets as well as institutions: surveillance of market activity can reveal emerging systemic risks. However, as market activity is increasingly driven by algorithms, it can become more opaque to regulators. Whether participants in financial markets should have to disclose their algorithms to regulators has already become a very thorny issue, particularly in the context of high frequency trading. In 2015, the Commodity Futures Trading Commission proposed a rule that would provide the agency with some access to the source code of high frequency trading firms' trading algorithms.[47] This proposal was met with a huge backlash from industry members who resisted giving up their "secret sauce," and the CFTC ultimately gave up on the proposal. It's not actually clear, though, that source code disclosure is the right fight for regulators to pick. As machine learning becomes more prevalent, the source code that teaches the algorithm how to learn will become much less relevant than the data it learns from. Furthermore, even experienced software engineers struggle to find flaws simply by looking at source code—it is usually more helpful for them, and certainly would be more helpful for financial regulators, to run the algorithm in beta mode to see how it works.[48] As such, regulators may not need source code to understand financial market activity—but they probably will need the authority to compel the disclosure of training data and beta tests of algorithms if they want to monitor the financial markets for new vulnerabilities. Unfortunately, when the market players using those algorithms are not banks, financial stability regulators often lack jurisdiction over them.

Even when it comes to banks, financial stability regulation will be strained as fintech innovations become increasingly popular. At the best of times, it is a challenging exercise (involving some guesswork) to figure out how risky financial assets are, and to determine the capital and liquidity requirements that should apply to those assets as a result. The rise of new classes of cryptoassets may make these types of calculations impossible. Before distributed ledgers and smart contracts came into existence, financial assets had to be tethered—even if very tangentially—to something real. Fintech innovations, however, have created the possibility of cryptoassets that have no such limiting factor. If unlimited numbers of cryptoassets can be created, there will be considerable uncertainty about the levels of regulatory capital and liquid assets that an institution with exposure to those assets should be required to maintain.

Even the regulatory capital and liquidity requirements that are applied to traditional assets may turn out to be wrong if those traditional assets unexpectedly turn out to be correlated with cryptoassets. One way of detecting these kinds of correlations is to subject a bank to a stress test, but if the scenario used for the stress test is based on experience with a pre-fintech financial system, it may not tell regulators much about how the system will fare when something goes awry today. For example, stress test hypotheticals might not anticipate the likelihood that algorithms will cause people to "hyperswitch" between financial products at a speed and on a scale that we have never seen before, making runs much worse than in the past.[49] If capital and liquidity requirements do turn out to be poorly calibrated for the fintech era, then that will increase the likelihood that financial institutions won't have enough of a cushion to survive a financial shock.

Regulators' supervision of bank management will also have to be adjusted to take into account the challenges that the bank's directors and senior managers will face in overseeing the operations of their firms in the fintech era. Most of these senior bank personnel won't have much expertise in the artificial intelligence-, distributed ledger- and data-driven technologies that are becoming increasingly central to their businesses, so regulators will have to assess if banks have enough institutional expertise to properly oversee their own operations. If banks are outsourcing key functions to third-party technology vendors, financial regulators may also need to supervise these vendors as well, which may be far out of their experience and comfort zone. Ultimately, financial regulators may find themselves in the unenviable position of having to supervise automated compliance systems instead of humans (more on this shortly).

Related to the issue of bank supervision is the issue of bank culture. Because the law can only do so much to rein in destabilizing financial risk-taking (it's impossible to prescribe rules that dictate how bank industry personnel should act in every potential context and contingency), central banks and financial regulators have increasingly been trying to reform the culture of the banking industry to encourage industry employees to take some responsibility for the ultimate impact of their decisions on the broader economy—particularly their decisions about risk-taking.[50] Trying to change an industry's culture is exceedingly challenging at the best of times, though, and as the industry increasingly relies on the newest technologies, the task is only going to get harder.

As risk-management decisions are increasingly delegated to algorithms, it's going to become even harder to convince the humans working in the financial industry that their individual decision-making matters to the stability of the financial system. Culture influences an individual's decision-making by shaming failure to comply with cultural norms, and by offering social approval for conforming. These are very human emotions and experiences, and as more and more decisions are automated, the disciplinary power of a good corporate culture will be diminished. Right now, the algorithms themselves aren't capable of human empathy or shame (although some are starting to learn to mimic them).[51] The people who program the algorithms may view their work as a purely technical exercise, allowing them to mentally distance themselves from the algorithm's output. As for those humans who work alongside the algorithms, it will often be easy for them to convince themselves that the responsibility for questionable risk-taking lies with the algorithm, which will allow them to avoid any shame they might otherwise experience.[52] As a result, decisions that disregard potential impacts on financial stability could become even more common as institutions increasingly rely on algorithms to manage risks.

Cultural reform, along with bank supervision and capital and liquidity requirements, is sometimes referred to as *ex ante* regulation, because these regulatory strategies try to prevent problems from occurring in the first place. *Ex ante* regulation is precautionary by nature, but *ex ante* approaches are not guaranteed to succeed. Precaution also requires us to plan in advance for how we will respond if *ex ante* regulation fails—these responses are sometimes referred to as *ex post* regulation. A central bank's lender of last resort function is a prime example of an *ex post* approach to financial stability—unfortunately, the rise of fintech may play havoc with this function, as well as with the rest of our *ex post* playbook for banks, non-bank institutions, and markets.

The emergency *ex post* measures that central banks and regulators take in a crisis are designed to calm down market turmoil and inspire confidence in the financial system. In the past, just communicating that emergency support was on the way was often enough to restore confidence and prevent a panic.[53] If algorithms will be making most of the financial decisions in the future, though, it is unclear how they will interpret communication strategies that are designed to appeal to humans (it is also unclear how algorithms will view other regulatory measures, like deposit insurance and special resolution mechanisms, that are designed to instill human confidence in banks). It is even unclear how algorithms will respond to the actual implementation of emergency measures: for an algorithm to respond favorably to government intervention, it would need to have been programmed (or in the case of machine learning algorithms, to have learned) that that government intervention is a good thing. Given that emergency measures are only used rarely, it would not be surprising if many algorithms had no clear rules about how to respond to them.

Market regulators have different kinds of *ex post* measures available to them—most notably, circuit breakers. In the stock market, for example, circuit breakers are sometimes used to pause panicked trading and allow market participants to take a collective breath and reset wildly erroneous stock prices.[54] These pauses can be important from a financial stability perspective, because if the prices of stocks fall dramatically and remain depressed, liquidity and solvency problems can ensue (financial institutions with significant exposure to stocks may need to sell other types of assets at a discount in order to raise cash for their immediate needs, potentially compromising their own solvency and depressing assets prices in other financial asset markets). The speed that algorithmic trading has now reached, however, means that deployment of circuit breakers may come too late to avoid transmitting harm from the stock market to other financial markets and institutions.

These are just some examples of ways that the rise of fintech could undermine existing financial stability regulation. We should always remain humble about our understanding of the workings of the financial system: fintech is likely to throw up many more unanticipated hurdles for our current approaches to promoting financial stability. It is already clear, though, that as financial stability regulators are increasingly forced to supervise "driverless finance," they will find themselves in the unenviable position of having to reassess much of what they know about how financial institutions and markets function. There is also an added degree of difficulty for the regulators that comes from increased industry reliance on so-called "regtech" solutions to automate their compliance with existing regulations.

## Industry reliance on regtech

In the financial industry, regulatory compliance personnel are charged with keeping abreast of and interpreting regulatory requirements, and then ensuring that their institution has the necessary policies and procedures in place to ensure compliance with those requirements. Compliance personnel are also tasked with ensuring that the adopted policies and procedures achieve the desired compliance outcomes, and addressing any deficiencies that may arise.[55] Over the last few years, the artificial intelligence, cloud computing, and other technological innovations that have been deployed by the financial industry to improve financial products and services have also been used to automate regulatory compliance—in this context, the technology is usually referred to as "regtech" rather than "fintech."[56]

Regtech solutions can make compliance more efficient (particularly when it comes to information reporting requirements, which have increased significantly over the last decade), and they can also eliminate a lot of the human errors associated with manual execution of compliance functions.[57] In addition to saving money on the labor costs associated with compliance functions, firms using regtech solutions also hope to avoid fines associated with regulatory violations. Automating compliance has some downsides, though, which should be somewhat familiar by this stage of the book.

Some of these downsides relate to potential technological malfunctions: if, as seems likely, financial institutions end up adopting a suite of specialized regtech solutions developed by different vendors and integrating them into their existing systems, there may be unanticipated interactions between the systems that could cause operational problems.[58] There is also a lot of interest in developing regtech solutions that are designed to be interoperable with the regulators' systems (particularly when it comes to data reporting).[59] While this interoperability would have a lot of benefits, it could also act as a pathway that allows technological failures originating in the private sector to cascade into problems with the regulators' systems—which could then cascade back out into the systems of other private sector entities that are linked to the regulators' systems.

Even when the technological aspects of a regtech solution are functioning as expected, we should be cautious about how regtech will be deployed. While automating compliance can avoid some types of human error, it can bake in other types of errors at the programming stage. For example, if an institution uses machine learning to determine which data to report to the regulator and the machine learning algorithm isn't trained right, the institution may systematically fail to report vital required information to the regulator. As we explored in Chapter 2, machine learned errors are more difficult to rectify than errors made by human beings, and if many financial institutions are buying regtech reporting solutions from the same vendor, the consequences of such a "baked in" error could be widespread.

Another drawback of regtech is that it's likely to engender automation biases that encourage compliance employees not to interrogate the processes or results of their regtech software (which means "baked in" errors are more likely to go undetected). One regtech proponent has spoken enthusiastically about the possibility of an automated compliance system that can be evaluated "based on how well it produces superior results, regardless of whether we know how it does so,"[60] but we have already explored the dangers inherent in relying unquestioningly on model output. The delegation of responsibility to automated processes can also undermine employees' sense of personal responsibility with regard to their work, and limit their opportunities to learn about the nuances of the broader compliance function. As a result, when it comes time to purchase a new regtech solution, compliance employees may lack a fundamental understanding of what they need that solution to do (they may also lack the technical expertise to determine how the solution should achieve the desired outcome). If this happens, most responsibility for compliance will be ceded to the regtech vendors, who may be more experienced in "tech" than "reg," and who may in some circumstances escape regulatory oversight.

For all of these reasons, regtech will not ensure perfect regulatory compliance, and regulatory supervision of financial institutions will continue to be needed. Regulatory supervision of regtech will be qualitatively different to the supervisory expertise that financial regulatory agencies have honed over the last few decades, though. While financial institutions have long used computer modeling to assist in their regulatory compliance, the final judgments about compliance were made by human beings, and financial regulatory agencies are used to supervising these human beings (who are capable of explaining and contextualizing their actions). Regulators are *not* used to supervising the unadulterated output of machine learning and other new technologies, nor are they used to regulating financial institutions' choices about which regtech solutions to adopt.

Taking enforcement action against noncompliant financial institutions also becomes more complicated when decision-making is automated. There is still a lot of uncertainty about who should be held legally liable for an algorithm's output, particularly when the algorithm is capable of machine learning and therefore has not been given any direct instructions by a human being.[61] If a financial institution is found to have violated a regulation because it delegated compliance to a defective machine learning algorithm, what kind of sanctions are appropriate? Should fines or other enforcement actions be levied against the programmer of the algorithm, or the data scientist who selected data sets used to train the algorithms? What if the technology was supplied by a third-party vendor?

These are important questions to ask, but the financial industry's interest and investment in regtech continues unhindered. Regulatory supervision and enforcement will be forced to adapt to accommodate regtech, despite the difficulties involved. Failure to adapt will allow rampant opportunities for new types of tech-savvy regulatory arbitrage. To get an idea of the flavor this arbitrage is likely to take, we can think back to the 2008 financial crisis, and the computer models that were used by the largest banks to determine how much regulatory capital they needed to absorb losses.

These large banks calculated their regulatory capital requirements using the VaR models we discussed in Chapter 2. These VaR models spit out a number that represented how much the banks could potentially lose on their investments, determined at a specified confidence level. The "determined at a specified confidence level" aspect of the VaR model was what invited arbitrage—if a VaR model was set at a 99% confidence level, there was a 99% chance that the bank would have enough regulatory capital to absorb the losses, but there remained a 1% chance that the bank could lose much more on its investments. Regulators accepted the output of these computer models anyway, and banks were able to calculate their regulatory capital requirements based on the 99% confidence level.[62] This encouraged banks to make investments that had a less than 1% chance of losses.

The fact that banks were seeking out investments with a low probability of losses might *seem* like a desirable outcome, but VaR models have nothing to say about the potential *size* of these low probability losses. Because taking on greater risks is compensated with greater returns, many banks made money by investing in things that could potentially suffer huge losses—but only in unlikely circumstances (this practice has been referred to as "stuffing risk into the tails").[63] When the unexpected did happen in 2007 and 2008—in the form of a nationwide housing crash—some banks didn't have enough capital to cushion their investment losses, and needed bailouts from national authorities in order to stay afloat.

The next generation of machine learning-enabled regtech tools may calculate regulatory capital requirements in ways that are completely unintelligible to financial regulators, hiding their assumptions and limitations. Knowing that regulators will face significant difficulties in understanding the logic of machine learning-capable risk management models, financial industry participants may try to arbitrage regulatory capital requirements by selectively exposing those models to data sets that neglect tail risks. Regulators would only be able to ferret out this type of arbitrage by developing their own machine learning applications, capable of surveying the data sets used to train the industry algorithms, and assessing whether that training data adequately takes into account the possibility of tail risks that could threaten the entire financial system.

This is just one example of the ways in which technologically sophisticated regtech applications could offer new ways of exploiting regulatory loopholes. Financial industry participants looking to confirm the legality of creative regtech arbitrage strategies might very well pressure regulators to certify that the output of a particular regtech tool constitutes sufficient compliance. Regulators need to be careful about endorsing specific regtech tools, though, because this will promote widespread adoption of the tool, ensuring that the impact of any errors in it are likely to be systemic.[64] Automation biases would probably become more entrenched as well, with the industry deferring without question to the output of any regtech tool that had been blessed by the regulators. Even if regulators hesitate to sign off on the use of any particular regtech tools, though, further reliance on regtech by the private sector seems inevitable.[65] As I have already said, regulators will have to adapt accordingly.

## The challenges of suptech

As regtech has become more popular, financial regulators have become increasingly interested in integrating technological solutions into their own supervisory practices. Financial regulators' own forays into technological tools have also been described as "regtech," but this can be confusing and so I prefer to use the term "suptech" (a portmanteau of "supervisory technology") to describe the use of machine learning, big data, and distributed learning technologies by financial regulators. While few suptech applications are operational yet, a survey conducted in October 2019 found that approximately twenty financial regulatory bodies were actively engaging in some type of suptech experimentation, and interest is expected to grow.[66]

So far, suptech experimentation has focused on developing tools that improve the collection and analysis of the voluminous amounts of data that regulated financial institutions are required to produce—data that are increasingly being generated and submitted by regtech applications.[67] The hope is that these tools will allow financial regulatory supervision to evolve from being a backward-looking historical exercise into something more predictive and proactive. For example, there has been significant interest in developing applications that allow for real-time surveillance of the financial markets, possibly even creating opportunities for regulators to intervene to prevent fraud and money laundering before the relevant transactions are completed.[68]

So far, there hasn't been much experimentation with using suptech to address threats to financial stability (although there have been a few exceptions, including efforts to apply artificial intelligence to detect deficiencies in stress testing models,[69] and to analyze real estate advertisements in an attempt to forecast housing prices and inflation).[70] There is a lot of unexplored potential, though, to develop technologies that help detect threats to individual institutions and the financial system as whole by aggregating new data sources and applying machine learning analysis techniques to them. Suptech innovation could also generate new ways of regulating that rely less on rules and more on technological interventions, which could be implanted into fintech products and services in order to ensure that they function in a way that is aligned with regulatory goals (Chapter 6 will suggest a number of possible interventions, including the addition of circuit breakers to smart contracts). There has been almost no experimentation with these types of technological interventions so far, though. When it comes to financial stability, suptech's potential has been almost entirely neglected.

There are a number of possible explanations for why there has been such limited experimentation with financial stability-related suptech.[71] First, as always, is the resources issue. Regulators will either have to develop the suptech technology in-house, or enlist someone to develop it for them. Most financial regulators don't have the expertise needed for in-house development, but outsourcing will only be an option if there is someone regulators can outsource to, and there are very few vendors who specialize in suptech technologies. Even when a suitable third-party vendor can be found, the quality of the technology that is developed will depend on the regulator's budget, and on its ability to monitor the vendor's programming process—which a regulator can only do if it has employees with enough technological savvy to communicate with the technical specialists at the vendor.

Reliance on vendors for suptech may also open up new avenues for regulatory arbitrage. Because relationships with government agencies may not be particularly lucrative for technology vendors, the vendors who do supply suptech software may try to leverage their work by providing related regtech tools to private firms who can pay more. This opens up the possibility that the vendors may skew the design of suptech solutions in a way that favors their private sector regtech clients.[72] Several financial regulatory agencies have already expressed concerns that adopting suptech will lead to more arbitrage, and as already discussed, sophisticated arbitrage strategies that are embedded in software may be particularly hard to detect.[73]

Conflicting regulatory mandates are also an issue for the development of suptech. While some types of suptech (such as using biometrics and big data analytics to detect money laundering more efficiently) are generally seen as a "win-win" for both industry and the regulator, the calculus won't be that simple for all suptech approaches. Stability-related suptech interventions could make some private sector technologies run less efficiently, which could conflict with a regulator's efficiency mandate. For example, algorithms work more quickly with fewer lines of code, and so adding technological requirements like circuit breakers to smart contracts could reduce the speed with which they can execute their functions.

Suptech innovations may also have unintended consequences that could ultimately undermine the financial stability they were designed to protect. For example, if a regulator were to mandate that all risk management algorithms capable of machine learning be trained using standardized data sets that recognize tail risk (a measure that will be discussed in detail in Chapter 6), the result might be that all of those algorithms learn to behave in identical ways during low-probability events—which could counterproductively make panics worse.

In short, the resource constraints, conflicting objectives, and fear of unintended consequences that make regulating new technologies difficult will be compounded when the regulatory intervention itself is not just words on a page, but a specific piece of technology that is designed to interact with technology developed by the private sector. While the enormity of these challenges explains regulators' limited embrace of suptech so far, relying on traditional financial regulatory approaches to protect the financial system from new fintech and regtech innovations is the regulatory equivalent of bringing a knife to a gunfight.

Suptech is becoming a practical necessity, and time is of the essence in developing it. The financial industry is only just beginning to apply technology like machine learning and smart contracts to financial services, and so there is still significant scope for regulators to require that suptech interventions be incorporated into privately developed financial products. If regulators wait too long, though, technological interventions into operational technologies will be far more difficult, and more likely to result in unexpected (and potentially negative) side effects. Regulators will also face an even steeper political battle against the financial industry if they wait until the new technologies are entrenched in the financial markets before taking action.

Given limitations on available resources, financial regulatory agencies should prioritize their own suptech experimentation over efforts to promote private sector innovation. They should also consider partnering with universities with strong data science and software engineering departments to develop suptech solutions: relationships with these publicly minded institutions can give regulators access to cutting edge technology that they otherwise might not be able to afford. Conversations with academics may also be fruitful in terms of identifying and prioritizing opportunities for suptech applications, although of course the regulators will also have their own ideas about the types of tools that could assist them in discharging their functions.

Developing suptech tools is only the first step, however. Financial regulators must then figure out how to use them. In the era of suptech, regulators will need to devote more resources to managing their own internal operational risks. Chapter 4 explored the many operational risks that come from relying on complex technological systems, and regulators are not immune from these. In particular, technology-driven regulatory tools might become a particularly attractive target for hackers looking to profit from disruptions in the financial markets—a similarly motivated cyberattack targeted the SEC's financial disclosure database in 2016, seeking market scoops that could be used for trading.[74]

In addition to making their technology secure, regulators need to reassess their institutional culture to ensure that new technologies are used appropriately. Like all human beings, financial regulators are susceptible to automation biases, so they must actively take steps to maintain some degree of skepticism and humility regarding their suptech solutions. Such steps should include policies that require agencies to regularly interrogate and reassess their suptech tools in light of the agency's broader understanding of the financial system and its regulatory goals. If it becomes clear that a tool has failed to achieve the agency's goals or requires substantial revision, it needs to be fixed or abandoned as a matter of priority—otherwise, the product will entrench and institutionalize flawed regulatory approaches. Above all, this is an exercise in humility. Regulators will need to learn to accept that trial and error is essential for developing suptech tools, and that some failure is inevitable. We will return to the necessary shift in mindset in Chapter 7.

* * *

Our current financial regulatory system is ill-equipped to deal with the rise of fintech and regtech, and new regulatory programs like sandboxes and innovation hubs are not going to fix this. Fresh approaches to financial stability regulation, including experimentation with suptech, are crucial if regulators wish to retain any control over the stability of our financial system. While implementing these new approaches will be fraught with challenges, the alternative—giving the fintech industry free rein to profit by taking risks that will ultimately be borne by the rest of us—is unacceptable. The next chapter will therefore provide some suggestions for new approaches to financial stability regulation.

# 6

# Precautionary Regulation of Fintech Innovation

It is not easy to diagnose the threats that driverless finance poses for financial stability—but proposing regulatory solutions is even harder. We have to try, though: the last chapter showed that we cannot stick with the regulatory status quo without risking the potentially catastrophic outcomes discussed in part II of this book. This chapter therefore makes precautionary regulatory proposals designed to apply to specific fintech innovations, as well as to the financial innovation process more broadly. This chapter also engages with the difficult resource and jurisdictional issues that will need to be addressed for these proposals to become a reality.

All of these proposals are experimental, and should be the subject of debate and criticism. Debate and criticism will help refine the proposals—and maybe come up with better alternatives—but we should be careful not to let the perfect be the enemy of the good. When we are dealing with significant uncertainty, any regulatory approach will inevitably have some unintended consequences, but we *can* design regulation in light of what we already know about the financial system and fintech innovations. We should not let fear of unintended consequences paralyze early regulatory action that has a good chance of preventing or containing worst-case outcomes. Remember that finance is not a neutral playing field: without regulation, financial technologies are likely to develop in ways that primarily benefit the developers of those technologies, often at the public's expense. The precautionary proposals outlined here try to ensure that the public's interest in a stable financial system is not neglected as these technologies evolve.

Precautionary regulation of fintech innovation can take many forms. As this chapter will explore, it can be applied at a particular point in time, as with a licensing procedure for new technologies, or it can be carried out through an ongoing process of supervisory oversight. Precautionary regulation can be targeted, like requiring a suptech intervention for a particular financial product, or it can be more diffuse and informational—simply researching

*Driverless Finance.* Hilary J. Allen, Oxford University Press. © Hilary J. Allen 2022.
DOI: 10.1093/oso/9780197626801.003.0007

technologies in order to understand their potential pitfalls is precautionary. Different forms of precautionary regulation will be better suited to different types of technologies, business models, and institutions. However, where possible, all approaches should offer regulators an opportunity for early intervention, when the technology is still in the development process. Financial stability regulators will therefore need the expertise to evaluate the technology involved and its likely impacts, and the legal authority to take action. Before they can exercise their expertise and authority, though, they will need ways of finding out when and how technological innovation is occurring.

## The need for information

As we explored in Chapter 1, precautionary regulation involves shifting the burden to the industry to show why they *shouldn't* be regulated. This involves requiring the industry to provide information about new technologies to the regulator, rather than requiring the regulator to ferret out whether any new technology is being adopted. Fintech regulatory strategies like innovation hubs and regulatory sandboxes bring some information to the regulators' attention, but these approaches only work if innovators "opt in" to cooperating with the regulators. As a result, they are (at best) a haphazard and incomplete method of providing information to regulators about the new technologies being used to deliver financial services. Instead, regulators need a comprehensive picture of the types of technologies being used.

To achieve this, regulators will need a new type of disclosure, a "Form T" if you will, that would require regulated financial institutions to disclose all of the technological systems that they rely upon to deliver financial services. This Form T should require disclosure of any technology that forms the backbone of a particular financial product offered by the institution, as well as any technological system used by an institution to manage its operations internally (for example, machine learning systems used for institutional risk assessment, or cloud computing for data storage). Form T should also require disclosure of the technological qualifications held by members of the institution's board of directors and senior management, to give regulators insight into whether the financial institution is capable of overseeing its own use of technology.

The form should be certified by the institution's Chief Technology Officer, and submitted quarterly.[1] The adoption of any new technological system should trigger an obligation to make a supplemental report.[2] Preparing a Form T for the first time will probably be a time-consuming and costly exercise for a financial institution, but updates won't be as onerous (just as preparing a company for an IPO is much more work than preparing later disclosures to investors). Looking on the bright side, preparing a Form T for the first time may actually have unanticipated benefits for a financial institution, providing it with an opportunity to understand its own technological systems better. After this exercise, a financial institution may even be able to streamline its use of technologies—and any steps that an individual financial institution takes to reduce its own technological complexity will help make the financial system as a whole more stable.[3]

Perhaps the most difficult part of determining the types of disclosures that should be required by Form T will be figuring out how granular they should be. For example, what constitutes a "technological system" for disclosure purposes? What level of information needs to be provided about that system? How significant does a change to existing technology have to be to trigger the obligation to make a supplemental report? In Chapter 5, I explained that disclosure of algorithmic source code is not likely to be particularly helpful to regulators—I'm not proposing that Form T require disclosures that are *that* granular. Still, regulators may need information about the choices a data scientist made in training a machine learning algorithm, or the opportunity to see how a smart contract functions in beta mode. Regulators may also need insight into even incremental changes to existing technological systems, because those incremental changes can ratchet up complexity and increase the chance of unexpected interactions and problems.

The developers of Form T could turn to the discipline of biology for help with figuring out when incremental changes (and new applications of existing technologies) need to be reported, and for general help with defining and categorizing financial technologies. As a science, biology embraces a world of living things that is much more complex than the universe of financial technologies, and manages to categorize all the various types of life in a way that leaves room for new discoveries. When those new discoveries are made, they are categorized in ways that show how they are similar to, and how they differ from, what has been discovered before. Form T could riff on the Linnaean biological taxonomy, which uses a hierarchy of kingdom, phylum, class, order, family, genus, and finally species to highlight where living organisms are similar and where they have important differences.[4] For example, machine learning could be a technology "kingdom," with supervised or unsupervised algorithms being phyla within that kingdom. The different types of algorithms (like neural networks, random forests of decision trees, partial least squares, and support vector machines) could be categorized at the class phase, and then differences between data, training, and testing strategies could be captured at the order, family, genus, and species level.

Ideally, the information provided on Form T would be detailed enough to alert regulators to where they need to probe further, but not so detailed as to place an overwhelming burden on the private sector—finding the right balance will probably involve trial and error, and so we should expect Form T's requirements to evolve over time. It is already clear, though, that the disclosures made on Form T should be kept secure and confidential by the regulators who receive them. The financial institutions and other firms using cutting-edge technologies certainly won't want this kind of information disclosed to their competitors.

## Regulatory expertise and culture

Any information disclosed to financial regulators using Form T will be largely useless to them unless they have some expertise in software engineering and data science. Without this expertise, regulators will be forced to rely on the private sector's explanations of how the technology works—and private sector innovators have no real incentive to look for (let alone report) problems that their technology could cause for financial stability. In order for regulators to take precautionary steps with regard to new technologies, those regulators need to be able to understand and contextualize technologies and their risks for themselves. Right now, financial regulatory agencies are mostly staffed with economists, lawyers, and accountants. Efforts to attract different kinds of expertise to these agencies face a number of hurdles—most obviously, government salaries.

Technologies like machine learning and distributed ledgers are both new and "hot," which means that the relatively few people that understand them are very expensive to hire. Regulatory agencies will be competing directly with established financial institutions, techfins, and fintech start-ups trying to attract these kinds of personnel. While start-ups typically lack the stability that a government job can provide, they offer excitement to their employees, and an outlet for their innovative creativity (start-ups also have the lure of the unlikely-but-still-very-real possibility of huge payoffs for their early employees if they succeed). The techfins can offer opportunities for creativity and innovation that rival a startup's, in combination with more job stability and salaries that are often extremely high. Established financial institutions may not always have the same innovative cachet as the start-ups and techfins, but they can offer job stability, and combine that stability with significant salaries that the government will not be able to compete with.

The sheer scale of demand from the private sector means that there will be a limited pool of people with computer and data science qualifications available to work for financial regulatory agencies (Goldman Sachs alone estimated in 2020 that it employed 10,000 software developers—a quarter of its total workforce).[5] However, agencies' ability to hire these kinds of employees will improve if they offer the highest salaries they can, as well as opportunities for employees to innovate (employees who want to create something new may be particularly attracted to jobs that involve suptech innovation, for example). Regulatory agencies may also be able to capitalize on generational shifts, attracting younger employees who both understand the relevant technologies and are attracted to public service.[6] As such, hiring data and computer scientists may not be impossible—but it will never be easy.

Financial regulatory agencies will have to figure out how to make the best use of the employees that they *are* able to attract. In the United States, this means consolidating expertise in one agency, rather than scattering it among the many different regulatory agencies (who sometimes try to poach employees from each other).[7] Consolidating a large group of experts in one agency will allow them to collaborate, instead of siloing them off in different agencies with few colleagues who understand or value what they do. Consolidating expertise in one agency is also more likely to yield consistent regulation of the same technologies (which can be hard to achieve when each financial regulatory agency devises its own approaches to a new technology in reliance on a few in-house experts).[8] Finally, creating a true hub of expertise can also serve as a recruiting tool: the promise of working with a collegial group of scientists and technologists on a cross-section of cutting-edge financial technologies should make it easier to attract new employees.

The most obvious US agency to serve as a scientific and technological expertise hub is the Office of Financial Research ("OFR"), which could become an interdisciplinary resource for the many different US financial regulatory agencies.[9] Although the OFR was created to serve as a data collection and analysis body, it already has wide-ranging research powers that would authorize it to investigate the threats that fintech poses for financial stability, and to engage in suptech innovation and experiment with other creative regulatory responses.[10] The OFR is also already authorized to collaborate with academic institutions, which may be particularly useful for developing cutting-edge suptech tools.[11] The OFR's staff and resources were decimated during the Trump administration, meaning that there is now an opportunity to rebuild the agency with a new focus on science and technology research. If the OFR is rebuilt in this way, it will be a valuable resource for other financial regulatory agencies to consult and collaborate with.

In addition to building the right expertise, financial stability regulators will also have to think about the type of culture that is needed to execute precautionary regulatory strategies. Expertise is not enough: humility, curiosity, and skepticism of conventional wisdom are also important because of the uncertainty surrounding the impact of new technologies on the financial system. Financial stability regulators should also try to foster a culture of innovation that could generate out-of-the-box solutions to regulatory problems—as this chapter explores, the increasing technological sophistication of the financial system may sometimes require regulation that takes the form of technological interventions (suptech) rather than rules.

In the private sector, a lot of thought has gone into the types of institutional cultures that are more likely to promote innovation.[12] This private sector experience can help guide senior management at financial regulatory agencies. For example, regulatory agencies can set up the kind of "agile" workflows popular in Silicon Valley, which involve "breaking complex projects into smaller ones and bringing together multi-disciplinary teams to do rapid building of solutions."[13] The most important aspect of any innovation-friendly culture, though, is a tolerance for failure, which means that regulatory agencies can't create a pro-innovation culture all on their own. Financial stability regulators also need to be given some leeway by the public to experiment, fail, take unpopular positions—and sometimes just to observe and study without taking any concrete action.

Financial regulatory agencies can be structured in a way that helps insulate them from short-term political pressures, but financial regulatory independence began to fall out of favor in the aftermath of the 2008 crisis.[14] Elected officials and their appointees started to be given more active roles in financial regulation around the world—but this trend raises some concerns. We've already discussed how the private sector lacks both the incentives and the ability to promote financial stability; elected officials and political appointees focused on the next election may also have too short-term a focus to do the hard work needed to prevent crises that may occur many years in the future. The unfortunate truth is that if financial regulators do not take steps to protect financial stability, there is no one else likely to step up. The public in general therefore needs a better appreciation of what financial stability regulators do, and to afford them more grace to do it. We will pick up this issue again in the next chapter; for now, we'll turn our attention to the third thing that financial stability regulators need in order to regulate new technological innovations—the legal authority to take action.

## Legal authority

Even the most expert and innovative financial regulatory agencies will be hamstrung if they don't have any jurisdiction over the firms that are developing or using innovative new technologies. Financial laws always have limits and gaps, and these limits and gaps are a particular problem in the United States because it has such a fractured system of financial regulatory authority (the United States has at least eight federal financial regulatory agencies, depending on how you count, and many more at the state level).[15] Different types of financial institutions and markets are subject to different types of regulatory oversight from different regulatory agencies—with some being more stringent than others. Firms often engage in regulatory arbitrage, purposely structuring a business model or technology to avoid the strictest regulatory requirements.

The regulation of banks, for example, is usually stricter than the regulation of markets for things like securities, and so securities products have been designed that carry out banking functions without the associated regulation—resulting in the "shadow banking" phenomenon we discussed in Chapter 3. Risks that developed in the shadow banking system helped cause the financial crisis of 2008,[16] but more than a decade later, we still have not made much headway in figuring out what authority financial stability regulators should have over shadow banking. The issue is becoming even more complicated with the rise of fintech.

Could financial institutions avoid regulation by outsourcing some of their activities to third-party technology vendors? Right now, vendors are typically regulated indirectly, with financial institutions being responsible for managing the operational and other risks arising out of their relationships with those vendors (who range from huge cloud providers like Amazon to much smaller niche providers). Given that financial institutions generally lack the incentives and capacity to address the systemic risks that might arise from their reliance on these vendors, systemic risks may fall through the cracks unless regulators are given direct jurisdiction over vendors. Risks may also fall through the cracks as Google, Amazon, Apple and Facebook—the so-called techfins—start to provide payments and other financial services. These techfins are not regulated financial institutions, but their vast size ensures that they could quickly scale up to be a significant threat to financial stability.

Regulatory arbitrage can also be geographical. The financial system is global, but financial regulation is typically administered at the national level. If one country adopts rules that are particularly stringent, that country runs the risk that financial institutions and fintech innovators will simply move their activities elsewhere—but the spillover effects of those activities can still harm the first country. This can make individual countries reluctant to adopt stringent financial regulation—why clamp down on your own fintech industry when you're likely to suffer from any global economic meltdown regardless?[17] In order to overcome this reluctance, countries around the world have sometimes come together to harmonize their financial rules: the most prominent example is the regulatory capital regime developed by the Basel Committee on Banking Supervision (a group of central bankers and financial regulators representing 28 different jurisdictions).[18] The process of coordinating fintech regulation across borders has barely begun, though.

In 2019, the UK's Financial Conduct Authority spearheaded a "Global Financial Innovation Network" of financial regulators, which is usually referred to as the "GFIN." The GFIN is intended to be a network and discussion forum for financial regulatory agencies who have demonstrated "a commitment to supporting financial innovation."[19] The main focus of the GFIN so far seems to be on developing cross-border regulatory sandboxes and other regulatory strategies to encourage private sector innovation.[20] There is no dedicated international forum for regulators who are skeptical about fintech and concerned about its cross-border impacts. However, another transnational network and discussion forum—the Financial Stability Board—has taken up the issue of fintech as part of its broader assessment of threats to financial stability.[21] The Financial Stability Board has not yet made any recommendations on how to address those threats at an international level, though.

Because there is no international coordination on fintech regulation, any country that pursues precautionary regulation of fintech runs the risk that innovators will move their activities to a more lightly regulated jurisdiction. Of course, moving jurisdictions may not always be practically feasible: doing so may cut an innovator off from the markets they need to access, or they may not be able to attract the necessary workforce in the new jurisdiction, or they may simply just not want to move.[22] Innovators may also find that they lose out by forfeiting the legitimacy and trust that comes from operating within a highly regulated environment. Still, the threat of geographical arbitrage—and more importantly from our perspective, the spillovers of risky fintech activity across national borders—is real, and so it makes sense for financial stability regulators to try to coordinate with their global counterparts as they pursue precautionary approaches. At least at the beginning, they could rely on the institutional framework of the Financial Stability Board for such collaboration.

Ultimately, the problems of geographical arbitrage and spillover effects will not be entirely solvable. That is not a good enough reason to abandon precautionary regulation of fintech, though. National financial systems face real threats from domestic financial activities as well as spillovers from other countries. Precautionary regulation is all about erring on the side of caution, and regardless of what other countries do, national financial stability regulations can help protect their national economy from an internally generated meltdown. The fact that such rules will also contribute to financial stability at the international level is an added bonus.

We will pick up the big picture question of jurisdictional limitations again in Chapter 7. For now, it suffices to say that even though there are loopholes that innovators can exploit, many fintech innovations are being implemented directly by financial institutions that are already regulated one way or another. We can start by focusing our precautionary regulation on the use of fintech by these institutions.

## Precautionary regulatory strategies for new technologies

With the necessary authority, expertise, and information, financial stability regulators can start considering new types of regulatory approaches to fintech innovations. These new regulatory approaches will often be most effective if they are applied *during the technological design process*. If regulators wait until after products have been introduced into the financial marketplace, a network of providers and users will already have developed vested interests in preserving the unregulated status quo. In addition to political challenges, there are also technical challenges inherent in trying to regulate a technology that is already "fully baked": changing the programming of a technology after its initial development is not only more expensive, but also more likely to produce unintended consequences, than incorporating interventions during the initial design process. A precautionary regulatory strategy should therefore target the technological development phase where possible. The best way to achieve this is through some form of preapproval or licensing process, like the processes that the US Food and Drug Administration uses for approving things like drugs and medical devices.[23]

Regulated financial institutions could be required to obtain licenses before they implement new technological systems. Sometimes, a license would be refused, which could keep the most problematic technologies out of the financial system altogether. More commonly, the licensing process would permit the use of a technology with conditions designed to protect financial stability—and these conditions could be imposed and addressed during the technological design process (of course, if no problems are apparent, unconditional use of technology could also be authorized). Implementing a licensing regime for financial technologies would also have incidental benefits for financial stability. For example, if innovators know that their technology is going to have to get through a licensing process, they may be encouraged to test for bugs more thoroughly, and perhaps even eliminate unnecessary (and potentially destabilizing) complexity from the technology in an attempt to make the approval process smoother.[24]

There are strong arguments for establishing a licensing regime for financial technologies, but it would not be practically possible to subject *all* technologies to such a regime. Regulators simply wouldn't have enough resources to review them all. Where a licensing regime is not feasible (or not appropriate), regulators can still take a precautionary approach to their more traditional regulatory functions of supervision, enforcement and rule-making. For example, when a financial institution uses technology to manage its operations internally—say, using machine learning for managing the risks in its investment portfolios—regulators can exercise precautionary oversight over these technologies as part of their ongoing supervision of firms' credit, market, and liquidity risks. However, it can be very hard to draft rules that set out detailed expectations about how regulated institutions should use evolving new technologies. Instead, a principles-based strategy is often the best starting position.[25]

In a principles-based regulatory system, high-level objectives are adopted through formal rule-making procedures, and then the industry has some flexibility as to how they comply with those objectives.[26] In the past, principles-based regulation has often been viewed as a "light-touch" approach to regulation, but it doesn't have to be that way. The overarching objective of a principles-based regime for fintech should be financial stability: if the technology poses a threat to the continuing ability of financial institutions or markets to help people manage risks, invest, borrow, or make payments, then intervention is justified. The developers and adopters of technology should be afforded some flexibility in how they satisfy this objective, but regulators will also provide them with informal guidance.

A principles-based approach like this would essentially give regulators an umbrella framework under which they could flexibly deploy new types of regulatory strategies as new technologies arose (this could also help minimize opportunities for regulatory arbitrage, because it is often harder to arbitrage the spirit of a principle than the letter of a narrower rule). Of course, no regulatory approach is perfect, and principles-based regulation certainly has its flaws. Unless the principles are well-crafted—and unless committed regulators ensure that there are real consequences for failing to uphold them—principles-based regulation can end up working as a form of deregulation. There is also the risk that enforcement actions for breaching high-level principles will be made with the benefit of hindsight, perhaps informally and non-transparently, which is not fair to regulated firms.[27] Enforcement actions and informal guidance can also "become rule-based regulation by the back door," which can deprive the regulatory regime of a lot of its flexibility.[28]

Despite these drawbacks, principles-based regulation—if it's administered by regulators who have the necessary technical expertise and are committed to promoting financial stability—will often be the best way of dealing with new technologies that are not yet fully understood. Because more formal rules can't keep up with these new technologies, the alternative is likely to be no regulation at all. If regulators have the expertise needed to properly assess compliance with principles on an ongoing basis, enforcement by hindsight is less likely, and the development of new technologies can be infused with the public interest. As technologies mature and their benefits and drawbacks become better understood, we can then transition to a more formal regulatory regime which provides more certainty.

Formal regulation can take the form of detailed rules, but regulators will increasingly need to explore other options as well. For example, when financial transacting is occurring too quickly for human intervention, regulators will sometimes need a nonhuman (read, technological) way of intervening. Or there might be a concern that trying to address an issue with a thicket of written rules will provide too many opportunities for arbitrage, whereas a targeted technological intervention could be designed that would introduce less complexity into the financial system. In these circumstances, regulators should consider designing suptech interventions. The rest of this chapter will consider some concrete applications of suptech (in addition to concrete applications of principles-based regulatory approaches, hard rules, and licensing regimes) that can respond to the concerns about fintech technologies and business models that we raised in part II of the book.

## Precautionary oversight of risk management algorithms

Chapter 2 illustrated some of the problems that can arise when financial institutions use machine learning technology for internal risk management purposes. The key takeaway from that chapter was that machine learning-based models are likely to underestimate low-probability but high-consequence tail events (like financial crises), leaving any financial institution that relies too heavily on those models vulnerable to massive losses in a time of stress. Many other financial modeling techniques also underestimate tail events, but we should be particularly concerned about machine learning-based models for a couple of reasons.

One worry is that people will be particularly likely to defer to the output of these new technological models, because it will be impossible to engage critically with their underlying decision-making processes. In addition to this concern about automation biases becoming more entrenched, the other big concern is increased coordination of financial decision-making during a tail event—if lots of financial institutions are relying on the same or similar machine learning algorithms exposed to the same or similar data, then they may all deal with similar financial assets in the same or similar ways. If reliance on machine learning for risk modeling not only neglects tail events, but also coordinates investment behavior so that the fallout from neglecting tail events is magnified, then this could pose a major threat to the stability of our financial system.

Both automation biases and destructive coordination will be less of a concern if the institutions using these kinds of models also employ human beings that understand the technology, and can override a model's output when appropriate. Financial institutions using these models should therefore be required to demonstrate their compliance with the principle that they have the institutional capacity and competency to use these models appropriately. It wouldn't be enough for a financial institution to show that it employed software engineers and data scientists to maintain the model—at the very least, the institution would need to have a more senior manager who understands both the technology *and* has a background in finance. Of course, human oversight could only do so much if the risk management model were tied to a trading execution algorithm that automatically adjusted the institution's investment portfolios in response to the output of the risk management model. Here, a hard rule is appropriate—trading execution algorithms should not be automatically linked to risk management algorithms; a human must have the opportunity to intervene and interrupt automated purchases and sales of assets. In fact, humans should be kept "in the loop" in all risk management decisions.[29]

Human oversight of risk management models will also be easier if the model is able to explain, at least to some degree, how it reached its conclusions. A regulatory principle could be adopted that requires financial institutions using machine learning in their risk modeling to consider the "explainability" of the algorithm's final output when they select and train their algorithms. This will give the institution itself, as well as financial stability regulators, some insight into the reasons why the algorithm made the risk determination it did.

Most of the work that has been done so far on improving algorithmic explainability has focused on explaining particular decisions by highlighting the variables that were relied upon and the weight given to them by the algorithm.[30] While this can be very helpful for other types of financial regulation (for example, determining whether a decision to refuse credit was based on a proxy for a persons' race, religion, or sex is important for enforcing anti-discrimination laws), when it comes to financial stability, an algorithm-generated explanation of how a particular decision was reached is not a substitute for understanding how the algorithm is likely to make decisions in the future—especially during stressed situations. There are some other approaches to explainability that would be more useful for a financial stability regulator. For example, it is sometimes possible to graph the relationships between input variables and outcome variables to help identify which correlations the algorithm has learned to rely on when making its decisions—but some types of machine learning algorithms aren't suited to this type of analysis.[31] Maximizing explainability may therefore require financial institutions to choose other, more compatible machine learning algorithms—but doing so can come at the expense of accuracy. As such, while the use of explainable algorithms should be encouraged to some degree, we should stop short of adopting any principle that requires financial institutions to *always* maximize the explainability of their risk management algorithms. Instead, explainability should be one of the many factors that regulated institutions must consider when choosing their machine learning algorithms.

A principles-based regime should, however, require that firms adopting machine learning models prioritize a focus on low probability but high consequence events, so that the models learn how to respond to the unexpected. This principle might be satisfied, for example, by preventing the data scientists responsible for training the algorithm from excluding outlier events of financial instability from their training data sets (or from failing to label those outlier events or tuning the algorithm to ignore them). As the use of machine learning in risk management becomes better understood, regulators might also decide to implement more concrete rules. One possibility is that regulation could require data scientists to emphasize tail events during the tuning process by mandating an asymmetric cost ratio that makes underestimates of losses in risk models far less common than overestimates. (As we explored in Chapter 2, an asymmetric cost ratio is a way of penalizing a machine learning algorithm more for some types of errors than others. For example, a cost ratio of 4:1 could be mandated for underestimates of potential investment losses in the risk management context so that for each underestimate generated, four overestimates will be generated).

## Suptech interventions for machine learning

While a principles-based regime can make machine learning algorithms less likely to ignore instances of tail events in their data sets, if these data sets are drawn from historical experience, the best-case scenario is that algorithms will learn how to respond to past episodes of financial instability. Machine learning algorithms can only learn if there is something to learn from, but the past is unlikely to be predictive of the future—we have no historical experience of how a financial crisis is likely to go down in a world of highly automated financial activity. This lack of historical precedent is a problem for human learning as well—law professor John Crawford has observed that it's hard for regulators to learn how to best respond to financial crises when they happen so infrequently.[32] Crawford has proposed a solution to this human experience deficit, though, and it could be adapted for machine learning algorithms as well: generating hypothetical scenarios of future crises for training purposes.

These kinds of training scenarios can be developed by borrowing from the military's experience with wargames.[33] Wargames have traditionally been performed by real human beings, responding to a hypothetical scenario in a way that suggests their likely approach to a real crisis in the future. Wargames involving humans are time-consuming and expensive to run, though, and machine learning algorithms need lots of data points to learn from. It would probably be too expensive to repeat this type of wargaming exercise enough times to generate enough data to train machine learning algorithms. A less costly and disruptive alternative might be to simulate the wargames using agent-based models: a hypothetical stressed scenario would still need to be created, but instead of humans responding to that scenario, computerized "agents" would be programmed with decision-making rules, and then let loose to interact within that scenario.[34] This can be repeated as often as necessary to generate more datapoints.

Unfortunately, these agent-based models are rife with assumptions about the type of stressed scenarios that could occur and how agents will behave when they do, and these assumptions may not be realistic. Where there are rich real-world data sets to draw from, machine learning would probably do a better job of predicting future behavior than an agent-based model.[35] However, where real-world data is lacking (as with financial system failures), agent-based models may be the only alternative. And the output of these models may not be all that unrealistic after all. The behavior of individual agents may actually be very predictable in some circumstances—we have seen time and time again that financial instability arises when people or firms behave in ways that are individually rational, but collectively destructive.[36] If our purpose is to determine how *collective* behavior can cause problems, agent-based modeling may actually give us a pretty good sense of the consequences of the interactions of a myriad of predictable responses.[37] And if agent-based models don't always do a good job of simulating how humans might respond to a given situation, they might do a better job of simulating how algorithms might behave in the same circumstances.

The outcomes of agent-based simulations, which could highlight previously unanticipated interconnections and spillover effects that could occur in the financial system during a tail event, could therefore serve as data points used for training machine learning algorithms in a way that discourages underestimates of financial risks. Again, this is by no means a perfect solution to machine learning algorithms' neglect of tail events. It would probably be cost prohibitive for each financial institution to run its own agent-based simulations, so they would often end up being developed by a regulatory agency as a form of suptech for broader dissemination. If everyone relies on the same data points to train their machine learning algorithms, that could be another avenue for generating destructive coordination in investment behavior—what may be a rational response to a tail event from one algorithm could have serious negative consequences for financial stability if multiple algorithms behave in the same way (for example, if they have all learned to dump the same kinds of assets at the same time). In some circumstances, it might be better to alert financial institutions to the outcomes of the agent-based simulations and give them some flexibility to figure out how to address the deficiencies that have been revealed, rather than giving them the output of the simulations to use as training data.

Given how complicated it will be to improve the quality of machine learning approaches to tail events, it would be a good idea to backstop these innovative, technologically driven regulatory interventions with very simple regulatory rules. The simplest regulatory response to machine learning-driven risk management models may be to simply limit the extent to which financial institutions are able to rely on them. As preeminent financial stability regulator Andrew Haldane has said, "[a]s you do not fight fire with fire, you do not fight complexity with complexity. Because complexity generates uncertainty, not risk, it requires a regulatory response grounded in simplicity, not complexity."[38]

Haldane was specifically criticizing complex regulatory capital regulations that allow financial institutions to use their own internal risk management models to help determine how much of their investments must be funded with their own (rather than borrowed) money—those regulations allowed financial institutions to rely far too heavily on borrowed money in the lead up to the 2008 financial crisis which made them vulnerable when that crisis hit.[39] Haldane argued that capital regulations should not refer to financial institutions' internal models at all;[40] at the very least, regulators should not make things worse by allowing regulatory capital requirements for financial institutions to be tied to the output of machine learning-based internal risk models (which will be more complex even than the most complicated VaR models used in 2008). If this caution is not heeded, though, and machine learning is incorporated into risk capital requirements, regulators should at the very least take steps—either the ones outlined here, or other creative approaches—to ensure that machine learning pays more attention to tail risk.

## Precautionary regulation of operational risks

A principles-based approach supplemented by suptech interventions could also help address the types of operational threats that are arising along with the increased technological complexity of finance, as explored in Chapter 4. While we haven't yet experienced a financial crisis caused by technological failures, experience with other complex systems suggests that the financial system as a whole will become more vulnerable as the technological complexity of the system components, and the interconnections among those components, increases.[41]

While much of this increased complexity is a result of private sector innovation, financial regulation also contributes to it. In particular, regulation that focuses on making individual financial institutions more reliable—without considering the consequences of that regulation for other parts of the financial system—can leave the system as a whole more fragile.[42] In the last decade, financial regulators have started to adopt a more systemic focus in their regulation of financial institutions' credit and liquidity risks, but they have largely stuck with letting financial institutions manage their own operational risks. This needs to change. We need to pay more attention to how the interactions of operational risks could potentially shut down the financial "plumbing" we rely on to process payments, as well as to clear and settle trades of stocks, bonds, commodities, and derivatives. The following are some strategies that could form the beginning of a more "macro" approach to the regulation of operational risk.

A complex system will be more robust if it can adapt to changes over time, and so regulators need to understand how technological systems are being used, and any problems that are occurring. The Form T discussed earlier in this chapter will inform regulators of the types of technology being used, but there also needs to be some kind of incident reporting system: the development of a real-time incident reporting system capable of alerting regulators to outages and other technological failures as they occur should be a priority for suptech innovation. The obligation to make reports using this system must, by necessity, be principles-based: it is not possible to specify in advance all of the types of technological failures that could occur, and so financial institutions should be directed to report any problem that they consider significant (although it may be worthwhile for the regulators to provide some guidance on some kinds of technological problems that are presumed significant and therefore should be reported).

With the benefit of this reporting system, regulators could take real-time action to respond to developing threats. This real-time intervention could take the form of another suptech innovation—circuit breakers that prevent a financial service provider from rerouting or transferring transactions to another provider or system, if regulators determine that that alternative could be compromised by the overload. In more extreme circumstances, regulators may need to consider shutting down *all* providers of a particular financial service for a brief period of time, if it seems likely that the entire system will otherwise be overwhelmed. The Electric Reliability Commission of Texas (known as ERCOT) was faced with a similar calculation in February 2021, when it had to choose between triggering outages for its customers (which ended up lasting for days) and the possibility of infrastructure catching on fire and becoming permanently damaged (which could have limited electricity supply for months).[43] ERCOT chose outages—the right decision, but one that came at significant human cost to the people of Texas.[44]

The financial equivalent of the outages that ERCOT triggered might look like the week-long "bank holiday" (a euphemism for forced suspension of banking services) that President Roosevelt imposed in 1933 to calm down a nationwide bank panic: a necessary step that nonetheless cuts people off from financial services on which they rely.[45] A broad-based shutdown would certainly be highly disruptive and should only be deployed in extreme circumstances, but it would have two advantages over a more targeted response. First, it would avoid the difficult distributional questions that arise when financial services are shut off for some customers but not others (there are problems associated with allowing unelected officials to decide who should continue to get critical services and who shouldn't—there was a significant controversy when PG&E selectively shut off power for some of its customers during the 2019 California wildfires, for example).[46] Second, selectively shutting down parts of the system assumes that regulators understand all of the pathways for contagion and can isolate the problem—in a complex system, this can be challenging and if regulators miss something, then the whole system could become compromised despite the shutdown.

Unless and until a real-time reporting system becomes a reality, though, real-time opportunities for shutdowns and other intervention will be limited. Reports of technological incidents will have to be delivered after the fact, but regulators can still conduct post-mortems based on these reports to better understand how technological problems are actually being transmitted through the system. With this information, regulators will be in a better position to understand the likely impacts of future technological failures, and to develop possible emergency responses to those future failures.

Right now, the go-to emergency response during financial crises is for central banks to make loans to ailing financial institutions, but these loans won't be able to fix a purely technical problem. New types of emergency responses are needed, and regulators can develop hypothetical scenarios to stress test the impact of possible technological failures on the system to help figure out what those emergency responses should be. Outside of finance, lots of other technology providers are experimenting with how to test for technological failures. Their experiments and approaches can inform technological stress testing of financial institutions. Netflix, for example, uses something called "chaos monkey" to randomly shut down parts of its system, in order to learn more about the connections between the components of its system, and the likelihood that those connections will transmit problems from one part of the system to another.[47] The consequences of *actually* shutting down parts of the financial system would be much more harmful than just an unavailable movie, so financial regulators should not follow Netflix's example to the letter. Simulations in this vein might assist in understanding pathways for contagion in the financial system, though, and there are some new technologies that could help design these simulations. For example, breakthroughs are being made in the field of novelty detection, where artificial intelligence is being used to find unexpected outcomes in a system.[48] Of course, the outputs of novelty detection technologies should be taken with the requisite grain of salt, but even though they will not be entirely predictive, their output can still be used as the basis for developing stress test hypotheticals.

The lessons learned from post-mortems, stress tests, and other simulations can inform the development of new emergency responses, so that they are ready to go when needed. These lessons may also suggest regulatory reforms that can be implemented so that systems are less likely to fail in the first place. However, we have to remember that these regulatory reforms will also increase the complexity of the system, and therefore make it more fragile in some ways. As we discussed in the context of machine learning algorithms, simple reforms should be prioritized, and if a regulation is only meant to make the components of the system incrementally safer while making the system as a whole much more complicated, the regulation may not be worthwhile from a financial stability perspective.

Understanding that all of these kinds of macro-operational measures will be new and experimental at first, regulators should make sure that there's some redundancy in the system to pick up the slack should key infrastructure fail—even if that redundancy makes the system a little less efficient. In the case of payments processing, for example, redundancy could be created by central banks creating a "payment system of last resort" that could pick up the slack if the ability of the private sector to process retail payments transactions were compromised (we explored some of the proposals for new public payments infrastructure in Chapter 4). Alternatively, or as a supplemental (and decidedly low-tech) approach, redundancy could be created by enacting laws that force businesses to accept physical cash payments, and central banks could plan to make cash reserves strategically available (just as the Federal Reserve did in preparation for Y2K).[49] This would prevent a transition to a wholly cashless society that would make us entirely dependent on technology for our ability to transact.[50]

## The scope of a licensing regime

This chapter's proposals for principles-based supervisory approaches and suptech innovations can mitigate some of fintech's threats to financial stability, but as we've already alluded to, they will inevitably add some complexity to the financial system. A licensing regime, however, can *limit* the complexity of the overall system: if there are significant concerns about how a new technology will interact with the rest of the financial system, a licensing regime can prevent the new technology from ever entering the system. Even when a licensing regime authorizes the use of new technology, the licensing process provides opportunities to ensure that the technology is designed from the start to comply with regulatory conditions—which avoids the complexity that comes from retrofitting an operational technology to satisfy regulatory requirements.

While there are a lot of benefits that would flow from a licensing regime for financial technologies, figuring out the appropriate scope of such a regime is challenging. It would be very disruptive to retroactively review technologies that are already being used by regulated financial institutions, and it won't even be feasible to review every new technology that will be adopted by regulated institutions in the future. Regulators just don't have enough resources. So where should we draw the line?

Technologies that are already in use pose some of the most difficult issues for a licensing regime. We have precedents, though, in how the US Congress phased in new approval requirements for drugs, medical devices, food additives, color additives, and tobacco products to be administered by the US Food and Drug Administration ("FDA"). Congress's approach to tackling FDA transitional issues has varied between and even within product types. In some instances, it granted blanket exemptions from the new approval requirements to an entire category of preexisting products, and in others it allowed preexisting products to be marketed until their approval process could be completed. In still others, it excluded preexisting products from the approval process if certain things could be demonstrated (things that were different—and often less stringent—than what new entrants needed to demonstrate as part of their approval process).[51]

Lawmakers and financial regulators can study these approaches to help inform their approach to reviewing existing financial technologies. One possibility would be to automatically grant a temporary authorization for all technologies adopted by financial institutions prior to the creation of the licensing regime (details of the date on which existing technologies were adopted and the uses to which they are applied could be collected using Form T). This temporary authorization would last until a financial regulator has an opportunity to review the technology. It has taken the FDA decades to review some existing drugs and medical devices;[52] a temporary authorization for financial technologies will often end up working as a de facto permanent authorization. Because authorizations for older technologies would remain nominally temporary, though, it would preserve the regulator's ability to review, regulate, or even ban the use of existing technologies if any concerns develop. The ever-present possibility of such review could also have the welcome side effect of encouraging more responsible use of technology by the financial industry.

When it comes to the adoption of new technologies, it will be easier to catch those technologies for review, but regulators will still face resource constraints and have to make determinations about which technologies deserve the most scrutiny. Regulators will also have to determine what to do about incremental changes to existing technologies, and new uses of existing technology: because such changes can ratchet up complexity and increase the chance of unexpected interactions, regulators should not presume that they're not worth looking at. Going forward, the best approach may be to adopt a regime that requires a regulated institution to seek a license for each technological application it adopts. Regulators could then grant temporary authorizations as a matter of course while retaining the power to revisit them later—unless they have an immediate concern about the technology.

Right now, the new technologies that seem to deserve the most scrutiny are machine learning technologies being incorporated into robo-investing models, and cryptoassets. Robo-investing platforms have the potential to coordinate investor behavior on a scale that has never been seen before—if these platforms rely on machine learning technology that is highly unpredictable during tail events, then tail events could have catastrophic outcomes. Outsized impact is also a concern when it comes to cryptoassets: because there is no natural limit on the number of cryptoassets that can be created, they are completely untethered to reality and can exponentially multiply the amount of risk in the financial system. A licensing regime that creates a bottleneck in the production of cryptoassets would benefit financial stability simply by reducing their numbers. Where the efficiencies associated with a particular type of cryptoasset are so great that regulators want to consider ways of authorizing the technology for those uses, the licensing process would provide an opportunity for regulators to make suptech interventions that could introduce some flexibility into the cryptoassets' operations in order to preserve financial stability (we will return to these shortly).

## The licensing review process

So what would the licensing process look like for technologies that are being subjected to higher scrutiny? For guidance, we can look to several law professors who have proposed frameworks for a financial product preapproval procedure, modeled on the precedent of the FDA.[53] Because these proposals predate the rise of fintech, it's not surprising that they don't pay much attention to the *technology* used in providing financial products and services—their focus is largely on financial products like credit default swaps that helped fuel the last financial crisis. Still, the proposals serve as useful starting points for a discussion about the type of regulatory regime that could authorize regulators to ban or conditionally license the use of new financial technologies.

In all of these proposals, the authors acknowledge that one of the biggest design challenges is determining exactly what should have to go through the preapproval process.[54] I have already recommended that *all* technologies adopted by a financial institution should be subject to a licensing regime, but that temporary authorizations be given speedily and as a matter of course unless the technology is one that raises obvious financial stability concerns (readily providing temporary authorizations has the added benefit of avoiding a scenario where the government is seen as "picking winners" from among the technologies submitted to regulators). When it comes to the review process itself, Saule Omarova recommends that the innovation be subjected to three tests: an economic purpose test, an institutional capacity test, and a systemic effects test.[55] These tests are well suited to assessing new financial technologies.

The economic purpose test is designed to show that a technology serves a real economic need—in other words, that it doesn't just exist to make money for the financial institution using it. There must therefore be real demand for a particular technology to better manage risk, intermediate capital, or process payments or other transactions, but that demand isn't enough in and of itself to justify approval. As the gap widens between the expertise of financial institution managers and the types of technology they use, the need for an "institutional capacity test" becomes more and more important. The preapproval process should seek to prevent technology from being used by a financial institution that "fails to prove its ability to understand, identify, measure, monitor, and manage potential risks [the technology] poses to the institution's own financial health, as well as to the financial well-being of the product's users and overall market stability."[56]

The last of the three tests is the systemic effects test. Given the uncertainty about the future behavior of the financial system, trying to predict the exact effects of a new technological application on the financial system is impossible. We do know, though, that the more widely used a technology is, the greater its systemic impact is likely to be. This book has also identified increased complexity, speed, and coordination as potentially destructive forces that could undermine financial stability, and these can also be used as proxies for systemic concerns. Technological applications that have the potential to exacerbate complexity, speed, or coordination while only making minimal contributions to the financial system's ability to facilitate risk management, capital intermediation, or payments processing should not survive the preapproval process—particularly if the technology has a wide footprint and the institution deploying the technology does not fully understand it.

Where there are systemic concerns but both the economic case and institutional capacity are strong, regulators face a difficult determination. They may decide to make approval of the technology conditional—some suggested conditions for the use of cryptoassets and machine learning-enabled robo-investing are discussed below. Or, if regulators still harbor concerns about a technology, approval might be conditioned on further testing and review (perhaps with a small group of users, to limit fallout). While regulatory sandboxes may not be the best use of regulatory resources (as discussed in Chapter 5), the processes used in those sandboxes for trialing products could be a model for this type of conditional rollout of new financial products.

## A licensing regime for robo-investing

How would these economic purpose, institutional capacity, and systemic effects tests be applied to robo-investing models that rely on machine learning for their customer risk assessment and asset allocation functions? With this business model, the economic purpose test will probably be satisfied, given the potential for robo-investing's cost efficiencies to make financial advice available to a much larger, previously underserved population. The institutional capacity test may prove a challenge, though. If the institution using the machine learning algorithm lacks the technical capacity to properly oversee its ongoing tuning and use, then approval will not be granted. Finally, even if the technical capacity is there, we still need to be mindful of systemic effects. There are a number of conditions that could be put on any approval of this application of financial technology to help mitigate concerns about complexity, speed, and correlation.

One important condition should be a "human in the loop" requirement: the machine learning algorithms that assess customers and recommend investment portfolios should *not* be automatically linked to any kind of automatic execution or rebalancing algorithm. Before any investments are purchased or sold, a human should have the opportunity to intervene to ensure that the machine learning algorithms haven't recommended anything wildly erroneous. This human intervention will come at some cost to efficiency, but the alternative is to subject far more assets to the wild gyrations in prices that have been caused by flash crashes over the last decade.[57] If robo-investing scales up significantly, the spillover consequences of such coordinated trading behavior—for other financial institutions and for financial markets generally—have the potential to be far more pronounced than those we've seen in previous flash crashes.

Speaking of scale and coordination, there should be a limit on the amount of assets under management that a single algorithm can be responsible for. This would put some outer bound on the coordinating effect of robo-investing powered by machine learning. With regard to the algorithm itself, it would be prudent to implement ongoing principles-based requirements, similar to those already discussed for machine learning algorithms used in internal risk management, to ensure the algorithms are trained to better focus on low probability but high consequence events. Remember that any institution using machine learning to power their robo-investing platform must have satisfied an institutional capacity test to get preapproval; these institutions should therefore have the technological wherewithal to comply with principles-based regulation.

## A licensing regime for cryptoassets

Many cryptoasset versions of existing financial products (like credit default swaps) may be unable to obtain a license under this chapter's proposed framework. The use of smart contract and distributed ledger technologies may not add much to the economic purpose of the existing product beyond incremental gains in efficiency, and the benefit of these incremental gains is likely to be outweighed by the product's complexity and speed (which would doom the cryptoasset in terms of the institutional capacity and systemic effects tests). While many kinds of cryptoassets could ultimately be banned—at least for regulated financial institutions—if a cryptoasset were to have enough utility to obtain a license, the licensing process would still offer regulators the opportunity to make some interventions.

Many of the dangers of driverless finance arise because of the potential speed of automated financial transactions. If the rights associated with financial assets are increasingly governed by smart contracts operating on distributed ledgers, transactions can be slowed down by regulating the smart contract, the ledger, or both. Regulation targeted at the smart contract itself could take the form of a requirement that each smart contract be programmed to consult an external oracle that is maintained by the relevant regulator. The frequency of required consultation would be determined by regulation, in light of the nature of the market for trading that type of asset—daily consultations would presumably be enough in some markets, but others would need to be far more frequent. Typically, this oracle would provide no information to the smart contract, which would allow the smart contract to process transactions without regulatory interference. However, in times of systemic distress, the regulator could activate the oracle so that when the smart contract consults the oracle, it ceases to execute its regular instructions. In this capacity, the oracle would work like a circuit breaker for the smart contract that allows the regulator to prevent any self-execution that could harm financial stability.

Regulations relating to the distributed ledger on which the cryptoasset is hosted could also protect financial stability by preventing a problematic transaction from being consummated. Remember that no cryptoasset can be transferred without changing the distributed ledger to record the transfer, and that any payment between the parties will also be effected by updating the ledger. As such, transactions will never take place if the people in charge of validating the distributed ledger refuse to accept a version of the ledger that reflects the executed transaction. As an alternative or complement to preventing the transaction from executing in the first place, there are some mechanisms that can be used to undo the execution of any smart contract operating on the ledger. While some proponents of smart contracts claim that they are "immutable," in the sense that they cannot be undone, this immutability only exists if the validators refuse to undo the transaction. In fact, the ledger can be "rewritten" to exclude the undesirable transaction if enough of the validators agree.

Getting this consensus from validators can be time-consuming and cumbersome—if not downright impossible—if a distributed ledger is set up to allow anonymous parties to validate transactions. However, if the distributed ledger were set up so that transactions could only be verified by an identifiable group of validators, then they might be relied upon to prevent or quickly correct erroneous transactions when necessary. Regulators should therefore consider a rule that establishes that certain types of financial assets may only take the form of a cryptoasset if the distributed ledger on which those assets are hosted is controlled by trusted, permissioned validators—or at the very least, that all the persons authorized to validate (and therefore to reverse) transactions on that distributed ledger be readily identifiable regulated institutions that will respond to regulatory requests.

To regulate distributed ledgers and smart contracts in this way, financial stability regulators will need a flexible authorization that allows them to pause or reverse transactions in unusual and exigent circumstances. However, some clarity and limitations on this regulatory authority will be needed to address concerns about regulators stopping or reversing transactions when it's not warranted. It's also possible that regulators will fail to intervene even when it is warranted, either because they fear push-back from the parties or public criticism, or because they believe that regulatory intervention will alarm the financial markets, causing a panic.[58] In the US equity markets, these kinds of problems are addressed by using circuit breakers that automatically kick in when an index like the S&P 500 declines by more than a specified percentage in a single day.[59] Because those circuit breakers are tied to a market indicator rather than regulatory discretion, they are seen as more objective and regulators are less likely to be criticized. Could a similar approach be taken to halting or reversing transactions involving cryptoassets?

One approach might be to tie the regulator's power to intervene to a market indicator, like the VIX (which reflects market expectations about volatility and is sometimes referred to as the "fear index"). Market indicators like the VIX are a reflection of the sentiments of private market participants, though, and because market participants have an incomplete understanding of systemic risks, a market-based indicator is not a perfect predictor of financial system failure. Ideally, triggers would be tied to an indicator maintained by a public sector body.

The Financial Stress Index, developed by the Office of Financial Research as a "daily snapshot of current stress in global financial markets," could serve as a prototype for such an indicator.[60] While this Financial Stress Index relies exclusively on publicly available information, if we implement mechanisms to encourage information-sharing among regulators, it could be updated with the benefit of confidential information.[61] Currently, lags in reporting would prevent any indicator from providing an entirely current picture of stress in the financial system, but this could be addressed as advances are made in real-time reporting and analysis technology (this is another example of an area where suptech innovation by the regulator could advance the goal of financial stability).[62]

Regardless of the indicator used, regulators might not want to automatically pause or undo *all* transactions in circumstances of heightened systemic risk. The indicator could serve as a baseline authorization for intervention, and then regulators would have discretion to intervene as needed. Such an approach is not perfect: regulators may still refrain from needed intervention, even with authorization, because they fear pushback on their decisions. Relying on an indicator that is disclosed to the public could also invite problematic market behavior: if the indicator starts to trend in a way that suggests that regulatory action is coming, market participants may panic, trying to transact ahead of any regulatory freeze.[63] This issue could be solved by keeping the indicator private, but tying regulatory action to a secret indicator brings us right back to the legitimacy concerns we started with.

Ultimately, tying regulatory authority to an indicator will always have some inherent problems (not least of which is that the indicator may not always catch emerging systemic risks). Perfection is not possible, though, when grappling with the thorny and multifaceted issue of systemic risk, and the adoption of circuit breakers and distributed ledger regulation that could be used in indicated circumstances would increase the chances of pausing threats to financial stability. Remember, though, that all of this complexity can and should be avoided if the cryptoasset in question does not satisfy the threshold economic purpose, institutional capacity, and systemic effects tests. In those circumstances, financial institutions should not be allowed to issue cryptoassets in the first place.

Finally, there is the issue of cryptoassets that are not issued by regulated financial institutions, and would therefore not be subject to this licensing regime at all. Regulators should give serious consideration to severely restricting the ability of regulated financial institutions to invest (directly or indirectly) in those crypotassets, and at the very least, they should prohibit crypotassets from being used as collateral for interbank loans or repo arrangements. This kind of precautionary approach is needed in order to prevent the seemingly inevitable cryptoasset bubbles, panics, and fire sales we discussed in Chapter 3 from destabilizing the established financial system's ability to provide financial services to the broader economy.

* * *

Adoption of the precautionary regulatory strategies explored in this chapter would be a significant departure from the status quo, which by and large allows financial technologies to be developed and launched without any regulatory oversight. As significant a shift as this would be, though, it won't address all of the deficiencies of financial regulation that are being exposed by the rise of driverless finance. Time is of the essence—not just in pursuing this chapter's reforms, but also in grappling with other bigger picture questions about fintech's impact on financial stability. That is what we will do in the next chapter.

# 7
# The Bigger Picture

We have just discussed a range of proposals that could help address the threats that driverless finance poses for financial stability. As I conceded at the beginning of Chapter 6, these proposals will all need to be debated and refined before they can be implemented. Some of the refinements will be technical, but this will also be a very political process. There will surely be pushback on ideological grounds (from those who see government as more of a problem than a solution), on more cynical grounds (from those who stand to profit from the unregulated proliferation of these technologies), and on timid grounds (from those who see the proposals as admirable, but too ambitious). Strong public support will be needed to overcome these kinds of pushback; none of this book's proposals will be implemented without that support.

There is a timeless passage from the novel *Phineas Finn*, which was published in the 1860s but still captures how public opinion evolves today:

> Many who before regarded legislation on the subject as chimerical, will now fancy that it is only dangerous, or perhaps not more than difficult. And so in time it will come to be looked on as among the things possible, then among the things probable;—and so at last it will be ranged in the list of those few measures which the country requires as being absolutely needed. That is the way in which public opinion is made.[1]

This book aims to raise public awareness of how fintech innovations could cause financial system collapse, and to show how regulatory solutions could help. In other words, I wrote this book to help move those regulatory solutions further from the "chimerical" and closer to the "absolutely needed." But public opinion does not always march in a single direction. The interests of those who are invested in preventing regulation can also become more entrenched over time. And so even though the political challenges involved in regulating driverless finance are formidable right now, the novelty of these technologies means that the so-called vested interests are not quite so vested

*Driverless Finance.* Hilary J. Allen, Oxford University Press. © Hilary J. Allen 2022.
DOI: 10.1093/oso/9780197626801.003.0008

as they will be in a year or two. That is why time is of the essence in kick-starting the debate about fintech and financial stability.

Time is also of the essence in responding to many other big picture questions that have been brought into sharp relief by the rise of fintech. The concrete proposals in Chapter 6 focus narrowly on addressing financial stability concerns, but the rise of fintech also begs broader questions about the role and limits of bureaucratic expertise in our society (particularly the ability of government experts to engage in public-serving innovation), which is in turn part of a bigger debate about the role of public versus private in our financial system.[2] In addition, the entrance of new technologies and new types of firms into the financial system exacerbate already difficult questions about regulators' jurisdiction, and those questions are tied (particularly in the case of Amazon, Google, Apple, and Facebook) to new types of market power and competition problems. Finally, no discussion of fintech would be complete without a discussion of the privacy and cybersecurity issues that plague the digital delivery of financial services. This chapter will engage with this bigger picture.

## Public sector innovation

Given that this book has spent a lot of time investigating the potential dangers lurking in new technologies, it is fair to ask why Chapter 6 recommends *more* technological innovation (this time, suptech innovation by the government). A superficial answer is that it is a defensive necessity—as I have already said, regulators overseeing a technologically sophisticated industry without technology of their own is like bringing a knife to a gun fight. A deeper answer is that technology is a means and not an end, and so technology will have a very different impact if it is developed by someone with different priorities. Technology developed in order to promote the regulatory goal of financial stability will be trying to do very different things than private sector technologies designed to maximize short-term profits.

It is true that we cannot predict exactly what the impact of suptech will be—that's why this book has suggested that these innovations should be taken with a grain of salt, and ideally be backed up by more analog forms of regulation. However, technological innovation developed to further public-minded goals has more potential to make our financial system stable than private sector technological innovation that is—at best—indifferent to financial stability concerns. Regulators developing new technologies can intentionally try to avoid the complexity and coordination associated with so many private sector fintech innovations (although suptech will often need to be just as speedy as fintech, if it is to have any impact on light-speed financial transactions). However, suptech can only be successful if it overcomes the obstacles that impede public sector innovation writ large.

In her excellent book *The Entrepreneurial State*, economist Mariana Mazzucato makes the case that a lot of the hard work of innovation falls to the state rather than the private sector, and yet the private sector tends to reap the reputational and financial rewards.[3] Mazzucato illustrates this dynamic with plenty of historical examples—ranging from the internet to new drugs—but she points out that this dynamic is not inevitable. Allowing the private sector to take credit for these innovations is in many ways a choice, and a problematic one at that. Because the word "innovation" has so many positive connotations, it is powerful to frame actions as "innovative."[4] Instead of ceding this power to the private sector, public sector bodies could choose to market themselves as innovators, and by doing so, kick-start a virtuous cycle where the government is seen as a solution rather than a problem.

Many public sector bodies have been too intimidated, though, to take proactive steps to innovate in their sphere of influence (perhaps they have internalized Ronald Reagan's adage that "I'm from the Government, and I'm here to help" are the nine most terrifying words in the English language).[5] If regulators do indeed fear that their own mistakes will be worse than private sector mistakes, then it shouldn't be surprising if they hold back[6]—and by "hold back", I mean observing and trying to understand developments in the private sector, rather than actively seeking to influence those developments in a way that promotes financial stability and other regulatory goals. Unfortunately, this works as a self-fulfilling prophecy about the limited usefulness of the government—government can't succeed if it doesn't try.

If we want regulatory solutions that address the latest generation of financial stability risks, and do so in an inclusive way that benefits society as a whole, this narrative needs to change—regulators need to become effective innovators of suptech solutions. Economists use the term "public goods" to describe public benefits that people cannot be excluded from even if they can't pay for them (like clean air—and financial stability). Because they aren't fully compensated for creating public goods, private sector entities generally lack the incentives to produce them—which means that it often falls to the government to provide these public goods.[7] The public goods problem is not a new one, but the problem has evolved when it comes to public goods that must be delivered by technological means. Technological innovation by the public sector will be needed to provide those public goods.

Government agencies can sometimes outsource the development of public-minded technologies to private sector vendors, but outsourcing is not a complete solution. Providing niche solutions for one or two regulatory agencies is unlikely to be a profitable business model for any vendor, and so the vendors will often need other customers from the private sector. As we alluded to in Chapter 5, the fact that there are more private sector clients than public sector clients could ultimately encourage any vendors who do develop public sector solutions to skew them in ways that benefit their private sector clients.[8] Regulators will therefore need some capacity to do their own innovation in-house.

In order to be able to achieve this, regulatory agencies will need to be able to attract the necessary expertise. Stereotypes of government agencies as stodgy and bureaucratic can make it difficult to attract innovative minds to government work, though. This is why Mariana Mazzucato's point about rebranding the public sector as mission-driven and innovative is so important. The public sector will always struggle to compete with the salaries offered by the private sector, but there are certainly civic-minded experts out there who might be convinced to take a pay cut for the right position. These experts are more likely to gravitate to the public sector if their work there has real meaning—and if they are able to actively create things, rather than just react to what the private sector is doing. New types of expertise can also be cultivated within the public sector if there are innovative technological projects underway for employees to cut their teeth on.

## Innovation, expertise, and permission to fail

Chapter 6 talked about the importance of financial stability regulators accumulating computer and data science expertise (complexity science experience would also be helpful). But it's quite possible that responding to driverless finance's threats to financial stability will require expertise that simply doesn't exist yet, and needs to be developed.[9] How should regulators build this kind of expertise? And at this high level of technical difficulty, when should society defer to regulatory expertise, and when should we eye it with suspicion? These questions aren't just relevant to the maintenance of financial stability. They are part of a much broader debate about the role of expertise in our society. Given how complex our society is these days, we simply cannot expect to understand everything on our own, and a degree of trust in expertise is needed to make the world go round.[10] But there should be some limits on that trust—delegation to experts only really works if people educate themselves enough to know when *not* to defer to experts.[11]

The 2008 financial crisis rightfully damaged trust in the expertise of financial regulators, but not all regulatory screw-ups are that big, and some tolerance of lower-level screw-ups is needed to allow financial stability regulators to develop their expertise: experts will never be perfect. Experts are particularly likely to be *im*perfect when they are trying to negotiate an uncertain future—but we'll all be in trouble if they abdicate responsibility for planning for that uncertain future. Expertise can take decades to develop, and so waiting until a problem occurs almost ensures that experts will fall hopelessly behind and will be forced to play a mad game of catch-up in order to respond when something goes wrong. It's better for experts to experiment along the way to develop the expertise needed to confront problems when they arise. This kind of experimentation will inevitably involve a process of trial and error, and if the only negative consequences of an expert's errors are a waste of time and money (and maybe a little embarrassment), that would be a reasonable price to pay for the development of expertise.[12] Failure is integral to the innovation process as well as the development of expertise, and so should be expected as part of any public sector innovation program as well. Even private sector innovators fail most of the time, and public sector innovators are often trying to solve thorny long-term problems—ones that the private sector won't even touch.[13] They will probably fail a lot more frequently.

In short, innovators and experts working for the government need to be afforded some—but not unlimited—permission to fail. When it comes to granting this permission internally, government agencies can borrow from the vast private sector literature on how to develop "agile workflows" where failure comes thick and fast and is accepted as part of the learning process.[14] Unlike the private sector, though, the government also has to answer to the public at large. So long as public sector experts and innovators learn from their mistakes, they *should* be afforded some grace—but we can't always count on elected officials or the public at large to be so gracious. Structures may be needed to protect public sector experts and experimentation: ideally, these structures would hit the sweet spot of creating an environment that insulates public sector actors from negative pushback for their initial mistakes, but creates consequences if they fail to correct or adapt in light of those mistakes.

When the experts and innovators in question are regulators who work for the government, we already have a body of law (known as administrative law) that tries to strike a balance between holding regulators accountable on the one hand, and giving them the freedom they need to do their jobs on the other hand. At a minimum, administrative law tries to ensure that regulators stay within their legal mandates. Even this may be challenging for regulators to negotiate during a period of rapid technological change, when it can sometimes be hard to figure out where the boundaries of a legal mandate lie (for example, if a regulator has a long-standing mandate to regulate "securities," should that extend to new technologies like cryptoassets?). But administrative law often requires regulators to do more than just establish this bare legal authority.

Regulatory agencies are sometimes required to satisfy a type of "cost-benefit analysis" that requires the agency to quantify both the costs and the benefits of its regulation, and then demonstrate that the benefits outweigh the costs. Unfortunately, the benefits of public goods like financial stability are often hard to quantify, and quantifying these benefits becomes even harder when suptech (or some other innovative technology) is the method chosen to achieve them. Chapters 5 and 6 explained why suptech innovation is needed to respond to the rise of driverless finance, but how do you put a dollar number on the benefits of suptech if no one knows precisely how it will work?[15]

Suptech innovation will be a trial-and-error process for the regulators involved, and the inevitable failures will need to be handled with some kind of public relations strategy. While it's seen as perfectly acceptable for nine out of ten investments by a private venture capital firm to fail, government investments that fail can become a public relations crisis that confirm preconceived notions of the government as inept and wasteful—even when the government is trying to do something bigger, harder, and more necessary than any venture capital firm would ever get behind. How do we leave behind the framing of financial regulation as a purely reactive response to market failures, and rebrand it (particularly suptech) as an exciting and innovative approach to protecting society from financial collapse? Just as importantly, how can we get people to accept experimental suptech innovations as a legitimate form of regulation?

The general public can only assess suptech if there is some transparency about how it works, and if they have some ability to engage with the technology in question. Transparency is no longer as simple as posting a proposed regulation for public comment; future transparency efforts may require disclosure of source code or the release of beta models of technology, but most people don't have the technological skills to engage with that kind of disclosure. As governments around the world start to use technology to regulate more and more kinds of behavior, the question of how to make the workings of that technology more accessible to the general public is becoming increasingly relevant to a working democracy—but unfortunately there aren't many good answers to this question yet. Once we do start to figure this out, though, it won't be enough for regulators to open up to the public when they first adopt a suptech intervention. Technology is continually refined through its development and implementation processes, and so ongoing transparency will be needed into how the suptech is performing. This type of ongoing transparency may well be an adjustment for financial regulators, many of whom are used to operating in a more secretive way.[16]

Any mistakes or failures that are revealed through this transparency will be more easily forgiven if they occur in the context of early-stage experimentation and the only negative consequence is wasted resources. The stakes are higher once experimental suptech strategies start compelling companies and people to act in a particular way.[17] However, trust in the use of suptech can be reinforced if its development is guided by several rules of thumb. One is not to overreach—suptech should be tailored as narrowly as possible to the problem at hand, and more familiar forms of regulation (like rule-making) can take care of the rest. This will limit the coercive impact of the regulatory experts' experimentation, and potentially limit the scope for unintended consequences—it will also preserve space for future regulatory innovation. Another rule is to ensure that both technology experts and policymakers are "in the room where it happens," actively involved in designing suptech so that the technology actually reflects the goals the policymakers are trying to achieve.[18] Before this can happen, the policymakers will need to have very deliberate discussions about the conflicting values at stake (for example, financial stability versus efficiency) so that the desired balance of those goals can be clearly articulated and communicated to the public, as well as the technical experts.[19]

## The role of finance in society

If we accept that public bodies like central banks and financial regulators shouldn't just be passive when it comes to innovation and developing expertise, that begs the question of whether they should play a more proactive role in our economy in other ways as well. People often get instinctively nervous at the thought of direct government participation in the economy—it can conjure up images of government-directed five-year plans—but that's not what I'm talking about here. Instead, we can think about situations where the private financial industry has failed to meet society's needs, and ask whether there's a role for the public sector to provide financial services more directly.

Questions about the limitations of private sector solutions are particularly relevant when it comes to fintech innovation, because so much of the impetus for that innovation (or, if we're being cynical, the spin justifying that innovation) is the push to provide financial services to underserved communities. While there are definitely people who are desperately in need of reasonably priced risk management, capital intermediation, and payments services, we should ask ourselves whether we have to depend *only* on private-sector fintech entrepreneurs to develop these services.

It's very possible that the private sector will develop new fintech products and services that exploit vulnerable populations just as previous generations of financial innovations like payday lending and check cashing services have.[20] Instead of indirectly (and often inefficiently and inadequately) promoting financial inclusion by adopting innovation hubs and regulatory sandboxes to support private sector fintech innovation, the state could consider creating and shaping new markets for financial services as a more direct response to financial inclusion problems. If the state can do this in ways that are less complex (and perhaps a fraction slower) than what the private sector is offering, then not only will previously underserved populations benefit, our financial system as a whole will benefit from increased stability.

There have been a couple of places in this book where we've touched on proposals for these kinds of public solutions, particularly in Chapter 4, when we talked about public payments processing infrastructure. If these types of policies turn out to be successful, that might help make other types of direct public involvement in the financial markets more politically palatable—including creating or supporting markets for financial assets that will pay off in the long-term, but won't deliver the short-term profits that investors in private sector firms often demand.[21] To give one example, there is a lot of discussion about whether central banks should buy so-called green bonds to create a market for debt that is being used to fund environmentally sustainable projects.[22] While the merits of this particular proposal need to be debated, before we can even get to that debate, we need to figure out our level of comfort with central banks picking and choosing investments in the capital markets.

Not only does the rise of driverless finance beg questions about how big a role the public sector should have in the financial markets, it also begs questions about the inverse: Should there be limitations on the supply of financial services by the private sector? The dynamic of privatized gains and socialized losses is unfortunately endemic in the financial system. Throughout this book, we've referred to the socially useful functions of risk management, capital formation, and payments provided by the financial sector, but these functions aren't automatically socially useful. They become useful if they result in broader economic growth, but if they are used primarily to generate profits for a financial industry that is increasingly untethered from the broader economy, then they will do little (public) good. Not only that, but they may very well do harm, if the public sector is expected to bail out the financial industry when a self-referential bubble bursts.

As we explored in Chapter 3, the line between investment and gambling is blurring into nonexistence as new types of cryptoassets are being developed. These crypotassets can be made out of whole cloth, without any link to a real economic function, and many of them seem to exist primarily to allow for speculation (and of course, cryptoasset trading also generates data and transaction fees that will be profitable for someone). The absurdity of the situation is best illustrated by Dogecoin, a cryptoasset which was developed as a joke in 2013, but has somehow evolved into a legitimate financial asset.[23] At what point should the public sector stop accommodating the risks that speculators and the financial industry are incurring in pursuit of profits from cryptoasset trading?

This book has already answered this question in a narrow way with its proposal for a licensing regime—at a certain point, the public sector should say no and refuse to license some kinds of cryptoassets. But how should we approach other financial products? Should they also be required to be tethered to some real-world economic use, to prevent a world where there are simply too many financial assets with too much associated risk? Should we adopt policies (like transaction taxes) that favor fewer transactions rather than more? Answering the specifics of these questions will be complicated, but adopting a precautionary approach to finance more broadly is one way to rebalance power between the private and public sector. Precautionary financial stability regulation is a way of reasserting that the public's welfare is more important than the financial industry's profits.

And financial stability isn't the only aspect of public welfare that is being threatened by fintech. In early 2021, Bitcoin mining alone was estimated to consume more electricity than the entire country of Argentina,[24] which seems particularly offensive as the world scrambles to mitigate climate change. If cryptoasset investments are in many respects just gambling, how can this level of environmental damage be justified? These environmental impacts could potentially be addressed by switching to permissioned blockchains or a "proof of stake" verification process (as the Ethereum blockchain is doing),[25] but finance also puts other drains on our society that are harder to fix. People have long bemoaned that many of the brightest minds have gone to work for a financial industry which has an increasingly tenuous relationship with broader economic growth.[26] With the rise of fintech, finance isn't just employing economists and mathematicians, it's also attracting data scientists and software engineers who could be solving more pressing social problems.

## International and cyberspace borders

Public opinion and political attitudes about how aggressively the government should regulate fintech will vary around the world. This will complicate any international effort to coordinate on the threats that fintech poses for financial stability. We discussed in Chapter 6 why international coordination is needed—the short version is that the financial system is global, and national legal systems have to do their best to match that. Unfortunately, there are reasons to think that coordination on fintech will face new challenges that weren't an issue during earlier rounds of international coordination (like international agreements on regulatory capital requirements).

First, there is the notion that fintech lives in cyberspace, and is therefore even less tethered to any geographical jurisdiction than traditional forms of capital. Second, coordination on fintech regulation will require countries to reach consensus positions on both finance *and* technology matters (and on vendor software developers as well as financial institutions), and so consensus will need to be reached by more and different types of experts tackling more and different kinds of problems. Finally, a new balance of power is emerging when it comes to fintech, which means that the existing relationships among policymakers and regulators that were forged during the development of regulatory capital requirements won't be enough to achieve the necessary consensus.

Chapter 6 discussed the regulatory arbitrage that is possible when geographical limits on regulators' jurisdiction don't reflect the international nature of the financial system, and when somewhat arbitrary borders are adopted even within a geographical locale to delineate what "counts" as a regulated financial institution or service. The rise of fintech creates a third kind of border that complicates jurisdictional issues—the border between cyberspace and the real world.[27] Technological advances (particularly in distributed ledger technology and cloud computing) mean that financial transactions can now occur in a cyberspace over which no nation has any obvious jurisdiction. Transactions in cyberspace can have spillover effects in the real world, though, just as activities undertaken in one country can have spillover effects in another.

The possibility of arbitraging the real world/cyberspace border has real implications for the licensing regime proposed in this book. If a national (or even coordinated international) licensing regime bans certain kinds of cryptoassets, can that ban exert its influence in cyberspace? Some of the more concrete "teeth" of that licensing procedure depend on national courts: for example, one consequence of transacting without a license would be that courts would refuse to enforce any contracts involving unlicensed financial products.[28] If the operation of cryptoassests is governed by smart contracts, though, and if people believe that these smart contracts are self-executing and therefore beyond the purview of the courts, then the unavailability of court remedies won't discourage them from using unlicensed cryptoassets (of course, we spent a lot of time in Chapter 3 talking about how smart contracts are not always as autonomous as they claim to be, but in this instance, if people buy the hype, their belief will be more important than the reality).

It's possible that if investors know that a cryptoasset is banned at the national level, that knowledge alone may be enough delegitimize the asset in cyberspace, relegating the cryptoasset to a class of fringe investments that probably wouldn't hurt financial stability. However, given how unpredictable investors can be, it doesn't seem particularly wise to put all our faith in this kind of market discipline. So how can our national legal systems extend their reach into cyberspace? Well, the individuals who trade banned cryptoassets could theoretically be tracked down and punished, but (just like pursuing people who illegally download copyrighted movies and music) this would probably result in an endless game of whack-a-mole. That probably wouldn't be the best use of law enforcement resources, although this kind of direct enforcement could probably succeed in at least preventing regulated financial institutions from investing in the banned assets.

Another approach could be to direct regulation at intermediaries like internet service providers, cloud service providers, and search engines. They could theoretically serve as pressure points where regulation could be applied, but trying to draft these types of internet infrastructure providers into policing cryptoasset markets would open up a Pandora's box of issues associated with government intervention in the internet.[29] A more modest approach would be to regulate the new kinds of intermediaries that are emerging specifically in connection with cryptoassets, including the people responsible for validating transactions on the distributed ledger and maintaining the software that supports that ledger. However, when the cryptoasset is hosted on a decentralized permissionless ledger, these people could be almost as dispersed and hard to target as the cryptoasset investors themselves (this is one reason why Chapter 6 proposed that regulated financial institutions only be allowed to invest in cryptoassets that are hosted on ledgers maintained by trusted, permissioned validators). For decentralized permissionless ledgers, the path of least resistance is to target the providers of the electronic wallets used to store cryptoassets, and the exchanges used to convert cryptoassets into sovereign currencies. This was the strategy adopted by the New York Department of Financial Services when it adopted its "BitLicense" in 2015: although some wallet providers and exchanges might be fly-by-night operations that could try to avoid regulation, others (like Coinbase, the cryptocurrency exchange that went public in April 2021) are established players that national regulators could pursue.

Cryptoassets pose particularly challenging jurisdictional issues, but even when regulators don't need to reach into cyberspace (as with business models like marketplace lending and robo-investing), there are new jurisdictional issues that have emerged in conjunction with the rise of fintech. In an insightful essay, law professor Yesha Yadav explored some of the new challenges that will arise in trying to achieve international coordination on matters that intertwine financial and technological elements.[30] Some of these relate to the potential cultural specificity of technology—for example, technology that is deemed compliant with international standards because it works well enough in a smaller country may end up buckling if it is applied at a much larger scale in a bigger country, creating unforeseen operational risks. Or a machine learning algorithm that is trained using data from one country may not work well when applied to another country's data (Yadav gives the example of regular purchases of cigarettes and alcohol, which may be perfectly acceptable in some cultures, but may negatively impact assessments of creditworthiness in others).[31]

Another issue for the formulation of international standards is that the traditional balance of power has shifted with the rise of fintech. The United States and Europe have historically had the most influence in developing international financial standards, but their fintech sectors are nowhere near as developed as in countries like China, India, and Kenya (this is not an accident—fintech firms have often found more room to grow in countries that had less established financial industries to begin with).[32] China, India, Kenya, and others should not be left out of any international discussion about fintech standards—and so the somewhat "clubby" relationships among US and European regulators and central bankers that helped facilitate previous generations of international agreements won't suffice this time. Truly international standards will have to be forged by countries that have very different cultures and policy objectives—particularly when it comes to how "free" cyberspace should be.

It may ultimately be that international consensus is impossible—if that happens, opportunities for arbitrage will persist, but they could be mitigated if standards were developed and adopted on a smaller scale (either regionally, or among countries that share political, economic, and cultural similarities). Or nations could go it alone, recognizing that regardless of spillover effects, internally generated financial meltdowns will hurt their own national economy. Then the burden of developing new approaches to regulating fintech will fall squarely on each individual country's financial stability regulators.

## Financial stability regulation in the United States

This book has consistently talked about "financial stability regulators," but it's sometimes hard to pin down who exactly the financial stability regulators are—particularly in the United States. It's easier in countries that have adopted the "twin peaks" model: these countries have two major financial regulatory agencies, with one acting as a general prudential regulator for all providers of financial services, and the other agency focusing on market conduct issues. The prudential regulator is the financial stability regulator: often working in conjunction with the central bank, it considers systemic issues as well as the solvency of individual regulated institutions.[33]

Versions of the twin peaks model have been adopted in countries like Australia and the United Kingdom, where the Australian Prudential Regulatory Authority and the Prudential Regulatory Authority (which is housed within the Bank of England) oversee the safety and soundness of all regulated financial institutions. Both of these bodies have statutory mandates to pursue financial stability.[34] In the United States, though, most of the financial regulatory agencies—including the Federal Reserve—have no explicit statutory mandate to protect financial stability.[35] The only US regulatory bodies that do have this kind of mandate are the ones that were created after the 2008 financial crisis: the Office of Financial Research, and the Financial Stability Oversight Council ("FSOC").

We talked about the Office of Financial Research in Chapter 6: while it could be very useful for some things (like innovating suptech solutions, for example), it's ultimately a research agency and couldn't administer a licensing regime or enforce violations of a principles-based regime on its own. A financial stability regulator needs the authority to compel action from regulated entities, but the OFR lacks that authority. Unfortunately, so does the FSOC. The FSOC is a council of other regulatory agencies that's supposed to keep an eye on emerging threats to financial stability, but it has very few legal powers and has not been allocated many resources. As a result, the FSOC can't do much without leveraging the powers and resources of other financial regulatory agencies—none of whom have a legislative mandate to protect financial stability themselves. To complicate things further, the different financial regulatory agencies that make up the FSOC sometimes find it hard to agree on consistent approaches to financial stability regulation.[36]

If we're thinking big picture, a complete overhaul of the US financial regulatory architecture, moving it in the direction of twin peaks, would be desirable. Unfortunately, numerous past efforts to restructure the US system have failed—it seems that there are just too many entrenched interests in the current system to make significant change. It's possible, though, that the advent of new fintech innovations could provide an opportunity to experiment with better ways of *coordinating* regulatory approaches to financial stability among the many United States agencies—at least when it comes to dealing with complex technologies.

The licensing regime for financial technologies proposed in this book would definitely require coordination across multiple regulatory agencies. To illustrate, consider a new robo-advisory service that depends on machine learning technology to provide consumers with comprehensive advice about financial products and services that are suitable for their unique financial situation. If the technology could recommend (for example) mortgage loan providers as well as investments in mutual funds, cryptoassets, certificates of deposit, and life insurance policies, the Securities and Exchange Commission; the Commodity Futures Trading Commission; the Federal Reserve; the Office of the Comptroller of the Currency; the Federal Deposit Insurance Corporation; the Consumer Financial Protection Bureau; and state banking, insurance, and securities regulators might all have an interest in how that technology worked. As a result, they would all need to be consulted in connection with any license application from that robo-advisory service.

The FSOC could establish a new committee comprised of representatives of all these regulatory agencies that would choose which agency should be primarily responsible for overseeing the licensing process for a particular technology. If this "committee plus delegation" structure worked well for the licensing process, it could serve as a blueprint for future coordination on things like the consistent application of principles-based regulation to new technologies. The OFR could provide technical assistance to the committee, and that technical assistance would be the glue that holds the committee together. Understanding fintech requires software engineering and data science expertise that are significantly underrepresented in all of the financial regulatory agencies right now. It would be prohibitively expensive for each of these agencies to build a deep bench in these fields. It might be feasible, though, for *one* agency—the OFR—to build that deep bench.

Even though an actual restructuring of the US financial regulatory architecture remains elusive, if each financial regulatory agency relies on the OFR for assistance in dealing with new technologies, then we could reasonably expect to see a more coherent and consistent response to those technologies from the various different regulatory agencies. Furthermore, because the OFR was created for the purpose of monitoring threats to financial stability, financial stability concerns will be baked into its analysis of new technologies. Other regulatory goals, like investor and consumer protection, wouldn't be drowned out, though, if agencies like the Securities and Exchange Commission and the Consumer Financial Protection Bureau that prioritize those concerns were also part of the conversation about how to approach those new technologies.[37]

We're now going to switch gears now to another set of related problems—concerns relating to competition, privacy, and cybersecurity. These concerns have been either been generated or exacerbated by the rise of the digital economy, and they are much broader in scope than the financial stability issues that are the subject of this book. With that said, there are some aspects of these problems that are deeply intertwined with threats to financial stability—in particular, Amazon, Google, Apple, and Facebook loom large as "too big to fail," and problems relating to privacy and cyberattacks can undermine confidence in the financial system. The rest of this chapter will focus on these interconnections.

## Competition and the techfins

Concerns about competition are particularly pressing in the context of Amazon, Google, Apple, and Facebook. While we've referred to these companies as "techfins" throughout this book, most of the world doesn't use that word to describe them—after all, their footprint is much larger outside of the world of finance, and they pose lots of problems that are unrelated to financial stability. In particular, the raw economic and political power of these firms (measured not just in terms of money but also in terms of the data they collect and their ability to dictate the information we receive) raises concerns, as does their ability to snuff out nascent competitors who might otherwise challenge their dominance in the future.[38] From a purely financial stability perspective, though, this concentration of market power will be most problematic if a firm like Amazon, Google, Apple, or Facebook becomes a dominant provider of financial service or a dominant provider of infrastructure on which financial services depend.

The lack of alternative infrastructure providers seems to be the more immediate threat. For example, Amazon Web Services already controls the lion's share of the cloud computing markets. This means that Amazon outages can have a significant impact: several times a year, there are headlines like "Prolonged AWS outage takes down a big chunk of the internet."[39] If financial institutions come to rely heavily on Amazon Web Services to store their core data, these outages will be a significant concern for financial stability: for example, an outage affecting a large bank's storage of account data could prevent it from processing payments (and if customers are unable to make payments for a prolonged period of time, that might ultimately spark a run on that bank and other banks that rely on Amazon for their cloud services). These types of concerns have already motivated calls for Amazon Web Services to be regulated as a systemically important financial market utility (like the clearinghouses we discussed in Chapter 4),[40] but financial stability could also be impacted more indirectly by other types of infrastructure monopoly. For example, because Google is so dominant as a search engine, its search results could theoretically steer consumers and investors toward or away from certain financial services and providers. This could potentially coordinate investor behavior, with the destabilizing consequences we discussed in Chapter 3.

There are therefore reasons to be concerned about the financial industry's dependence on a few tech firms for much of their infrastructure. Even more concerns will be raised if the largest tech firms become dominant providers of financial services themselves. We have already discussed Facebook's controversial foray into finance with its proposed Diem currency, but it is by no means the only tech firm interested in financial services. In China, the giant e-commerce platform Alibaba launched the ubiquitous and lucrative AliPay. In the United States, Amazon, Apple and Google (together with Intuit, Paypal, Square, and Stripe) have joined together to form the lobbying group "Financial Innovation Now," which they describe as "an alliance of technology leaders working to modernize the way consumers and businesses manage money and conduct commerce."[41] These tech firms' interest in financial services is not surprising: they already have a lot of users, and financial services often become more valuable when there are more users (this increased value is often described as a "network externality").[42] Payments services demonstrate particularly strong network externalities—a payments service is better when there are more people you can pay with it—and so a firm that already has a large user base has a significant advantage in this space.

A payments service is therefore likely to be many tech firms' first foray into finance, but they won't necessarily stop there. As more users adopt the payment service, more user data is generated (about the customers and their transactions), which the tech firm can use not only to target advertising or identify potential customers for its non-financial services (which will yield yet more data) but also to expand into financial services that involve some data-dependent risk assessment (such as making loans or offering insurance). Offering more types of financial services will create new networks and generate yet more user data in a cycle that is virtuous for the tech firm, but not necessarily for a competitive marketplace or stable financial system.[43]

The techfins have a potential advantage over even the largest banks here, because they can exploit large troves of customer data (like social media posts or search histories or shopping patterns) that they have collected through their non-financial activities. In the United States, banks are prevented from engaging in non-financial activities, so the types of data that banks can collect are more limited (Goldman Sachs can't purchase a search engine, and Citibank can't start up an e-commerce platform). This legal divide only keeps deposit-taking banks and their affiliates out of commercial activities, though.[44] There is nothing to keep the techfins out of financial activities like lending or payments processing.

Because of the competitive advantages that come from their data supremacy (and because they are already huge), Google, Amazon, Facebook, and Apple could quickly become "too big to fail" providers of financial services. "Too big to fail" is used to describe a firm that is so critical to the provision of financial services (because of factors like its size, a lack of substitute providers, or interconnections with other parts of the financial system) that a government simply will not allow it to fail. Unfortunately, firms that recognize that they are "too big to fail" are perversely encouraged to take extra risks: they will profit if those risks turn out well, but they know that any disastrous failures will probably be covered by a government bailout. Profit therefore comes at the expense of the public, which is left holding the bag if the firm's risks don't pan out.[45] And in some ways, that's a best-case scenario. What if a government bailout isn't actually feasible?

Google, Amazon, Facebook, and Apple are so big that in many ways, they make our existing notions of "too big to fail" seem quaint. A recent government report concluded that Facebook and Google have monopoly power in their defined markets, and that Amazon and Apple have "significant and durable market power."[46] If any of these behemoths were to add payments or lending services to their existing markets, they could outcompete many of the alternatives, leaving few substitutes if they were to fail. In the absence of substitutes, a bailout seems inevitable—but what would a bailout on this scale look like? For example, might the government have to bail out Amazon's e-commerce business as well as any lending arm? And which country's government would be responsible? Some smaller countries (like

Iceland and Switzerland) have already had to grapple with the issue that their banks might be too big for them to bail out, but when it comes to the techfins, even large countries like the United States might find them "too big to save."[47]

Given the challenges and costs involved in bailing out a techfin, we need to confront the risks inherent in techfins' provision of financial services before they get too deep into the business. Are there existing financial regulations that can be repurposed to address the provision of financial services by techfins, or do we need new financial regulations that prevent commercial firms from entering finance at all (or at least prevent the techfins from offering payments services)? Is this a problem that is too big for financial regulation to solve on its own—does it need to be addressed by competition law? These are questions that need to be addressed as a matter of urgency.

In the aftermath of the 2008 crisis, several new regulatory approaches were adopted to proactively address the threat of "too big to fail" firms and avoid future bailouts. Among these was a new power to designate large non-bank financial firms as "systemically important," and subject them to heightened bank-like regulation. Although this designation process has not been used in recent years, the framework remains in place, which begs questions about how it might be applied to the techfins. For example, while a techfin's size and the availability of substitutes would obviously be relevant to determining its systemic importance, should the breadth of its non-financial services also be taken into account in the determination? Is unique access to certain kinds of data something that demonstrates systemic significance?

Tech firms' unique access to large troves of data is certainly beginning to be scrutinized as a potential source of market power, but competition law is only just beginning to consider how to respond to this kind of market power.[48] Privacy and data security regulations might be part of the solution, but they are not direct or complete responses to data supremacy. However, if competition law evolves in a way that prevents the techfins from leveraging their large pools of data into a broader platform, then that could rein in the techfins' ability to expand into financial services. This breed of competition law could improve financial stability, and it's also worth considering the flip side of this discussion—whether financial stability regulation could be used to respond to anticompetitive behaviors by these firms. For example, could the financial regulatory technique of separating deposit-taking from commercial activities be deployed in service of competition goals, setting up at least one kind of barrier to the expansion of Amazon, Facebook, Apple, and Google?[49] Should the designation process we discussed (which subjects systemically important firms to heightened regulation) be used not only to keep an eye on any risks building in these firms, but also as a way of discouraging or punishing their "bigness"?[50]

## Competition and smaller fintechs

Even putting aside the particular problems associated with the largest tech firms, the regulatory goals of financial stability and competition have always had an uneasy relationship that may be complicated further by the influx of fintech start-ups.[51] In most industries, encouraging more market entrants is generally seen as a good thing, because it will promote efficiency and innovation. However, because of the rippling economic impact of bank failure, competition that reduces the profitability of a bank—or innovation that disrupts a bank's business model—may sometimes be considered undesirable from a financial stability perspective. As a result, financial regulators will sometimes take steps to limit competition, for example by refusing to let a bank open in what they consider to be an oversaturated market.[52] However, these limits on bank competition can be a double-edged sword for financial stability. For example, they can allow existing banks to grow extremely large, exacerbating the "too big to fail" problem. Tight controls on the number of banks can also have the effect of pushing financial services out into the shadow banking sector, where there are fewer barriers to entry but also less regulation.

Balancing competition and financial stability therefore involves a complex series of trade-offs, and it is not yet clear how these trade-offs will play out with respect to fintech start-ups. If the largest banks were to face increased competition from these start-ups, this could theoretically help erode their "too big to fail" status, which would in turn discourage these huge banks from taking outsized risks.[53] However, while we are starting to see an uptick in the number of fintechs seeking their own banking charters, the largest banks still seem to be partnering with or acquiring fintechs rather than competing with them.[54] As a result, a lot of the innovation produced by fintech start-ups seems to be entrenching the market dominance of the largest banks instead of disrupting it, exacerbating the largest banks' systemic importance.

If fintech start-ups were disrupting the larger financial institutions, however, and making them smaller as a result, then financial stability regulators would face some thorny trade-offs. Important questions would need to be asked about whether this book's proposed technology licensing regime could stymie the growth of fintech start-ups (the institutional capacity test articulated in Chapter 6 would be a particular challenge for small firms). There would also be a stronger justification for programs like regulatory sandboxes, which seek to lower regulatory barriers to entry that could otherwise prevent fintechs from entering the marketplace. As we just noted, these issues are largely moot right now, but regulators might need to start engaging with fintechs as a potentially disruptive force if more fintech start-ups start seeking their own bank charters.

Fintechs could also become a more disruptive force as a result of competition law reform. United States Senator Amy Klobuchar recently introduced a bill that would place the burden on established firms to demonstrate that their proposed acquisition of a nascent competitor would not lessen competition in the market.[55] If this kind of effort were to gain traction, then established banks would have a harder time acquiring fintech start-ups—and so reforms related to acquisitions of nascent competitors could impact financial stability. Any effort to protect nascent competitors would also need to have a data-related component: while banks don't have as much data as the largest tech companies, they can still weaponize the data they *do* have to make it harder for fintech start-ups to enter the market. For example, robo-advisory business models depend on access to a consumer's financial data. If the consumer in question has a bank account and that bank refuses to make account information available to third parties like the robo-advisor (even if the customer wants it to be released), then the advice that the robo-advisor generates will be incomplete at best and wrong at worst.[56] New varieties of data-centric competition law could ultimately make this and other kinds of data sharing easier—however, data sharing always raises issues of privacy.

## Data and privacy

As I observed in the Introduction to this book, a lot of the debate about the dangers of fintech has focused on misuses of consumer information and invasions of privacy, and rightly so. There are potentially dystopian "Minority Report"-style implications for individuals whose access to financial services could be cut off by algorithmic interpretations of new types of data.[57] Machine learning models may end up dividing the world into haves and have-nots, with a permanent underclass being charged more for their credit, or excluded from insurance markets. Information about transactions could also be used as a form of surveillance that could lead to problematic profiling by law enforcement.[58] Some have even suggested that governments launching central bank digital currencies have the ulterior motive of collecting more transactional data about their citizens—this kind of financial transaction data could then be used by the government for a host of reasons, ranging from immigration enforcement to determining public benefits eligibility. These very important issues are outside the scope of this book, though; we will focus instead on whether collective individual harms stemming from the misuse of information could add up to problems for the stability of the financial system.

One of the big selling points of fintech is that it can harness more and better consumer data to provide financial services more efficiently and inclusively. Some fintech business models, particularly marketplace lending but also robo-advisory, already rely on personal data that goes far beyond what we might traditionally think of as relevant to consumer assessments (including information drawn from social media and geolocation data).[59] This type of data can certainly make the provision of financial services more efficient, but its relationship with financial inclusion is a little more complicated. As Shoshana Zuboff observed in her book *The Age of Surveillance Capitalism*, there are limits on how much money can be made by simply collecting data. More profits can be generated if that data can be used to nudge people into acting in a way that is profitable for the data collectors.[60]

If fintech business models are using consumer data to nudge previously underserved populations toward financial products that have high rates of interest and associated fees, consumer protection advocates should certainly be concerned—and we should also be wary of the systemic implications of these predatory behaviors. After all, predatory residential mortgages with high fees and interest rates were some of the building blocks of the financial crisis of 2008.[61] That experience illustrated that predatory financial products can be so profitable that people are happy to turn a blind eye to the risks involved, with financial products and services (particularly credit) being extended in a way that not only harms the affected consumers, but can ultimately result in losses for those who issue and invest in those products and services as well.[62] New sources of consumer data could allow for even more fine-tuned consumer manipulation, pushing people into expensive loans replete with confusing features that make them harder to repay[63]—which may ultimately backfire for the issuers of those financial products, their investors, and the financial system more broadly.

Financial stability can be threatened by predatory behaviors that occur on a systemic scale; it can also be threatened by markets that are based on inaccurate information, or accurate information that is used incorrectly. In Chapter 2, we discussed how machine learning models with garbage data make garbage decisions, and how even machine learning models with good data can make poor decisions (particularly in unusual circumstances). When the data in question is consumer data, some privacy regimes provide ways of identifying and addressing these problems. The EU's General Data Protection Regulation, for example, gives consumers a right to require the correction of some kinds of inaccurate personal data, as well as a right to contest certain decisions if they were made solely by algorithms.[64] However, while it's theoretically possible that the large-scale exercise of these rights could help identify widespread errors in data collection and analysis, the regime was really designed to protect individual rights, not to pick up systemic problems (and, as we explored in Chapter 2, the question of what to do with a machine learning algorithm after errors have been identified is a separate and difficult issue). We simply don't have a good solution to the problem of systemically inaccurate information yet.

So far, we've focused on the potential systemic consequences of data misuse and mistakes by the financial industry, but personal information can also be a target for hackers from the outside. Stealing sensitive financial information can be particularly attractive to hackers looking to engage in identity theft. Compromising the availability of data can also be a tactic used to extort money from a financial institution. These types of hacks can damage confidence in financial institutions because their customers expect that data will be kept safe; if a hack damages this expectation and destroys customer confidence, then that could ultimately lead to a run on an affected institution.[65]

Consumer data is not the only vulnerable information. The confidential information that financial institutions provide to their supervisors is also an attractive target for hackers. As a result, there has been interest in developing innovative technological solutions that move regulators away from maintaining centralized (and therefore vulnerable) repositories of reported data, and toward methods that allow regulators to access regulated firms' own records. This of course begs questions about how much of a firm's data regulators should be allowed to see. Too narrow a slice could skew regulators' understanding of what is happening in the financial system, including budding systemic risks. But many regulated institutions would revolt at the thought of regulators having full access to *all* of their internal data. The optimal degree of regulatory access to information, as well as the optimal way of encrypting that data, remain important questions for the development of suptech.[66]

## Cybersecurity

Just like antitrust and privacy, cybersecurity is far too big a subject to do justice to here. Cyberattacks threaten to compromise infrastructure systems as well as the confidentiality, availability, and integrity of data—and not just within the financial system. All industries and public services need to prepare for these kinds of attacks. Governments and private sector companies do so by monitoring possible threats, sharing information about them (to the extent permitted by law), and developing patches when a vulnerability is detected.[67]

In many respects, the rise of fintech doesn't so much raise new questions about cybersecurity as underline its importance. Cybersecurity is already recognized as one of the top threats to financial stability,[68] but as fintech innovation makes the provision of financial services even more digital, it creates new points of vulnerability. For example, some of the hesitancy that central banks have expressed about adopting central bank digital currencies relates to concerns about them becoming a new target for cyberattacks.[69] When it comes to privately issued cryptoassets, decentralized distributed ledgers (like those used by Bitcoin and Ethereum) have been designed to be resistant to cyberattacks, but there are now concerns that quantum supercomputers could crack those ledgers.[70] The permissioned ledgers operated by financial institutions or techfins (like the one used for JPMCoin) typically have fewer nodes capable of validating and recording transactions, and will be vulnerable as a result.[71]

Machine learning algorithms are also vulnerable to new types of cyberthreats. One group of researchers found that machine learning algorithms could be attacked by bad actors that wanted to steal the algorithm's training data, steal the algorithm itself, or manipulate the workings of the algorithm.[72] From a financial stability perspective, the potential for manipulation is the greatest cause for concern. In what are sometimes called "adversarial attacks," bad actors can fool machine learning algorithms with false data inputs, either in the training data or in the data being processed by a live algorithm. These attacks made through the submission of inaccurate data points are a lot harder to detect and address than cyberattacks that target a line of software code.[73] As a result, if financial institutions increasingly rely on machine learning algorithms to automate their risk management, this will create serious vulnerabilities for those institutions. Imagine the havoc that would be created if BlackRock's Aladdin risk management system were unwittingly tricked into, say, recommending that all of its clients engage in widespread asset sales if the price of a meme stock like GameStop fell below a certain dollar amount.

Even if a cyberattack only targets a single financial institution, the consequences may not be limited to that institution. In 2020, several Federal Reserve economists issued what they called a "pre-mortem," exploring the many paths a cyberattack could take in compromising the interbank payments system in the United States. In it, they discuss potential mechanisms for contagion that should be familiar to us by this stage of the book: traditional forms of panics and runs brought on by the uncertainty surrounding a cyberattack, and technologically compromised systems or infrastructure freezing people's ability to transact. The authors conclude that:

> [I]f a cyber attack were to compromise the integrity of banks' systems, the reconciliation and recuperation process would be an unprecedented task. This could have severe implications on the stability of the broader financial system vis-à-vis spillovers to investors, creditors, and other financial market participants.[74]

Financial stability regulators must think about the different types of cyber preparedness that will be needed to limit contagion if a cyberattack does in fact occur. Sharing information about threats and attacks is ordinarily a key part of the coordinated response to cyberattacks, but could such disclosures inspire panics and runs? Panics and runs could be mitigated by traditional forms of emergency responses like loans from the central bank, but different types of responses will be needed for operational problems. Creating dedicated back-up facilities that can support the system in an emergency could be a fertile area for suptech innovation.

* * *

While this chapter has raised more questions than it has answered, it's important to recognize that driverless finance is adding new dimensions to many long-standing debates that implicate the stability of our financial system. Ultimately, the ongoing resilience of the financial system may depend as much on how these debates are resolved as on the implementation of the proposals outlined in Chapter 6.

# Conclusion

Technological innovation moves quickly—so quickly, that some of the technical details in this book will probably be out of date by the time it is printed. Still, this book's exploration of fintech business models and technologies has many constant themes, and financial stability regulation should be designed to respond to these enduring themes. In particular, financial stability regulation should respond to the increased speed, complexity, and coordination associated with many fintech business models and technologies—and financial stability regulation should do so before these dynamics get out of control and threaten the stability of our entire financial system.

Unfortunately, in the United States, the default position on new financial innovation is often "wait and see." That kind of approach saves regulators and policymakers the embarrassment that can come from regulation's unintended consequences, but doing nothing in the face of developing risks is its own kind of failure. We need to make "wait and see" an uncomfortable option for those regulators and policymakers. There are certainly valuable elements of fintech business models and technologies, but their harmful elements should not be ignored. We need to assess fintech with a critical eye, not be overwhelmed by unbridled enthusiasm about it, and make our concerns known to regulators and our elected representatives. Expressing those concerns will require "mythbusting" the conventional wisdom about fintech.

The first myth to bust is that innovation is somehow inherently good. Looking skeptically at financial innovation may go against our romanticized ideal of the innovation process, but if we really stop to think about it, why would we expect the activities of profit-driven private sector innovators to always benefit society as a whole? Of course there will be win-wins where profitable innovation is good for everyone, but economists and policymakers have long recognized that the private sector lacks the incentives to produce public goods like financial stability. It should therefore come as no surprise that private sector innovation can sometimes hurt financial stability (and that regulators' hasty embrace of regulatory sandboxes and other structures

*Driverless Finance.* Hilary J. Allen, Oxford University Press. © Hilary J. Allen 2022.
DOI: 10.1093/oso/9780197626801.003.0009

that promote private sector innovation may be a little misguided). We can flip the script on fintech innovation, though, and judge it as a means to an end, rather than as an end in itself. Fintech innovation is good if it achieves good things—and public sector suptech (and other, less technologically oriented public sector solutions) will sometimes be the more direct way of achieving those good things.

Speaking of "achieving good things," our second myth is that efficiency is always a good thing. Sometimes it is, but sometimes a more efficient system is a more fragile system, and we would be better off with a slightly clunkier system that we can rely upon to keep doing what it needs to do. Sometimes, a more efficient system is a more unequal system, because although overall increases in economic benefits are usually viewed as "more efficient," those economic benefits are not always distributed equally, and some people may end up bearing a lot of economic costs associated with others' benefits.[1] Efficiency is important, but "increased efficiency" should not be a trump card that allows fintech innovators to avoid regulatory scrutiny.

Third, fintech isn't "too small to care" about. Regulators' current "wait and see" approach is sometimes justified on the grounds that fintech is too niche a sector to have a real impact on financial stability, but this view is misinformed at best, and disingenuous at worst. Fintech business models and technologies are already being eyed by the largest tech companies and used by the largest financial institutions. If we wait until fintech has scaled up to the point where it could undeniably impact the entire financial system, we will have forfeited our ability to use regulation to guide its development in a way that protects financial stability. Implicit in the "too small to care" narrative is the idea that we can always clean up any messes afterward. But if the messes become bigger, governments won't always be able to fully clean them up—and the costs of the incomplete clean-up are likely to fall disproportionately on the most vulnerable members of society.

This relates to the fourth piece of mistaken conventional wisdom: that financial crises are once-in-a-generation events. This claim is used as a kind of cost-benefit justification for not regulating the financial industry. Sure, the industry may cause a major crisis every 50 or 100 years, this line of thinking goes, but is that really a good enough reason to tamp down on 50 or 100 years of possible economic growth? Financial crises haven't always been rare, though (major banking panics were a regular occurrence in the United States until deposit insurance was adopted in 1933), and as new technologies and business models edge their way around the banking regulation that provided stability for much of the 20th century, they could become common again. There is truth in the quip that "to err is human, but to really foul things up requires a computer"—as fintech innovations make the operations of the financial system faster, more complex, and more coordinated than ever before, crises may become even more common than they were before the 1930s.

A dose of history is also needed to bust our fifth myth: that "this time is different." Economists Carmen Reinhart and Kenneth Rogoff titled their history of financial crises *This Time Is Different* because that's what people say every time they want to believe that innovation has transformed financial risk.[2] The "this time is different" story is a bit like the *Emperor's New Clothes*, with everyone afraid to admit that they can't understand what's so new and transformative about the innovation—but with added financial incentives to keep going along with the story so that you can profit from it.[3] Fintech innovations make for a particularly dazzling "this time is different" story, wedding financial engineering with stories of the digital revolution. But cryptoassets aren't really that different from previous generations of investments—their underlying technological sophistication doesn't exempt them from the laws of financial gravity. They *are* different in the sense that there is potentially a limitless supply of them, but that just means they generate more risk, not eliminate it. Right now, the cryptoasset markets look for all the world like another asset bubble. Similarly, while machine learning may improve risk management models in some ways, they're still likely to underestimate the impact of low-probability events, just like their forebears were. Fintech innovations may make real strides in making payments services faster and more widely available, but new e-wallets are vulnerable to runs that look a lot like the runs banks faced before deposit insurance was adopted. And one payments provider recently highlighted the perils of believing that when it comes to fintech, this time really is different: the German fintech Wirecard used stories of its transformational business model to deflect attention from what turned out to be "one of Germany's biggest postwar accounting frauds."[4]

Our final myth is that the financial markets will somehow take care of fintech's threats to financial stability on their own, without any need for regulatory intervention. This myth is so persistent (despite having so little evidentiary support) that I have tried to bust it in almost every chapter of this book (sometimes multiple times). But to quickly restate what I have already said so many times, private market participants lack the incentives, the information, and the ability to coordinate behavior needed to address the systemic risks emerging from the rise of fintech. Policymakers and regulators must step up.

If these myths aren't busted and fintech's threats to financial stability remain unchecked, the consequences could be catastrophic. We often use science fiction to help us think through the implications of things that haven't happened yet; if those implications seem too dystopian, we have an opportunity to course correct. That's why this book has a fictional prologue—a kind of financial *Black Mirror* episode—to help make the dystopian possibilities of driverless finance more real while there is still time to change its trajectory.

The stakes are high. If nothing else, this book has tried to convey that financial stability isn't a niche issue. It is a matter of enormous civic importance, and should be treated as such. Just how high are the stakes? Sir Paul Tucker, when he chaired the group of former top central bankers, regulators, and academics known as the Systemic Risk Council, pointed out that a financial crisis was narrowly averted at the outset of the COVID-19 pandemic in March and April of 2020. He put it bluntly: "The west cannot afford another financial crisis. It would be a disaster in every possible way domestically, and a geopolitical gift to strategic competitors in Beijing and elsewhere."[5] The fabric of democracy in the United States is already stretched thin—if fintech causes a financial crisis, it may not just be our economy that falters.

# Notes

## Introduction

1. *2001: A Space Odyssey* (Metro-Goldwyn-Mayer 1968).
2. Andrei A. Kirilenko & Andrew W. Lo, *Moore's Law versus Murphy's Law: Algorithmic Trading and Its Discontents*, 27 J. Econ. Perspectives 51, 52 (2013).
3. Majority Staff of Comm. on Transp. & Infrastructure, Final Committee Report: The Design, Development & Certification of the Boeing 737 Max 13 (Sept. 2020).
4. Although "autonomous vehicle" is the preferred industry term, "driverless car" is both more colloquial and more evocative. "Driverless car" is therefore a better metaphor for conveying the risks inherent in new types of fintech innovations.
5. For a thorough history of financial crises, *see* Carmen M. Reinhart & Kenneth S. Rogoff, This Time Is Different: Eight Centuries of Financial Folly (2009).
6. Oxford Essential Quotations (Susan Ratcliffe ed., 4th ed. 2016).
7. *Equitable Algorithms: Examining Ways to Reduce AI Bias in Financial Services: Hearing Before the Task Force on A.I. of the Comm. on Fin. Serv.*, 116th Cong. (2020).
8. *Robots on Wall Street: The Impact of AI on Capital Markets and Jobs in the Financial Services Industry: Hearing Before the Task Force on A.I. of the Comm. on Fin. Serv.*, 116th Cong. (2019).
9. *Banking on Your Data: The Role of Big Data in Financial Services: Hearing Before the Task Force on Fin. Tech. of the Comm. on Fin. Serv.*, 116th Cong. (2019).
10. *AI and the Evolution of Cloud Computing: Evaluating How Financial Data Is Stored, Protected, and Maintained by Cloud Providers: Hearing Before the Task Force on A.I. of the Comm. on Fin. Serv.*, 116th Cong. (2019).
11. *Examining the Use of Alternative Data in Underwriting and Credit Scoring to Expand Access to Credit: Hearing Before the Task Force on Fin. Tech. of the Comm. on Fin. Serv.*, 116th Cong. (2019).
12. Financial Services Act, 2012, § 2A (UK).
13. Articles of Agreement of the International Monetary Fund art. 5, Dec. 27 1945, 1 U.N.T.S. 39.
14. Bank for International Settlement, Central Bank Governance and Financial Stability 31 (2011).
15. For a discussion of the systemic dimension of fire sales, *see* Anil K. Kashyap et al., *The Macroprudential Toolkit*, 59 IMF Econ. Rev. 145 (2011).
16. Karen Ho, Liquidated: An Ethnography of Wall Street 10–11 (2009).
17. Deloitte, Marketplace Lending 2.0: Bringing on the Next Stage In Lending 7 (2017).

18. Benjamin P. Edwards, *The Rise of Automated Investment Advice: Can Robo-Advisers Rescue the Retail Market?*, 93 CHI.-KENT L. REV. 97, 103 (2018).
19. There is still considerable uncertainty regarding the identity of the creator or creators of Bitcoin. CRAIG K. ELWELL ET AL., CONG. RSCH. SERV., R43339, BITCOIN: QUESTIONS, ANSWERS AND ANALYSIS OF LEGAL ISSUES 1 (2015).
20. RENA S. MILLER & GARY SHORTER, CONG. RSCH. SERV., R44443, HIGH FREQUENCY TRADING: OVERVIEW OF RECENT DEVELOPMENTS, 1 (2016).
21. A recent survey of financial institutions regarding their use of artificial intelligence found that "FinTechs are more widely using AI to create new products and services, while Incumbents predominantly harness AI to enhance existing ones." CAMBRIDGE CENTRE FOR ALTERNATIVE FINANCE & WORLD ECONOMIC FORUM (hereinafter CAMBRIDGE CENTER), TRANSFORMING PARADIGMS: A GLOBAL AI IN FINANCIAL SERVICES SURVEY 33 (2020).
22. Raghav Bharadwaj, *Machine Learning in Investment Management and Asset Management—Current Applications*, EMERJ (Apr. 3, 2020), https://emerj.com/ai-sector-overviews/machine-learning-in-investment-management-and-asset-management/ (last visited Sept. 24, 2020).
23. J.P. Morgan, *J.P. Morgan Creates Digital Coin for Payments*, J.P. MORGAN (Feb. 14, 2019), https://www.jpmorgan.com/solutions/cib/news/digital-coin-payments.
24. "[M]achine learning algorithms can be clearly distinguished from traditional computer programs which follow a static set of predetermined instructions." CAMBRIDGE CENTRE, *supra* note 21, at 17.
25. Representative publications from the Financial Stability Board include the following: FIN. STABILITY BD., FINANCIAL STABILITY IMPLICATIONS FROM FINTECH (2017); FIN. STABILITY BD., ARTIFICIAL INTELLIGENCE AND MACHINE LEARNING IN FINANCIAL SERVICES (2017); FIN. STABILITY BD., FINTECH AND MARKET STRUCTURE IN FINANCIAL SERVICES: MARKET DEVELOPMENTS AND POTENTIAL FINANCIAL STABILITY IMPLICATIONS (2019); FIN. STABILITY BD., BIGTECH IN FINANCE: MARKET DEVELOPMENTS AND POTENTIAL FINANCIAL STABILITY IMPLICATIONS (2019).

## Chapter 1

1. "There is a fundamental distinction between the reward for taking a known risk and that for assuming a risk whose value itself is not known"; "true uncertainty [is] . . . "not susceptible to measurement." FRANK H. KNIGHT, RISK, UNCERTAINTY AND PROFIT 21 (1921).
2. Guido Calabresi, *Transaction Costs, Resource Allocation and Liability Rules—A Comment*, 11 J.L. & ECON 67, 70 (1968).
3. For a thorough account of the genesis of the crisis of 2008, *see* FIN. CRISIS INQUIRY COMM'N, THE FINANCIAL CRISIS INQUIRY REPORT: FINAL REPORT OF THE NATIONAL COMMISSION ON THE CAUSES OF THE FINANCIAL AND ECONOMIC CRISIS IN THE UNITED STATES (2011).

4. Ben Bernanke, *The Real Effects of Disrupted Credit: Evidence from the Global Financial Crisis*, Brookings Papers Econ. Activity, Fall 2018, at 251, 253–54.
5. Fin. Crisis Inquiry Comm'n, *supra* note 3, at 390.
6. *Id.* at 391.
7. Regis Barnichon et al., *The Financial Crisis at 10: Will We Ever Recover?* (Fed. Res. Bank S.F. Econ. Letters Working Paper, 2018), https://www.frbsf.org/economic-research/publications/economic-letter/2018/august/financial-crisis-at-10-years-will-we-ever-recover/.
8. US Gov't Accountability Off., GAO-13-180, Financial Crisis Losses and Potential Impacts of the Dodd-Frank Act (2013).
9. Janet L. Yellen, Vice Chairwoman, Board Governors of the Fed. Res. Sys., Remarks at "A Trans-Atlantic Agenda for Shared Prosperity": A Conference Sponsored by the AFL-CIO, Friedrich Ebert Stiftung, and the IMK Macroeconomic Policy Institute, A Painfully Slow Recovery for America's Workers: Causes, Implications, and the Federal Reserve's Response 10 (Feb. 11, 2013).
10. Ronald A. Wilson, *The View from South Tucson: How the Economic Crisis Affects Defendants in My Courtroom*, 48 Judges' J. 14 (2009).
11. Mona Fiuzat et al., *United States Stock Market Performance and Acute Myocardial Infarction Rates in 2008–2009 (from the Duke Databank for Cardiovascular Disease)*, 106 Am. J. Cardiology 1545 (2010); Aaron Reeves et al., *Increase in State Suicide Rates in the USA during Economic Recession*, 380 Lancet 1813 (2012); Annamaria Lusardi et al., *The Economic Crisis and Medical Care Use: Comparative Evidence from Five High-Income Countries*, 96 Soc. Sci. Q. 202 (2015).
12. Fin. Crisis Inquiry Comm'n, *supra* note 3, at 391.
13. Lowell Ricketts, *When the Stock Market Rises, Who Benefits?*, Fed. Res. Bank St. Louis On the Econ. Blog (Feb. 27, 2018), https://www.stlouisfed.org/on-the-economy/2018/february/when-stock-market-rises-who-benefits.
14. Nelson D. Schwartz, *The Recovery Threw the Middle Class Dream Under a Benz*, N.Y. Times (Sept. 12, 2018), at BU3.
15. *Id.*
16. Inci Otker-Robe & Anca Maria Podpiera, *The Social Impact of Financial Crises: Evidence from the Global Financial Crisis* (World Bank Pol'y Res., Working Paper No. 6703, 2013), http://documents.worldbank.org/curated/en/498911468180867209/pdf/WPS6703.pdf.
17. Jeffrey N. Gordon, *"Dynamic Precaution" in Maintaining Financial Stability: The Importance of FSOC, in* Ten Years After The Crash (Sharyn O'Halloran & Thomas Groll eds., 2019).
18. Jonathan B. Wiener, *Whose Precaution After All? A Comment on the Comparison and Evolution of Risk Regulatory Systems*, 13 Duke J. Comp & Int'l L. 207, 210 (2003).
19. *Id.*
20. Sharon LaFraniere & Noah Weiland, *White House Blocks New Coronavirus Vaccine Guidelines*, N.Y. Times (Oct. 5, 2020), https://www.nytimes.com/2020/10/05/us/politics/coronavirus-vaccine-guidelines.html.

21. For a discussion of the FDA approval process as a potential model for financial regulation, *see* Saule T. Omarova, *License to Deal: Mandatory Approval of Complex Financial Products*, 90 Wash. U. L. Rev. 64 (2012).
22. David E. Adelman, *A Cautiously Pessimistic Appraisal of Trends in Toxics Regulation*, 32 Wash. U. J.L. Pol'y 377 (2010).
23. Daniel Kahenman, *Maps of Bounded Rationality: Psychology for Behavioral Economics*, 93 Am. Econ. Rev. 1449, 1459 (2003).
24. Neal E. Boudette, *Despite High Hopes, Self-Driving Cars Are "Way in the Future,"* N.Y. Times (Jul. 17, 2019), https://www.nytimes.com/2019/07/17/business/self-driving-autonomous-cars.html.
25. For further discussion of the limitations of cost-benefit analysis in financial stability regulation, *see* John C. Coates IV, *Cost-Benefit Analysis of Financial Regulation: Case Studies and Implications*, 124 Yale L. J. 882 (2014–2015); Hilary J. Allen, *A New Philosophy for Financial Stability Regulation*, 45 Loy. U. Chi. L.J. 173 (2013).
26. Clayton Christensen, *Key Concepts: Disruptive Innovation*, Clayton Christensen, http://claytonchristensen.com/key-concepts/.
27. Joseph Schumpeter, Capitalism, Socialism and Democracy 119 (1st ed. 1975).
28. Dan Awrey, *Complexity, Innovation and the Regulation of Modern Financial Markets*, 2 Harv. Bus. L. Rev. 235, 259 (2012).
29. Fed. Deposit Ins. Corp., 2019 FDIC Survey of Household Use of Banking and Financial Services: Executive Summary (2020).
30. Richard Cordray, Director, CFPB, Prepared Remarks of CFPB Director Richard Cordray at Money 20/20 (Oct. 23, 2016).
31. *Id.*
32. *Examining the Fintech Landscape: Hearing Before the Comm. on Banking, Hous., & Urb. Aff. US Sen.*, 115th Cong. 80-1 (2017) (statement of Frank Pasquale, Prof. of Law, Univ. of Md. Francis King Carey Sch. of L.).
33. Simon Johnson & James Kwak, *Is Financial Innovation Good for the Economy?*, 12 Innovation Pol'y & Econ 1, 4 (2012).
34. *See*, for example, John Chapman, *CDS: Modern Day Weapons of Mass Destruction*, Financial Times (Sept. 11, 2011), https://www.ft.com/content/1c81fdf8-d4b9-11e0-a7ac-00144feab49a.
35. International Swaps and Derivatives Association (hereinafter ISDA) & Linklaters, Smart Contracts and Distributed Ledger—A Legal Perspective, ISDA (Aug. 3, 2017), https://www.isda.org/a/6EKDE/smart-contracts-and-distributed-ledger-a-legal-perspective.pdf; ISDA & King & Wood Mallesons, *Smart Derivatives Contracts: From Concept to Construction*, ISDA (Oct. 2018), https://www.isda.org/a/cHvEE/Smart-Derivatives-Contracts-From-Concept-to-Construction-Oct-2018.pdf.
36. This definition is taken from Kevin Werbach & Nicolas Cornell, *Contracts Ex Machina*, 67 Duke L. J. 313, 320 (2017).
37. For a discussion of the contractual rigidities in MBS, and the harm they caused during the crisis of 2008, *see* Anna Gelpern & Adam J. Levitin, *Rewriting Frankenstein Contracts: Workout Prohibitions in Residential Mortgage-Backed Securities*, 82 S. Cal. L. Rev. 1075 (2009).

38. Rena S. Miller & Kathleen Ann Ruane, Cong. Rsch. Serv., R41398, The Dodd-Frank Wall Street Reform And Consumer Protection Act: Title VII, Derivatives 5 (2012).
39. Fin. Crisis Inquiry Comm'n, *supra* note 3, at 266.
40. Miller & Ruane, *supra* note 38, at 5. For further discussion of AIG's obligations to post collateral under its CDSs, *see* Fin. Crisis Inquiry Comm'n, *supra* note 3, at 265–74.
41. Fin. Crisis Inquiry Comm'n, *supra* note 3, at 394–95.
42. ISDA & King & Wood Mallesons, *supra* note 35, at 27.
43. Allen, *supra* note 25, at 181.
44. Eric Lipton, *As Scrutiny of Cryptocurrency Grows, the Industry Turns to K Street*, N.Y. Times (May 9, 2021), https://www.nytimes.com/2021/05/10/us/politics/as-scrutiny-of-cryptocurrency-grows-the-industry-turns-to-k-street.html.
45. Jen Wieczner, *A Bitcoin Billionaire on When to Sell vs. HODL and Dogecoin "Nihilism,"* N.Y. Magazine (May 13, 2021), https://nymag.com/intelligencer/2021/05/bitcoin-billionaire-mike-novogratz-on-when-to-sell.html.
46. Lipton, *supra* note 44.

## Chapter 2

1. For a discussion of the "social contract" between banks and society, see Mehrsa Baradaran, *Banking and the Social Contract*, 89 Notre Dame L. Rev. 1283 (2014).
2. This categorization of risks, as well as much of the discussion of VaR models in this chapter, is drawn from Erik F. Gerding, *Code, Crash, and Open Source: The Outsourcing of Financial Regulation to Risk Models and the Global Financial Crisis*, 84 Wash L. Rev. 127 (2009).
3. The foundation of modern portfolio theory is Harry Markowitz's *Portfolio Selection*, 7 J. Fin. 77 (1952).
4. BCG estimated in 2019 that the global asset management industry had $89 trillion worth of assets under management. Lubasha Heredia et al., Global Asset Management 2020: Protect, Adapt and Innovate (2020), available at https://www.bcg.com/en-us/publications/2020/global-asset-management-protect-adapt-innovate.
5. Fin Crisis Inquiry Comm'n, The Financial Crisis Inquiry Report: Final Report of the National Commission on the Causes of the Financial and Economic Crisis in the United States 44 (2011).
6. *See, e.g.*, European Central Bank, ECB Guide to Internal Models (2019).
7. Bd. of Governors, Fed. Res. Sys., SR 11-7, Guidance on Model Risk Management (Apr. 4, 2011).
8. Lael Brainard, Governor, Fed. Res., Speech at Fintech and the New Financial Landscape titled What Are We Learning about Artificial Intelligence in Financial Services (Nov. 13, 2018); *See also* Bernhard Babel et al., Derisking Machine Learning and Artificial Intelligence, McKinsey & Company (Feb. 29, 2019), https://www.

mckinsey.com/business-functions/risk/our-insights/derisking-machine-learning-and-artificial- intelligence#.

9. Cambridge Centre for Alternative Finance & World Economic Forum (herein after Cambridge Center), Transforming Paradigms: A Global AI in Financial Services Survey 40 (2020).
10. Louie Woodall, *Model Risk Managers Eye Benefits of Machine Learning*, Risk.Net (Apr. 11, 2017), https://www.risk.net/risk-management/4646956/model-risk-managers-eye-benefits-of-machine-learning.
11. A recent survey of fintech firms and incumbent financial institutions reported that "59% of all surveyed investment managers are currently using AI in their investment process" and that among them, "portfolio risk management is currently the most active area of AI implementation at an adoption rate of 61%, followed by portfolio structuring (58%) and asset price forecasting (55%). Often these uses cases are combined, leveraging the economies of scale of AI." Cambridge Center, *supra* note 9, at 100.
12. "The internal (back-office) applications of AI and machine learning could improve risk management, fraud detection, and compliance with regulatory requirements, potentially at lower cost. In portfolio management, the more efficient processing of information from AI and machine learning applications could help to boost the efficiency and resilience of financial markets." Financial Stability Board, Artificial Intelligence And Machine Learning In Financial Services: Market Developments And Financial Stability Implications 33 (2017).
13. Much of this discussion of the variations in machine learning approaches is drawn from David Lehr & Paul Ohm, *Playing with the Data: What Legal Scholars Should Learn about Machine Learning*, 51 U.C. Davis L. Rev. 653 (2017); and Vishal Maini & Samer Sabri, *Machine Learning For Humans*, Medium (Aug. 19, 2017), https://medium.com/machine-learning-for-humans.
14. For example, some new credit scoring algorithms seek to draw on data like information from social media profiles, but relevant features need to be pulled out from these profiles before they can be used to assess whether an applicant is likely to default on a loan or not. *See* Woodall, *supra* note 10.
15. Cambridge Center, *supra* note 9, at 50.
16. For example, there is interest in using information from social media profiles to improve the assessment of market risks. *See* US Sec. & Exch. Comm'n, Investor Bulletin: Social Sentiment Investing Tools—Think Twice Before Trading Based On Social Media (Apr. 3, 2019).
17. Cambridge Center, *supra* note 9, at 115.
18. *Id.*
19. For further critiques of VaR modeling, see Gerding, *supra* note 2.
20. During the crisis of 2007 to 2008, systemic problems flowed from a nationwide housing downturn that was far more consequential than anyone had thought possible. Fin. Crisis Inquiry Comm'n, *supra* note 5, at xxi. For Long-Term Capital Management, the tail event was Russia's default on its sovereign debt. Gerding, *supra* note 2, at 168–69.

21. "Having only a few hundred to a few thousand observations may often be insufficient. Beyond that, tens of thousands could be sufficient for some applications, and other applications operate optimally on hundreds of thousands or even millions of observations." Lehr & Ohm, *supra* note 13, at 678–79.
22. Nazneen Sherif, *Academics Warn against Overuse of Machine Learning*, RISK.NET (Mar. 15, 2017), https://www.risk.net/risk-management/4120236/academics-warn-against-overuse-of-machine-learning.
23. Andrew G. Haldane & Vasileios Madouros, Speech at the Federal Reserve Bank of Kansas City's 366th economic policy symposium, "The Changing Policy Landscape" titled The Dog and the Frisbee (Aug. 31, 2012).
24. US SEC. & EXCH. COMM'N, *supra* note 16.
25. BlackRock, *Artificial Intelligence and Machine Learning in Asset Management*, BLACKROCK (Oct. 2019), https://www.blackrock.com/corporate/literature/whitepaper/viewpoint-artificial-intelligence-machine-learning-asset-management-october-2019.pdf.
26. IBM, *10 Key Market Trends for 2017*, IBM MARKETING CLOUD (2016).
27. For an overview of the enthusiasm for applying AI to risk management, *see* CAMBRIDGE CENTER, *supra* note 9.
28. Linda J. Skitka et al., *Accountability and Automation Bias*, 52 INT. J. HUMAN-COMPUTER STUDIES 701 (2000).
29. Daniel A. Effron & Paul Conway, *When Virtue Leads to Villainy: Advances in Research on Moral Self-Licensing*, 6 CURRENT OP. IN PSYCHOLOGY 32 (2015).
30. BD. OF GOVERNORS, FED. RES. SYS., *supra* note 7, at 4.
31. Rich Caruana et al., *Intelligible Models for HealthCare: Predicting Pneumonia Risk and Hospital 30-Day Readmission*, *in* PROCEEDINGS OF THE 21TH ACM SIGKDD INTERNATIONAL CONFERENCE ON KNOWLEDGE DISCOVERY AND DATA MINING 1721 (2015).
32. Excellent examples of the behavioral finance literature include ROBERT J. SHILLER, IRRATIONAL EXUBERANCE (2000) and ANDREW W. LO, ADAPTIVE MARKETS: EVOLUTION AT THE SPEED OF THOUGHT (2017).
33. Andrew D. Selbst & Solon Barocas, *The Intuitive Appeal of Explainable Machines*, 87 FORDHAM L. REV. 1085, 1091 (2018).
34. For further discussion of possible approaches to improving the explainability of machine learning algorithms, see *id.*
35. For a discussion of new advances that may help banks interpret their machine learning models, see Babel et al., *supra* note 8.
36. BD. OF GOVERNORS, FED. RES. SYS., *supra* note 7, at 4.
37. CAMBRIDGE CENTER, *supra* note 9, at 68.
38. For a discussion of the behavioral dynamics of bubbles and busts, see SHILLER, *supra* note 32.
39. Brett McDonnell, *Don't Panic! Defending Cowardly Interventions During and After a Crisis*, 116 PENN. ST. L. REV. 1, 13 (2011).
40. For a discussion of the systemic dimension of fire sales, *see* Anil K. Kashyap et al., *The Macroprudential Toolkit*, 59 IMF ECON. REV. 145 (2011).

41. Gerding, *supra* note 2, at 167–68.
42. "The three credit rating agencies were key enablers of the financial meltdown." Fin. Crisis Inquiry Comm'n, *supra* note 5, at xxv.
43. For further discussion of Moody's (and Standard & Poor's) role in precipitating the crisis of 2008, *see id.* at 46–50.
44. Antoine Gara, *Wall Street Tech Spree: With Kensho Acquisition S&P Global Makes Largest A.I. Deal in History*, Forbes (Mar. 6, 2018), https://www.forbes.com/sites/antoinegara/2018/03/06/wall-street-tech-spree-with-kensho-acquisition-sp-global-makes-largest-a-i-deal-in-history/?sh=3eff288b67b8.
45. "As institutions find algorithms that generate uncorrelated profits or returns, there is a risk these will be exploited on a sufficiently wide scale that correlations actually increase." Financial Stability Board, *supra* note 12, at 31.
46. Cambridge Center, *supra* note 9, at 107.
47. FINRA, Report on Digital Investment Advice 2 (2016).
48. Cambridge Center, *supra* note 9, at 87.
49. Deloitte, The Next Frontier: The Future of Automated Financial Advice in the UK 22 (2017).
50. Barbara A. Friedberg, *Robo-Advisors with the Most Assets Under Management—2020*, Robo-Advisor Pros (Oct. 2, 2020), https://www.roboadvisorpros.com/robo-advisors-with-most-aum-assets-under-management/.
51. Vanguard, *Fast Facts about Vanguard*, Vanguard, https://about.vanguard.com/who-we-are/fast-facts/.
52. Charles Schwab, *Schwab Facts*, Charles Schwab, https://www.schwab.com/system/file/P-8770544.
53. John Courmarianos & Leslie P. Norton, *BlackRock Passes a Milestone, with $7 Trillion in Assets Under Management*, Barrons (Jan. 15, 2020), https://www.barrons.com/articles/blackrock-earnings-assets- under-management-7-trillion-51579116426.
54. Friedberg, *supra* note 50.
55. FINRA, *supra* note 47, at 6.
56. Lawrence White, *HSBC Signs Deal to Use BlackRock's "Aladdin" Software Worldwide*, Reuters (Mar. 21, 2019), https://www.reuters.com/article/us-hsbc-blackrock/hsbc-signs-deal-to-use-blackrocks-aladdin-software-worldwide-idUSKCN1R21NO.
57. BlackRock, *supra* note 25.
58. BlackRock, 2019 Annual Report 6 (2019).
59. Will Dunn, *Meet Aladdin, The Computer "More Powerful Than Traditional Politics,"* New Statesman (Apr. 6, 2018), https://www.newstatesman.com/spotlight/2018/04/meet-aladdin-computer-more-powerful-traditional-politics.
60. Stanley Pignall, *BlackRock: The Monolith and the Markets*, The Economist (Dec. 7, 2013), https://www.economist.com/briefing/2013/12/07/the-monolith-and-the-markets.
61. Dunn, *supra* note 59.
62. Jody Kochansky, *The Promise of Artificial Intelligence and What It Means to BlackRock*, Seeking Alpha (Mar. 13, 2018), https://seekingalpha.com/article/4156072-promise-of-artificial-intelligence-and-what-means-to-blackrock.

63. Financial Stability Board, *supra* note 12, at 13–14.
64. *See*, for example, Maximilien Baudry & Christian Y. Robert, *A Machine Learning Approach for Individual Claims Reserving in Insurance*, 35 Applied Stochastic Models Bus. & Indus. 1127 (Sept./Oct. 2019); Gopal Swaminathan, *Deploying Deep Learning in Claims Reserving*, InsurAnalytics.AI (Feb. 6, 2019), https://insuranalytics.ai/blogs/deploying-deep-learning-in-claims-reserving/.
65. For a discussion of the systemic risks posed by the insurance industry, *see* Daniel Schwarcz & Steven L. Schwarcz, *Regulating Systemic Risk in Insurance*, 81 U. Chi. L. Rev. 1569, 1620 (2014).
66. In 2019, the size of the insurance-linked securities market was estimated to be $30.28 billion. Swiss Re, *Insurance-Linked Securities Market Update: March 2020*, Swiss Re (Mar. 2020), https://www.swissre.com/our- business/alternative-capital-partners/ils-market-update-march-2020.html.
67. *Id.* at 1596.
68. Financial Stability Board, *supra* note 12, at 14.
69. Lin Lin & Christopher Chen, The Promise and Perils of Insurtech, 2020 Sing. J. Legal Stud. 115, 123 (2020).

## Chapter 3

1. John Armour et al., Principles of Financial Regulation, 26 (1st ed. 2016).
2. This chapter's discussion of banks, the services they provide, and their importance to the broader economy, draws from Richard Scott Carnell et al., The Law of Financial Institutions, 65 et seq. (6th ed. 2017). *See also* E. Gerald Corrigan, *Are Banks Special?*, *in* Fed. Res. Bank of Minneapolis Annual Report, 121 (1983).
3. Douglas W. Diamond & Philip H. Dybvig, *Bank Runs, Deposit Insurance, and Liquidity*, 91 J. Political Economy 401, 401 (1983).
4. The introduction of deposit insurance in the United States followed banking panics in 1873, 1884, 1890, 1893, 1907, and 1929. *See* Carnell et al., *supra* note 2, at 15, 19. Deposit insurance in the United States is capped at a fixed amount, but that amount has been increased several times over the decades. The cap is now $250,000 per account. *Id.* at 226.
5. Similar fears were expressed as people shifted to online banking in the 1990s and early 2000s. *See* Douglas W. Arner et al., *The Evolution of FinTech: A New Post-Crisis Paradigm?*, 47 Geo. J. Int'l L. 1271, 1284 (2016).
6. This discussion of runs on money market mutual funds relies heavily on the work of Gary Gorton and Andrew Metrick, leading scholars on so-called "shadow banking" runs that occur outside the regulated banking system. *See* Gary Gorton & Andrew Metrick, *Regulating the Shadow Banking System*, Brookings Papers Econ. Activity, Fall 2010, at 261.
7. Ben Bernanke, Chairman, Bd. Governor Fed. Res. Sys., Speech at the National Association for Business Economics 50th Annual Meeting: Current Economic and Financial Conditions (Oct. 7, 2008).

8. For a summary of the post-crisis conventional wisdom on the inadequacy of bank-centric financial stability regulation, *see* ARMOUR ET AL., *supra* note 1, at 434.
9. In 2009, the G-20 agreed that member countries would increase their regulatory focus on the most systemically important financial institutions (banks and non-banks). Grp. 20 [G20], *Leaders' Statement, The Pittsburgh Summit,* Sept. 24–25, 2009, posted here: https://www.oecd.org/g20/summits/pittsburgh/G20-Pittsburgh-Leaders-Declaration.pdf. In the United States, Title I of the Dodd-Frank Act of 2010 implemented a new regulatory regime for systemically important non-bank financial institutions. For a summary of this regime, *see* MICHAEL S. BARR ET AL. FINANCIAL REGULATION: LAW AND POLICY 704–05 (1st ed. 2016).
10. "[W]e should note, the weakest link in the financial stability chain might be *small,* rather than large, financial intermediaries." Eric S. Rosengren, President & Chief Executive Officer, Fed. Res. Bank of Bos., Keynote Remarks at the Stanford Finance Form, Graduate School of Business: Defining Financial Stability, and Some Policy Implications of Applying the Definition (Jun. 3, 2011).
11. Douglas W. Arner et al., *FinTech, RegTech, and the Reconceptualization of Financial Regulation*, 37 NW. J. INT'L L. & BUS. 371, 404 (2017).
12. TECH. COMM., INT'L ORG. OF SEC. COMM'NS, MITIGATING SYSTEMIC RISK: A ROLE FOR SECURITIES REGULATORS 24 (2011).
13. For a discussion of the systemic dimension of fire sales, see Anil K. Kashyap et al., *The Macroprudential Toolkit*, 59 IMF ECON. REV. 145 (2011).
14. In the United States, financial market infrastructure is regulated by the Federal Reserve pursuant to Title VIII of the Dodd-Frank Act of 2010.
15. LOUIS D. BRANDEIS, OTHER PEOPLE'S MONEY AND HOW THE BANKERS USE IT 92 (1914)
16. For a discussion of the inability of market discipline to protect financial stability, *see* David Min, *Understanding the Failures of Market Discipline*, 92 WASH. U. L. REV. 1421 (2015).
17. For further discussion of this phenomenon, *see* Tom C.W. Lin, *Infinite Financial Intermediation*, 50 WAKE FOREST L. REV. 643 (2015).
18. DAVID W. PERKINS, CONG. RSCH. SERV., R44614, MARKETPLACE LENDING: FINTECH IN CONSUMER AND SMALL-BUSINESS LENDING 1 (2018).
19. One industry participant observed that "We have gone from an industry dominated by retail investors in 2009 to one dominated by institutional investors in 2019. Self-directed individual investors now make up significantly less than 10% of the total volume at LendingClub and Prosper and that percentage continues to fall." Peter Renton, *Ten Years of Investing in Marketplace Lending*, LENDIT FINTECH NEWS (Jul. 3, 2019), https://www.lendacademy.com/ten-years-of-investing-in-marketplace-lending/.
20. Glen Fest, *Using AI to Make Secondary Market for Online Consumer Loans*, AM. BANKER (Aug. 11, 2020), https://www.americanbanker.com/news/using-ai-to-make-secondary-market-for-online-consumer-loans.
21. Perkins, *supra* note 18, at 5.

22. LendingClub, *Why Institutional Investors are Turning to Marketplace Loans*, LENDINGCLUB (Mar. 6, 2018), https://blog.lendingclub.com/institutional-insights-into-marketplace-lending.
23. Although some institutional investors deserted the marketplace lending market early in the pandemic, they began to return and "credit quality has held up better than expected." Kevin Wack, *Online Loans Are Holding Up Better Than Expected*, AM. BANKER (Sept. 8, 2020), https://www.americanbanker.com/news/online-loans-are-holding-up-better-than-expected.
24. There is increased interest in nontraditional data sources like "social media, public records (property transactions, births, deaths, marriage, divorce, criminal and civil legal matters, and the like), GPS and satellite tracking, and cameras." Jo Ann S. Barefoot, *Disrupting FinTech Law*, FINTECH LAW REP. (Mar./Apr. 2015) at 5.
25. Similar incentive problems arose in connection with the "originate-to-distribute" mode of mortgage origination in the lead-up to the financial crisis of 2007-08. FIN. CRISIS INQUIRY COMM'N, THE FINANCIAL CRISIS INQUIRY REPORT: FINAL REPORT OF THE NATIONAL COMMISSION ON THE CAUSES OF THE FINANCIAL AND ECONOMIC CRISIS IN THE UNITED STATES 89 (2011).
26. On November 19, 2008, Citigroup announced that it was "going to bring the remaining $17.4 billion in off-balance-sheet SIV assets onto its books." By doing so, Citigroup effectively guaranteed payments to investors in some of its affiliated investment funds, even though those investors had no legal claim against Citigroup. *Id.* at 380.
27. Lalita Clozel, *Could Online Lending Become the Next Systemic Risk?*, AM. BANKER (Oct. 13, 2017), https://www.americanbanker.com/news/could-online-lending-become-the-next-systemic-risk.
28. Geoffrey P. Miller and Gerald Rosenfeld, *Intellectual Hazard: How Conceptual Biases in Complex Organizations Contributed to the Crisis of 2008*, 33 HARV. J. L. & PUB. POL'Y 807, 819–20 (2010).
29. *See* Eleanor Kirby & Shane Worner, *Crowd-Funding: An Infant Industry Growing Fast*, 41–42 (Int'l Org. Sec. Comm'n, Working Paper No. SWP3/2014, 2014), https://www.iosco.org/research/pdf/swp/Crowd-funding-An-Infant-Industry-Growing-Fast.pdf.
30. For further background on high frequency trading, *see* Rena S. Miller & Gary Shorter, CONG. RSCH. SERV., R44443, HIGH FREQUENCY TRADING: OVERVIEW OF RECENT DEVELOPMENTS (2016). For a popular account, *see* MICHAEL LEWIS, FLASH BOYS: A WALL STREET REVOLT (2014).
31. High frequency trading is thought to account for at least 50% of all trading in the US equity markets. Johannes Breckenfelder, *Competition among High-Frequency Traders, and Market Quality* (Eur. Cent. Bank, Working Paper No. 2289, 2019), https://www.ecb.europa.eu/pub/pdf/scpwps/ecb.wp2290~b5fec3a181.en.pdf. For discussions of high frequency trading in other markets, *see* Yesha Yadav, *How Algoirthmic Trading Undermines Efficiency in Capital Markets*, 68 VAND. L. REV. 1607; 1622 (2015); Anna Baydakova, *High-Frequency Trading Is Newest Battleground in Crypto Exchange Race*, COINDESK (Jul. 8, 2019), https://www.coindesk.com/high- frequency-trading-is-new-battleground-in-crypto-exchange-race.

32. *See* Paul Golden, *FX: Machine Learning Use Grows, but Lags in HFT*, EUROMONEY (Aug. 2, 2018), https://www.euromoney.com/article/b19b36yppj92q5/fx-machine-learning- use-grows-but-lags-in-hft.
33. Merritt B. Fox et al., *The New Stock Market: Sense and Nonsense*, 65 DUKE L.J. 191, 202–03 (2015).
34. For further discussion of this flash crash, *see* US CFTC & SEC, FINDINGS REGARDING THE MARKET EVENTS OF MAY 6, 2010 1 (2010).
35. Kara M. Stein, Commissioner, SEC, Remarks before Trader Forum 2014 Equity Trading Summit (Feb. 6, 2014) (transcript available at https://www.sec.gov/news/speech/2014-spch020614kms).
36. Matt Levine, *Algorithms Had Themselves a Treasury Flash Crash*, BLOOMBERG (July 13, 2015), https://www.bloomberg.com/opinion/articles/2015-07-13/algorithms-had-themselves-a-treasury-flash-crash; William Watts, *What Caused the Ethereum Flash Crash?*, MARKETWATCH (Jun. 24, 2017), https://www.marketwatch.com/story/what-caused-the-ethereum-flash-crash-2017-06-22.
37. For example, on April 1, 2015, a "Tesla press release jokingly announced a new "W" model for a watch. It was clearly intended as a joke. However, it was taken all too seriously by computers dutifully executing their algorithms in response to the press release. The algorithms didn't quite get the joke, trading hundreds of thousands of shares and spiking the stock price within one minute of the issuance of the release." Kara M. Stein, Commissioner, SEC, Remarks at the SIFMA Operations Conference: The Dominance of Data and the Need for New Tools (Apr. 14, 2015) (transcript available at https://www.sec.gov/news/speech/2015-spch041415kms.html).
38. During the Flash Crash of 2010, for example, "[o]ver 20,000 trades across more than 300 securities were executed at prices more than 60% away from their values just moments before. Moreover, many of these trades were executed at prices of a penny or less, or as high as $100,000, before prices of those securities returned to their "pre-crash" levels." US CFTC & SEC, *supra* note 34, at 1.
39. "Faster trades means more trading." Saule T. Omarova, *Technology v Technocracy: Fintech as a Regulatory Challenge*, 6. J. FIN. REG. 75, 89 (2020).
40. Deutsche Bundesbank, *High-Frequency Trading Can Amplify Financial Market Volatility*, DEUTSCHE BUNDESBANK (Oct. 25, 2016), https://www.bundesbank.de/Redaktion/EN/Topics/2016/2016_10_25_monthly_report_october_high_frequency_trading.html.
41. For an excellent introduction to all things cryptoasset, *see* PRIMAVERA DE FILIPPI & AARON WRIGHT, BLOCKCHAIN AND THE LAW: THE RULE OF CODE (2018).
42. Benjamin Hart & Jen Wieczner, *What the Mainstreaming of Crypto Means for Normies*, N.Y. MAGAZINE (May 13, 2021), https://nymag.com/intelligencer/2021/04/what-the-mainstreaming-of-crypto-means-for-normies.html.
43. Shaanan Cohney et al., *Coin-Operated Capitalism*, 119 COLUM. L. REV. 591, 594 (2018).
44. Saule T. Omarova, *New Tech v. New Deal: Fintech as a Systemic Phenomenon*, 36 YALE J. REG. 735, 774 (2019).
45. ROBERT J. SHILLER, IRRATIONAL EXUBERANCE 123 *et seq.* (3rd ed. 2015)

46. For an account of Wirecard's failure, *see* Arthur E. Wilmarth, *Wirecard and Greensill Scandals Confirm Dangers of Mixing Banking and Commerce*, 40 BANKING & FIN. SERVICES POL'Y REP. No. 5 (May 2021).
47. Robert J. Shiller, *What Is Bitcoin Really Worth? Don't Even Ask*, N.Y. TIMES (Dec. 15, 2017), at BU2.
48. John Detrixhe, *Robert Shiller Wrote the Book on Bubbles. He Says "The Best Example Right Now Is Bitcoin,"* QUARTZ (Sept. 5, 2017), https://qz.com/1067557/robert-shiller-wrote-the-book-on-bubbles-he-says-the-best-example-right-now-is-bitcoin/#:~:text=Robert%20Shiller%20wrote%20the%20book,example%20right%20now%20is%20bitcoin.%E2%80%9D&text=One%20pinch%20and%20it%20might%20pop.&text=New%20technology%20is%20upending%20everything,to%20trading%20to%20making%20payments.
49. For detailed discussion of ICOs, *see* Cohney at al., *supra* note 43.
50. Christine Kim, The 'Hot Swap' Plan to Switch Ethereum to Proof-of-Stake Explained, COINDESK (Sept. 19, 2020) (available at https://www.coindesk.com/the-hot-swap-plan-to-switch-ethereum-to-proof-of-stake-explained).
51. For further discussion of the DAO hack, *see* Carla L. Reyes, *If Rockefeller Were a Coder*, 87 GEO. WASH. L. REV. 373, 388 (2019).
52. Cohney et al., *supra* note 43, at 596.
53. Ana Alexandre, *Research: ICO Market Down Almost 100% From a Year Ago, Raised $40 Million in Q1 2019*, COINTELEGRAPH (May 13, 2019), https://cointelegraph.com/news/research-ico-market-down-almost-100-from-a-year-ago-raised-40-million-in-q1-2019.
54. Scott Reyburn, *JPG File Sells for $69 Million, as 'NFT Mania' Gathers Pace*, N.Y. TIMES (Mar. 24, 2021), https://www.nytimes.com/2021/03/11/arts/design/nft-auction-christies-beeple.html.
55. Kevin Roose, *Buy This Column on the Blockchain!*, N.Y. TIMES, Mar. 24, 2021, https://www.nytimes.com/2021/03/24/technology/nft-column-blockchain.html.
56. Omarova, *supra* note 44, at 775.
57. For an explanation of repo, *see* Gary Gorton & Andrew Metrick, *Securitized Banking and the Run on Repo*, 104 J. FIN. ECON. 425 (2012).
58. James Tobin, *On the Efficiency of the Financial System*, 153 LLOYDS BANK REV. 1, 15 (1984).
59. MICHAEL ASHTON, WHAT'S WRONG WITH MONEY?: THE BIGGEST BUBBLE OF ALL, 43 (2016).
60. Zheping Huang, *Bitcoin Cash "Hard Fork": Everything You Need to Know about the Latest Cryptocurrency Civil War*, SOUTH CHINA MORNING POST (Nov. 15, 2018), https://www.scmp.com/tech/blockchain/article/2173389/bitcoin-cash-hard-fork-everything-you-need-know-about- latest.
61. For a discussion of foreign exchange crises and how they can lead to banking crises, *see* Frederic S. Mishkin, *Lessons from the Tequila Crisis*, 23 J. BANKING & FIN. 1521, 1523–24 (1999).
62. For discussion of 2008's run on repo, *see* Gorton & Metrick, *supra* note 57.
63. Cohney et al., *supra* note 43, at 639.

64. Anna Gelpern & Adam J. Levitin, *Rewriting Frankenstein Contracts: Workout Prohibitions in Residential Mortgage-Backed Securities*, 82 S. Cal. L. Rev. 1075, 1128–29 (2009).
65. Ryan Molecke, *How to Learn Solidity: The Ultimate Ethereum Coding Tutorial*, https://blockgeeks.com/guides/solidity/). For further background on Solidity, *see* Cohney et al., *supra* note 43, at 617–18.
66. Molecke, *supra* note 65.
67. Katharina Pistor, *A Legal Theory of Finance*, 41 J. Comparative Econ. 315, 321 (2013).
68. De Filippi & Wright, *supra* note 41, at 188.
69. Fin. Stability Bd., Regulation, Supervision and Oversight of "Global Stablecoin" Arrangements 1 (2020)
70. One of the progenitors of the initial Libra proposal confirmed that "[i]f Libra is successful, Facebook will first benefit from it by enabling more commerce across its family of apps. More commerce means ads will be more effective, and advertisers will buy more of them to grow their businesses." David Marcus, *Libra, 2 Weeks In*, Facebook (Jul. 3, 2019), https://www.facebook.com/notes/david-marcus/libra-2-weeks-in/10158616513819148/.
71. Diem Association, *An Introduction to Libra*, Diem Ass'n (June 2019), https://sls.gmu.edu/pfrt/wp-content/uploads/sites/54/2020/02/LibraWhitePaper_en_US-Rev0723.pdf,
72. Diem Association, *Welcome to the Official White Paper*, Diem Ass'n (Apr. 2020), https://www.diem.com/en- us/white-paper/.
73. Diem Association, *supra* note 72, at 12.
74. Diem Association, *supra* note 71, at 3.
75. Diem Association, *supra* note 72, at 14.
76. William McChesney Martin, Jr., Chairman, Fed. Reserve Sys. Bd. of Governors, Address before the New York Group of the Investment Bankers Association of America 12 (Oct. 19, 1955) (transcript available at https://fraser.stlouisfed.org/title/statements-speeches-william-mcchesney-martin-jr-448/address-new-york-group-investment-bankers-association-america-7800).
77. Saule Omarova & Graham Steele, *There's a Lot We Still Don't Know About Libra*, N.Y. Times (Nov. 4, 2019), https://www.nytimes.com/2019/11/04/opinion/facebook-libra-cryptocurrency.html.
78. *J.P. Morgan Creates Digital Coin for Payments*, J.P. Morgan (Feb. 14. 2019), https://www.jpmorgan.com/global/news/digital-coin-payments [https://perma.cc/L52T-B9S7].

## Chapter 4

1. On payments as accounting transactions, *see* Richard Scott Carnell et al., The Law of Financial Institutions 73 (6th ed. 2017).

2. This explanation of the interbank payments system draws from JOHN ARMOUR ET AL., PRINCIPLES OF FINANCIAL REGULATION, 393–97 (1st ed. 2016).
3. This description of payments settlement in the United States is based on MICHAEL S. BARR ET AL., FINANCIAL REGULATION: LAW AND POLICY 773–76 (2016).
4. *Bank for Int'l Settlements, Comm. on Payment and Settlements Sys.*, PAYMENT, CLEARING, AND SETTLEMENT SYSTEMS IN THE CPSS COUNTRIES 489–90 (2012), https://www.bis.org/cpmi/publ/d105.htm.
5. "In general, settlement risk is the possibility that the completion or settlement of individual transactions or settlement at the interbank funds transfer or securities settlement level more broadly, will not take place as expected." FED. FIN. INST. EXAMINATION COUNCIL, WHOLESALE PAYMENTS SYSTEMS IT EXAMINATION HANDBOOK 20 (2004), https://ithandbook.ffiec.gov/it-booklets/wholesale-payment-systems.aspx.
6. BANK FOR INT'L SETTLEMENTS, BASEL COMM. ON BANKING SUPERVISION, REVISIONS TO THE PRINCIPLES FOR THE SOUND MANAGEMENT OF OPERATIONAL RISK 2 (2021), https://www.bis.org/bcbs/publ/d515.htm.
7. Stacy Cowley, *RushCard Ordered to Pay $13 Million for Disruption of Prepaid Card Service*, N.Y. TIMES (Feb. 1, 2017), https://www.nytimes.com/2017/02/01/business/rushcard-cfpb.html.
8. This discussion of M-Pesa outages is drawn from Hilary J. Allen, *Payments Failure*, 62 B.C. L. REV. 453, 470–71 (2021).
9. *See* Nat'l Treasury, Republic of Kenya, MEDIUM TERM 2017 BUDGET POLICY STATEMENT: CONSOLIDATING ECONOMIC GAINS IN AN ENVIRONMENT OF SUBDUED GLOBAL DEMAND 83 (2016), https://www.treasury.go.ke/wp-content/uploads/2021/03/2017-Budget-Policy-Statement.pdf.
10. THOMAS M. EISENBACH ET AL., FEDERAL RESERVE BANK OF NEW YORK STAFF REPORTS, NO. 909: CYBER RISK AND THE US FINANCIAL SYSTEM: A PRE-MORTEM ANALYSIS 8 (2020), https://www.newyorkfed.org/research/staff_reports/sr909.
11. FIN. CRISIS INQUIRY COMM'N, THE FINANCIAL CRISIS INQUIRY REPORT: FINAL REPORT OF THE NATIONAL COMMISSION ON THE CAUSES OF THE FINANCIAL AND ECONOMIC CRISIS IN THE UNITED STATES 389 et seq. (2011).
12. This discussion of payment system operations after September 11 draws heavily from JEFFREY M. LACKER, FEDERAL RESERVE BANK OF RICHMOND WORKING PAPER 03-16: PAYMENT SYSTEM DISRUPTIONS AND THE FEDERAL RESERVE FOLLOWING SEPTEMBER 11, 2001 (2003), https://www.richmondfed.org/publications/research/working_papers/2003/wp_03-16.
13. In addition to these operational challenges, it has been suggested that other banks might have purposely held back making interbank payments because they were worried about not receiving the payments they were owed. *Id.* at 7.
14. EISENBACH ET AL., *supra* note 10, at 38–39.
15. ARMOUR ET AL., *supra* note 2, at 282–83.
16. BANK FOR INT'L SETTLEMENTS, BASEL COMM. ON BANKING SUPERVISION, *supra* note 6; BANK FOR INT'L SETTLEMENTS, BASEL COMM. ON BANKING SUPERVISION, PRINCIPLES FOR OPERATIONAL RESILIENCE (2021), https://www.bis.org/bcbs/publ/d516.pdf.

17. Bank for Int'l Settlements, Comm. on Payment and Settlement Sys. & Tech. Comm. of the Int'l Org. of Securities Commissions, Principles for Financial Market Infrastructures (2012), https://www.bis.org/cpmi/publ/d101.htm.
18. *See* Principles 4–7. *Id.* at 1–2.
19. *Id.* at 3.
20. Andrei A. Kirilenko & Andrew W. Lo, *Moore's Law versus Murphy's Law: Algorithmic Trading and Its Discontents*, 27 J. Econ. Perspectives 52 (Spring 2013). In 2003, Lacker observed that "technology-shock-indued interbank payment disruptions are a phenomenon of the last few decades." Lacker, *supra* note 12, at 24.
21. Bank for Int'l Settlements, Basel Comm. on Banking Supervision, *supra* note 6, at 8.
22. Bank for Int'l Settlements, Basel Comm. on Banking Supervision, *supra* note 16, at 7.
23. *See* Lacker, *supra* note 12, at 33–34.
24. Complex systems have been defined as "large networks of components with no central control and simple rules of operation give rise to complex collective behavior, sophisticated information processing, and adaptation via learning or evolution." Melanie Mitchell, Complexity: A Guided Tour 13 (2009).
25. For more on cascade failures, *see* Charles Perrow, Normal Accidents: Living with High-Risk Technologies 5 (1999); Dirk Helbing, *Globally Networked Risks and How to Respond*, 497 Nature 51 (2013).
26. *See*, for example, Eisenbach et al., *supra* note 10, at 7.
27. This description of a cascade failure in power transmission systems is drawn from Ian Dobson et al., *Complex Systems Analysis of Series of Blackouts: Cascading Failure, Critical Points, and Self-Organization*, 17 Chaos 026103 (2007).
28. The inadequacies of our current approach to operational risk regulation can be illustrated with an analogy to the failures of capital regulation in the lead-up to the 2008 crisis. Capital regulation at that time has been described as purely "microprudential," meaning that rules were set up to limit the solvency and liquidity risks of individual financial institutions, without thinking about how the risk management strategies of those individual institutions, and the defensive measures they took to maintain regulatory compliance, might interact to cause systemic problems. In the wake of the 2008 crisis, we developed an appreciation for the need for a "macroprudential" perspective on financial regulation, which would take into account the systemic consequences of actions taken by individual institutions to address their own credit, solvency, and liquidity risks. We haven't yet though through how defensive measures that individual firms take to address their own operational risks might have systemic consequences.
29. Bank for Int'l Settlements, Basel Comm. on Banking Supervision, *supra* note 16, at 7.
30. This description of complexity science draws heavily on David L. Alderson & John C. Doyle, *Contrasting Views of Complexity and Their Implications for Network-Centric Infrastructures*, 40 IEEE Transactions on Systems, Man & Cybernetics 839, 839 (*2010*), as well as on J.B. Ruhl's interpretation of their complexity science work for a legal audience. *See* J.B. Ruhl, *Managing Systemic Risk in Legal Systems*, 89 Ind. L.J.

559, 570 (*2014*); J.B. Ruhl, *Governing Cascade Failures in Complex Social-Ecological-Technological Systems: Framing Context, Strategies, and Challenges*, 22 VAND. J. ENT. & TECH. L. 407 (2020).

31. BANK FOR INT'L SETTLEMENTS, COMM. ON PAYMENTS AND MARKET INFRASTRUCTURES, DISTRIBUTED LEDGER TECHNOLOGY IN PAYMENT, CLEARING AND SETTLEMENT 15 (2017), https://www.bis.org/cpmi/publ/d157.htm.
32. For further discussion of the different types of mobile payments services available, and the vulnerability of mobile wallets to runs, *see* Dan Awrey & Kristin van Zwieten, *The Shadow Payment System*, 43 J. CORP. L. 775 (2018).
33. *Id.* at 805.
34. With regard to Venmo's transaction volume, *see* Statista, *Venmo's Total Payment Volume*, available at https://www.statista.com/statistics/763617/venmo-total-payment-volume/. With regard to Visa's transaction volume, *see* Daniel Keyes, *Visa's Payments Volume Plummeted in Its Most Recent Quarter Due to the Pandemic*, BUSINESS INSIDER (Jul. 30, 2020), https://headtopics.com/us/visa-s-payments-volume-plummeted-in-its-most-recent-quarter-due-to-the-pandemic-business-insider-14682192.
35. Caixin, *Chart of the Day: China's Mobile Payment Volume Hits $41.51 Trillion in 2018*, CAIXIN (Mar. 22, 2019), https://www.caixinglobal.com/2019-03-22/chart-of-the-day-chinas-mobile-payment-transaction-volume-hits-4151-trillion-in-2018-101395789.html.
36. AARON KLEIN, THE BROOKING INSTITUTION, IS CHINA'S NEW PAYMENT SYSTEM THE FUTURE? 7 (2019), https://www.brookings.edu/research/is-chinas-new-payment-system-the-future/.
37. For a discussion of regulatory reforms introduced by the People's Bank of China in response to the prominence of mobile payments providers, *see* BANK FOR INT'L SETTLEMENTS, ANNUAL ECONOMIC REPORT 70 (June 19).
38. Amy O'Leary, *Tech Companies Leave Phone Calls Behind*, N.Y. TIMES (Jul. 6, 2012), https://www.nytimes.com/2012/07/07/technology/tech-companies-leave-phone-calls-behind.html.
39. Peter Rudegeair, *Venmo to Users: If You Owe Us Money, We're Coming for It*, WALL ST. J. (Mar. 25, 2019), https://www.wsj.com/articles/venmo-to-users-if-you-owe-us-money-were-coming-for-it-11553518800.
40. "[T]he Federal Reserve Act dictates that only banks and other similar depository institutions have access to the Federal Reserve master accounts that represent the fastest, most convenient, and most reliable means of final settlement in our current payment system. And since the current payment system is built around these master accounts, this effectively excludes financial institutions other than banks from direct access to the major clearing networks." Dan Awrey, *Unbundling Banking, Money and Payments*, GEO. L. J. (forthcoming).
41. KLEIN, *supra* note 36.
42. Caitlin Long, *Framework for Understanding Blockchain's Next Chapter: Hybrid Financial Instruments*, FORBES (Nov. 17, 2018), https://www.forbes.com/sites/caitlinlong/2018/11/17/framework-for-understanding-blockchains-next-chapter-hyb

rid-financial-instruments-part-1/?sh=143163445649. There may be some lingering uncertainty about when settlement occurs as a legal matter, because many legal regimes don't cater for a consensus approach to verifying transactions. Bank for Int'l Settlements, Comm. on Payments and Market Infrastructures, *supra* note 31, at 16.

43. Bank for Int'l Settlements, Comm. on Payments and Market Infrastructures, *supra* note 31, at 14.
44. Diem Association, *Welcome to the Official White Paper*, Diem Ass'n 5 (Apr. 2020), https://www.diem.com/en- us/white-paper/.
45. Allen, *supra* note 8, at 473.
46. These questions were posed by Professor Chris Brummer in his testimony before the House Financial Services Committee. *See Examining Facebook's Proposed Cryptocurrency and Its Impact on Consumers, Investors, and the American Financial System: Hearing Before the H. Comm. on Fin. Servs.* 7, 116th Cong. (2018) (statement of testimony by Chris Brummer, Agnes N. Williams Research Professor Director, Institute of International Economic Law, Georgetown University Law Center), https://financialservices.house.gov/uploadedfiles/hhrg-116-ba00-wstate-brummerc-20190717.pdf.
47. Diem Association, *supra* note 44, at 1.
48. This description of the Bitcoin civil war is drawn from Zheping Huang, *Bitcoin Cash "Hard Fork": Everything You Need to Know About the Latest Cryptocurrency Civil War*, South China Morning Post (Nov. 15, 2018), https://www.scmp.com/tech/blockchain/article/2173389/bitcoin-cash-hard-fork-everything-you-need-know-about-latest.
49. Allen, *supra* note 8, at 496.
50. Samuel Arbesman, Overcomplicated: Technology at the Limits of Comprehension 39–40 (2016).
51. Tom Sullivan, *Looking for Job Security? Try Cobol*, N.Y. Times (Oct. 23, 2008), https://archive.nytimes.com/www.nytimes.com/external/idg/2008/10/23/23idg-Looking-for-job.html.
52. René M. Stulz, *FinTech, BigTech, and the Future of Banks*, 31 J. App. Corp. Fin. 86, 93 (2019).
53. Press Release, Office of Kirsten Gillibrand, Senators Gillibrand and Sanders, Representatives Ocasio-Cortez, Pascrell, and Kaptur Call on Congress to Implement Postal Banking Pilot Programs (Apr. 15, 2021), *https://www.gillibrand.senate.gov/news/press/release/senators-gillibrand-and-sanders-representatives-ocasio-cortez-pascrell-and-kaptur-call-on-congress-to-implement-postal-banking-pilot-programs-*. *See also* Mehrsa Baradaran, *It's Time for Postal Banking, 127* Harv. L. Rev. F. 165 (2014),
54. For further elaboration on these proposals, *see* John Crawford et al., *FedAccounts: Digital Dollars*, 89 Geo. Wash. L. Rev. 113 (2021); Saule T. Omarova, *The People's Ledger: How to Democratize Money and Finance the Economy*, Vand. L. Rev. (forthcoming).
55. About the FedNow Service, https://www.frbservices.org/financial-services/fednow/about.html (last visited *June 17, 2021*).

56. Usually referred to as "CBDCs," these have been defined as "a digital payment instrument, denominated in the national unit of account, that is a direct liability of the central bank," and contrasted with balances in traditional central bank reserve accounts. BANK FOR INT'L SETTLEMENTS, CENTRAL BANK DIGITAL CURRENCIES: FOUNDATIONAL PRINCIPLES AND CORE FEATURES 3 (2020).
57. *See* Baradaran, *supra* note 53; Crawford et al., *supra* note 54.
58. For further discussion of the difficulties faced by those living paycheck to paycheck, *see* AARON KLEIN, THE BROOKINGS INSTITUTION, HOW THE FED CAN HELP FAMILIES LIVING PAYCHECK TO PAYCHECK (2017), https://www.brookings.edu/research/how-the-fed-can-help-families-living-paycheck-to-paycheck/.
59. BANK FOR INT'L SETTLEMENTS, *supra* note 56, at 5–7.
60. The Federal Reserve has a "longstanding commitment to operational and financial support for the smooth functioning of the payment system." Peter Conti-Brown & David A. Wishnick, *Private Markets, Public Options, and the Payment System*, 37 YALE J. REG. 380, 419 (2020).
61. As Conti-Brown and Wishnick commented in connection with the development of FedNow, "the Fed's ability to manage systemic risks imposed by a giant actor in the payment system is much higher when the Fed owns the entity, rather than when it merely supervises it." *Id.* at 420. Some payments clearinghouses outside of the United States are owned and operated by their central bank, presumably for these reasons. ARMOUR ET AL., *supra* note 2 at 400.
62. BANK FOR INT'L SETTLEMENTS, *supra* note 56.
63. Crawford et al., *supra* note 54, at 142–43.
64. Omarova, *supra* note 54.
65. BANK FOR INT'L SETTLEMENTS, *supra* note 56, at 8.
66. This approach to CBDCs is an adaptation of Crawford et al., *supra* note 54, at 142–43.
67. BANK FOR INT'L SETTLEMENTS, *supra* note 56, at 8–9.
68. This description of clearing and settlement processes in the stock market is drawn from David A. Wishnick, *Reengineering Financial Market Infrastructure*, 105 MINN. L. REV. 2379 (2021). For a discussion of equivalent processes in the derivatives market, *see* Emilios Avgouleas & Aggelos Kiayias, *The Promise of Blockchain Technology for Global Securities and Derivatives Markets: The New Financial Ecosystem and the "Holy Grail" of Systemic Risk Containment*, 20 EUR. BUS. ORG. L. REV. 81 (2019).
69. Press Release, US SEC. & EXCH. COMM'N, SEC ADOPTS T + 2 SETTLEMENT CYCLE FOR SECURITIES TRANSACTIONS (Mar. 22, 2017), https://www.sec.gov/news/press-release/2017-68-0.
70. For a discussion of the risk that a clearinghouse like the NSCC might default, *see* Felix B. Chang, *The Systemic Risk Paradox: Banks and Clearinghouses under Regulation*, 2014 COLUM BUS. L. REV. 747 (2014).
71. Avgouleas & Kiayias, *supra* note 68, at 83.
72. Ben S. Bernanke, *Clearing and Settlement during the Crash*, 3 REV. FIN. STUD. 133, 146 (1990).
73. *Id.* at 146–47.
74. *Id.* at 149.

75. J. Travis Laster & Marcel T. Rosner, *Distributed Stock Ledgers and Delaware Law*, 73 Bus. Lawyer 319, 333–34 (2018).
76. Primavera De Filippi & Aaron Wright, Blockchain and the Law: The Rule of Code, 93 (2018).
77. Avgouleas & Kiayias, *supra* note 68, at 107.
78. Caitlin Long, *Settlement Risks in Crypto/Legacy Hybrid Instruments*, Forbes (Nov. 19, 2018), https://www.forbes.com/sites/caitlinlong/2018/11/19/settlement-risks-in-cryptolegacy-hybrid-instruments/?sh=786082562422.
79. This discussion of vendors draws heavily on Fin. Stability Bd., Regulatory and Supervisory Issues Relating to Outsourcing and Third-Party Relationships: Discussion Paper (2020).
80. "All supervisory authorities rely primarily on [financial institutions] to manage the risks in their outsourcing and third-party relationships. They do so through regulatory requirements and supervisory expectations regarding how FIs should oversee these relationships, with a particular focus on those that are critical or important to financial stability; the safety and soundness of FIs; or the provision of critical or important functions." *Id.* at 5.
81. For further discussion of issues associated with private sector certification of technology vendors for the financial industry, *see* Comment Letter from Americans for Financial Reform Education Fund & Demand Progress Education Fund regarding Request for Information on Standard Setting and Voluntary Certification for Models and Third-Party Providers of Technology and Other Services (Sept. 22, 2020), https://ourfinancialsecurity.org/wp-content/uploads/2020/09/AFR-Education-Fund-DPEF-Comment-FDIC-Docket-RIN-3064-ZA181.pdf.
82. Fin. Stability Bd., Third-Party Dependencies in Cloud Services: Considerations on Financial Stability Implications (2019).
83. Cloud services providers invest heavily in security, their servers are often housed in different geographical locations to diversify threats of natural disasters and the like, and they lack many of the problems of legacy systems. *Id.* at 1.
84. *Id.*
85. American Bankers Association, Sheltered Harbor, https://www.aba.com/banking-topics/technology/cybersecurity/sheltered-harbor (last visited June 17, 2021).

## Chapter 5

1. This classification of possible regulatory approaches draws from Matthew D. Adler, *Regulatory Theory*, *in* A Companion to Philosophy of Law and Legal Theory 595 (Dennis Patterson ed., 2nd ed. 2010).
2. Jeffrey S. Lubbers, *Administrative Law in the United States*, *in* Administrative Law of The European Union, Its Member States, and the United States: A Comparative Analysis 373 (René J.G.H. Seerden ed., 4th ed. 2018).

3. For a discussion of a principles-based approaches to financial regulation, *see* Julia Black et al., *Making a Success of Principles-Based Regulation*, 1 L. & Fin. Mkt. Rev. 191 (2007).
4. For examples of literature dealing with the difficulties in applying regulation to other types of innovation, *see* Tim Wu, *Agency Threats*, 60 Duke L.J. 1841, 1847 (2011); Eric Biber et al., *Regulating Business Innovation as Policy Disruption: From the Model T to Airbnb*, 70 Vand. L. Rev. 1561 (2017).
5. "Many of today's entrepreneurs live by Facebook founder Mark Zuckerberg's now-famous motto: "Move fast and break things." Hemant Taneja, *The Era of "Move Fast and Break Things"* is over, Harv. Bus. Rev. (Jan. 22, 2019), https://hbr.org/2019/01/the-era-of-move-fast-and-break-things-is-over. The concept of "failing fast" is also endemic in the tech sector, and reflects a perspective that "speed of execution is a lot more important than perfect execution." Sunnie Giles, *How to Fail Faster—and Why You Should*, Forbes (Apr. 30, 2018), https://www.forbes.com/sites/sunniegiles/2018/04/30/how-to-fail-faster-and-why-you-should/?sh=259348d6c177.
6. JoAnn Barefoot, *A Regtech Manifesto: Redesigning Financial Regulation for the Digital Age*, Alliance for Innovative Regulation 10 (Jul. 2020), https://www.dcfintechweek.org/wp-content/uploads/2020/10/Barefoot_Jo-Ann_AIR-Regtech-Manifesto-July-2020.pdf.
7. For a discussion of the regulatory quandaries posed by the increasing autonomy of vehicles, *see* Sarah E. Light, *Advisory Nonpreemption*, 95 Wash. U. L. Rev. 325, 328–29 (2017).
8. Wu, *supra* note 4, at 1844.
9. With regard to the ease with which financial assets can cross borders, *see* Chris Brummer *How International Financial Law Works (and How It Doesn't)*, 99 Geo. L.J. 257, 266 (2011). With regard to the lack of physical presence associated with many tech business models, *see* Elizabeth Pollman, *Tech, Regulatory Arbitrage, and Limits*, 20 Eur. Bus. Org. L. Rev. 567, 569 (2019).
10. For a discussion of the counterproductive potential of regulatory complexity, *see* Andrew G. Haldane & Vasileios Madouros, *The Dog and the Frisbee*, at Federal Reserve Bank of Kansas City's 366th Economic Policy Symposium: The Changing Policy Landscape 109 (2012), http://www.kansascityfed.org/publicat/sympos/2012/ah.pdf.
11. John Armour et al., Principles of Financial Regulation 62–68 (1st ed. 2016).
12. For a discussion of how salient features of financial products are sometimes hidden from consumers, *see* Oren Bar-Gill & Elizabeth Warren, *Making Credit Safer*, 157 U. Pa. L. Rev. 1 (2008). For an analogous discussion of how product features can be hidden from sophisticated investors, *see* Nicola Gennaioli et al., *Financial Innovation and Financial Fragility* (Fondazione Eni Enrico Mattei Nota Di Lavoro, Working Paper No. 114.2010, 2010).
13. An example of a product ban can be found in the UK's legislative restrictions on high-cost payday loans, as discussed in Armour et al, *supra* note 11, at 262–64.
14. "Early critiques of sandboxes focused on the risk of allowing new companies to operate in the market without appropriate oversight." UNSGSA FinTech Working

Group & CCAF, *Early Lessons on Regulatory Innovations to Enable Inclusive FinTech: Innovation Offices, Regulatory Sandboxes, and RegTech* 30 (2019).

15. This catalogue of different forms of regulatory support for financial innovation is drawn from Hilary J. Allen, *Experimental Strategies for Regulating Fintech*, 3. J. L. & INNOVATION 1, 22 (2020).
16. *Id.* at 21.
17. Ross P. Buckley et al., *Building Fintech Ecosystems: Regulatory Sandboxes, Innovation Hubs and Beyond*, 61 WASH. U. J. L. & POL'Y 55, 58 (2020).
18. OFF. OF COMPTROLLER OF CURRENCY, POLICY STATEMENT ON FINANCIAL TECHNOLOGY COMPANIES' ELIGIBILITY TO APPLY FOR NATIONAL BANK CHARTERS (Jul. 31, 2018).
19. The most prominent of the cases challenging the OCC Charter is Lacewell v. OCC Case 19–4271 SDNY.
20. Gregory Roberts, *OCC Fintech Charter May Be a Poor Fit for Fintechs*, BUREAU NAT'L AFFAIRS (Feb. 2, 2017), https://bnanews.bna.com/tech-and-telecom-law/occ-fintech-charter-may-be-a-poor-fit-for-fintechs?context=search&index=3.
21. Press Release, FIN. CONDUCT AUTH., FINANCIAL CONDUCT AUTHORITY'S REGULATORY SANDBOX OPENS TO APPLICATIONS (May 9, 2016), https://www.fca.org.uk/news/press-releases/financial-conduct-authority's-regulatory-sandbox-opens-applications.
22. *Id.*
23. For a listing of all of the firms who have participated in the FCA's sandbox together with a short description of their business models, *see Regulatory Sandbox*, FINANCIAL CONDUCT AUTHORITY, https://www.fca.org.uk/firms/innovation/regulatory-sandbox (last visited Feb. 22, 2021).
24. Hilary J. Allen, *Regulatory Sandboxes*, 87 GEO. WASH. L. REV. 579, 592 (2019). Buckley et al. have observed that regulatory sandboxes are unlikely to be effective in facilitating private sector innovation unless they are coupled with some sort of innovation hub. Buckley et al., *supra* note 17, at 59.
25. *Key Data from Regulatory Sandboxes Across the Globe*, THE WORLD BANK (Nov. 1, 2020), https://www.worldbank.org/en/topic/fintech/brief/key-data-from-regulatory-sandboxes-across-the-globe.
26. *See* The GFIN Cross-Border Testing, GLOBAL FINANCIAL INNOVATION NETWORK (GFIN), https://www.thegfin.com/crossborder-testing.
27. In the United States, the Consumer Financial Protection Bureau has adopted a policy creating a national-level "Compliance Assistance Sandbox," but its sandbox has not been utilized—likely due to uncertainty about its legality and scope. As a result, sandbox options in the United States are practically limited to state-sponsored sandboxes like those adopted by the States of Arizona, Utah, and Wyoming. Allen, *supra* note 15, at 21–22.
28. For further discussion of sandbox design features, *see* Allen, *supra* note 24, at 579.
29. With regard to international coordination in developing best practices, *see* Brummer, *supra* note 9, at 274.
30. The Financial Stability Board promotes the use of supervisory colleges of bank supervisors as the best way to monitor financial institutions with significant

trans-border operations. These colleges have "the primary objective of exchanging information and establishing a dialogue in order to ensure that they are able to identify and address the main risks across a banking group." Katia D'Hulster, *Cross Border Banking Supervision: Incentive Conflicts in Supervisory Information Sharing between Home and Host Supervisors* 1 (World Bank Pol'y Rsch., Working Paper No. 5871, 2011).

31. UNSGSA FinTech Working Group & CCAF, *supra* note 14, at 31.
32. *Id.*; Buckley et al., *supra* note 17, at 72.
33. The Financial Stability Board has observed that "stability was not often cited as an objective for recent or planned regulatory reforms with regard to FinTech." Financial Stability Board, Financial Stability Implications from FinTech, 5 (2017).
34. For a discussion of sunsetting financial regulation, *see* Roberta Romano, *Regulating in the Dark and a Postscript Assessment of the Iron Law of Financial Regulation*, 43 Hofstra L. Rev. 25, 38–39 (2014).
35. Michael S. Barr et al. Financial Regulation: Law And Policy 234 (1st ed. 2016).
36. Carnell et al., The Law of Financial Institutions 226 (6th ed. 2017).
37. For a summary of the rationales for special resolution mechanisms for banks, *see* Armour et al, *supra* note 11, at 341.
38. *See id.* at 324–25.
39. National regulatory capital and liquidity requirements are typically based on international standards set by the Basel Committee on Banking Supervision. The most recent iteration of these standards (first published in 2010, then subsequently amended) is referred to as "Basel III." Basel Committee on Banking Supervision, Basel III: A global regulatory framework for more resilient banks and banking systems, Bank for International Settlements (2011), https://www.bis.org/publ/bcbs189.pdf.
40. "For an accessible discussion of the inadequacies of existing bank regulation, particularly regulatory capital requirements, see Anat Admati & Martin Hellwig, The Bankers' New Clothes: What's Wrong with Banking and What do Hellweg About It (2013).
41. For a summary of the post-crisis conventional wisdom on the inadequacy of bank-centric financial stability regulation, *see* >Armour et al, *supra* note 11, at 434.
42. *Id.* at 416–18.
43. To give one example, the Financial Stability Oversight Council in the United States has the power to designate non-bank institutions as systemically important and subject them to heightened regulation by the Federal Reserve. This power has not been utilized in recent years, though—for an overview of the creation of this designation power and its subsequent erosion, *see* Jeremy C. Kress et al., *Regulating Entities and Activities: Complementary Approaches to Nonbank Systemic Risk*, 92 S. Cal. L. Rev. 1455, 1473 et seq. (2019).
44. Martin Hellwig, *Financial Stability and Monetary Policy*, MPI Collective Goods Preprint 20 (Aug. 2015), https://www.coll.mpg.de/pdf_dat/2015_10online.pdf.

45. For further discussion of macroprudential stress tests, *see* Viral Acharya et al., *Testing Macroprudential Stress Tests: The Risk of Regulatory Risk Weights*, 64 J. Monetary Econ. 36 (2014).
46. For a discussion of the difficulties fintech firms face in obtaining bank charters, *see* Rory Van Loo, *Making Innovation More Competitive: The Case of Fintech*, 65 UCLA L. Rev. 232, 244 (2018).
47. The original proposed rule would have required high frequency trading firms to maintain "a source code repository to manage source code access, persistence, copies of all code used in the production environment, and changes to such code" that the CFTC could access. Regulation Automated Trading, 80 Fed. Reg. 78,857 (Dec. 17, 2015).
48. On the limitations of reviewing source code, *see* Joshua A. Kroll et al., *Accountable Algorithms*, 165 U. Pa. L. REV. 633, 638, 647 (2017).
49. See the discussion of artificial intelligence-driven "hyperswitching" between financial products in Rory Van Loo, *Digital Market Perfection*, 117 Mich. L. Rev. 815, 879 (2019).
50. For an overview of these efforts, *see* John M. Conley, *Can Soft Regulation Prevent Financial Crises: The Dutch Central Bank's Supervision of Behavior and Culture*, 51 Cornell Int'l L.J. 773, 777; 780 (2019). For example, the UK Financial Conduct Authority has suggested that the efforts of the financial industry might be better channeled toward the public good if firms take steps "to enhance employees' understanding of how their work has a real world impact. . . to ensure that employees do not regard their work as simply "numbers on a screen," but acknowledge the importance of a well-functioning finance sector for the wider economy." *Behaviour and Compliance in Organisations*, Financial Conduct Authority 35 (Dec. 2016), https://www.fca.org.uk/publication/occasional-papers/op16-24.pdf.
51. Natasha Lomas, *Can an Algorithm Be Empathetic? UK Startup EI Technologies Is Building Software That's Sensitive to Tone of Voice*, TechCrunch (Aug. 4, 2013), https://techcrunch.com/2013/08/04/empathy/.
52. For a discussion of the ethical fading and moral licensing phenomena that can contribute to unethical behavior, *see* Ann E. Tenbrunsel & David M. Messick, *Ethical Fading: The Role of Self-Deception in Unethical Behavior*, 17 Soc. Just. Rsch. 223, 224 (2004); Daniel A. Effron & Paul Conway, *When Virtue Leads to Villainy: Advances in Research on Moral Self-Licensing*, Current Op. In Psych. 6 (2015).
53. For a discussion of (human) communications strategies used by central banks to inspire confidence, *see* Douglas R. Holmes, *Communicative Imperatives in Central Banks*, 47 Cornell Int'l L.J. 15 (2014).
54. Currently, in the United States, "a 15-minute pause kicks in when the price of the S&P 500 index declines by 7% or more before 3:25 p.m. Another is triggered if it declines by 13% or more. If it crosses 20%, all trading is halted. If there is a 7% or 13% decline at or after 3:25 p.m., trading continues unless it reaches 20%." Bradley Hope & Dan Strumpf, *The Problem with Circuit Breakers*, Wall St. J. (Jan. 7, 2016), https://www.wsj.com/articles/the-problem-with-circuit-breakers-1452205576.
55. "Compliance" refers to the processes by which an organization polices its own behavior to ensure that it conforms to applicable rules." Geoffrey P. Miller, The Law of Governance, Risk Management, and Compliance 4 (2019).

56. For an explanation of the various meanings of the term "regtech," *see* Luca Enriques, *Financial Supervisors and RegTech: Four Roles and Four Challenges*, REVUE TRIMESTRIELLE DE DROIT FINANCIER 53 (2017).
57. For a discussion of regtech's aspirations to be both better and cheaper than current compliance systems, *see* JoAnn Barefoot, *supra* note 6, at 23–24.
58. Barefoot anticipates that "Users could deploy multiple vendors even for a single use, in order to compare results, tap into more information and avoid the pitfalls inherent in one-size-fits-all models." *Id.* at 58.
59. *Id.* at 44, 46.
60. *Id.* at 46.
61. For a discussion of the challenges in assigning liability to autonomous machines, *see* David C. Vladeck, *Machines Without Principals: Liability Rule and Artificial Intelligence*, 89 WASH L. REV. 117 (2014).
62. Erik F. Gerding, *Code, Crash, and Open Source: The Outsourcing of Financial Regulation to Risk Models and the Global Financial Crisis*, 84 WASH L. REV. 127, 155 (2009).
63. See Joe Nocera, *Risk Mismanagement*, N.Y. TIMES MAG. (Jan. 2, 2009), https://www.nytimes.com/2009/01/04/magazine/04risk-t.html.
64. For a cautionary tale of how international regulatory capital standards coordinated bank behavior in a way that ultimately contributed to financial instability, *see* Roberta Romano, *For Diversity in the International Regulation of Financial Institutions: Critiquing and Recalibrating the Basel Architecture*, 31 YALE J. ON REG. 1 (2014).
65. For an argument that the development of ubiquitous regtech is inevitable, *see* Barefoot, *supra* note 6 at 98.
66. UNSGSA FinTech Working Group and CCAF, *supra* note 14 at 8.
67. A 2018 report found that "Suptech is currently found in two areas of applications: data collection and data analytics." Dirk Broeders & Jermy Prenio, *Innovative Technology in Financial Supervision (Suptech)—The Experience of Early Users*, BANK FOR INTERNATIONAL SETTLEMENTS 1 (2018).
68. *Id.*
69. Yueh-Ping (Alex) Yang & Cheng-Yun Tsang, *RegTech and the New Era of Financial Regulators: Envisaging More Public-Private Partnership Models of Financial Regulation*, 21 U. PA. J. BUS. L. 354, 367 (2018).
70. Simone de Castri et al., *The Suptech Generations*, BANK FOR INTERNATIONAL SETTLEMENTS 14 (2019).
71. The Bank for International Settlements suggested the following explanations for regulators' hesitancy to experiment with suptech: "(i) concerns among financial authorities about the uncertain value and risks of suptech [particularly operational risks]; (ii) resource constraints; and (iii) a limited product offering for suptech solutions from a small pool of specialised technology vendors. The inertia inherent in legacy IT systems is another factor." *Id.*
72. Enriques, *supra* note 55, at 55.
73. For a discussion of regulators' concerns about suptech and arbitrage, see Broeders & Prenio, *supra* note 66 at 2.

74. "In August 2017, the Commission learned that an incident previously detected in 2016 may have provided the basis for illicit gain through trading. Specifically, a software vulnerability in the test filing component of our EDGAR system, which was patched promptly after discovery, was exploited and resulted in access to nonpublic information." Public Statement on Cybersecurity from Jay Clayton, Chairman, US Sec. & Exch. Comm'n (Sept. 20, 2017) (on file at https://www.sec.gov/news/public-statement/statement-clayton-2017-09-20).

## Chapter 6

1. The officer certification suggested here is modeled on the requirement for CEOs and CFOs of US public companies to certify the accuracy of financial information. For a discussion of these requirements, *see* Lisa M. Fairfax, *Form Over Substance?: Officer Certification and the Promise of Enhanced Personal Accountability Under the Sarbanes-Oxley Act*, 55 RUTGERS L. REV. 1 (2002).
2. This aspect of Form T is modeled on the 8-K report that must be submitted by publicly -traded companies in the United States when one of the events specified in Form 8-K occurs. For further explanation of Form 8-K, *see* COX ET AL., SECURITIES REGULATION: CASES AND MATERIALS 557 (9th ed. 2020).
3. An analogy can be drawn with the "living wills" required of the largest US banking conglomerates by Section 165(d) of the Dodd-Frank legislation. These conglomerates are required to explain how they could be resolved in a bankruptcy situation, and the hope was that this requirement would encourage banking conglomerates to voluntarily simplify and rationalize their own corporate structures. One observer commented (somewhat sardonically) in 2014, "I suspect the systemically important financial institutions think they have made substantial progress rationalizing their structures — at least that's what I hear at conferences and other public events." Stephen J. Lubben, *Do "'Living Wills"' for Banks Even Make Sense?*, N.Y. TIMES (Aug. 11, 2014), https://dealbook.nytimes.com/2014/08/11/do-living-wills-for-banks-even-make-sense/. Even incremental steps toward a more rational corporate structure would help financial stability, and the same is true of rationalizing the use of technological systems.
4. Jim Chen, *Biolaw: Cracking the Code*, 56 U. KAN. L. REV. 1029, 1030 (2008).
5. Jia Len Low, *Developers Now Make Up a Quarter of Goldman Sachs' Workforce*, TECHHQ (Feb. 14, 2020), https://techhq.com/2020/02/developers-now-make-up-quarter-of-goldman-sachs-workforce/.
6. *The Millennial Problem—Banks Are Finding It Harder to Attract Young Recruits*, THE ECONOMIST (May 4, 2017), https://www.economist.com/special-report/2017/05/04/banks-are-finding-it-harder-to-attract-young-recruits.
7. For example, in 2014, the head of the OCC's quant staff said "his team recently poached a senior quant from another agency." Reuters, *US Banking Regulators Hire Quants of Their Own*, NEWSWEEK (Aug. 5, 2014), https://www.newsweek.com/us-banking-regulators-hire-quants-their-own-250375.

8. "Placing regulatory jurisdiction in multiple agencies would only make the problems of tunnel vision, random agenda selection, and inconsistency more acute." Andrew Tutt, *An FDA For Algorithms*, 69 ADMIN. L. REV. 83, 114 (2017).
9. For a more fulsome discussion of the benefits of consolidating interdisciplinary expertise in the OFR, *see* Hilary J. Allen, *Resurrecting the OFR*, 47 J. CORP. L. (2021).
10. The OFR is authorized to engage in "performing applied research and essential long-term research" (Section 153(a)(3) of Dodd-Frank), and to engage in "performing other related services" (Section 153(a)(5) of Dodd-Frank). The OFR's Research and Analysis Center is also authorized by Section 154(c)(1)(C) of Dodd-Frank to "maintain expertise in such areas as may be necessary to support specific requests for advice and assistance from financial regulators."
11. The OFR has the power to hire academic fellows under Section 152(i) of Dodd-Frank.
12. For a survey of some of these approaches, *see Inspiring Innovation*, HARV. BUS. REV. (Aug. 2002), https://hbr.org/2002/08/inspiring-innovation.
13. JoAnn Barefoot, *A Regtech Manifesto: Redesigning Financial Regulation for the Digital Age*, ALLIANCE FOR INNOVATIVE REGULATION 63 (Jul. 2020), https://www.dcfintechweek.org/wp-content/uploads/2020/10/Barefoot_Jo-Ann_AIR-Regtech-Manifesto-July-2020.pdf.
14. Stavros Gadinis, *From Independence to Politics in Financial Regulation*, 101 CALIF. L. REV. 327, 332 (2013).
15. US federal financial regulatory agencies include the Federal Reserve, the Office of the Comptroller of the Currency, the Securities and Exchange Commission, the Commodity Futures Trading Commission, the Federal Deposit Insurance Corporation, the Consumer Financial Protection Bureau, the National Credit Union Administration, and the Federal Housing Finance Authority. The Office of Financial Research, the Financial Stability Oversight Council, and the Federal Insurance Office could also be included in this list. For a discussion of how financial stability regulation in the United States is hampered by having so many financial regulators, *see* Hilary J. Allen, *Putting the "Financial Stability" In Financial Stability Oversight Council*, 76 OHIO ST. L. J. 1087, 1120 et seq. (2015).
16. The Financial Crisis Inquiry Commission, which was formed by Congress to study the causes of the Financial Crisis of 2008, concluded that "widespread failures in financial regulation and supervision proved devastating to the stability of the nation's financial markets . . . [including] gaps in oversight of critical areas with trillions of dollars at risk, such as the shadow banking system and over-the-counter derivatives markets." FIN. CRISIS INQUIRY COMM'N, THE FINANCIAL CRISIS INQUIRY REPORT: FINAL REPORT OF THE NATIONAL COMMISSION ON THE CAUSES OF THE FINANCIAL AND ECONOMIC CRISIS IN THE UNITED STATES xviii (2011).
17. This discussion of international collective action problems is largely drawn from Chris Brummer *How International Financial Law Works (and How It Doesn't)*, 99 GEO. L. J. 257, 267–68 (2011).
18. For more on the Basel Committee on Banking Supervision and its output, *see id.* at 277–78.

19. *Terms of Reference for Membership and Governance of the Global Financial Innovation Network (GFIN)*, Global Financial Innovation Network (GFIN) 3, https://www.fca.org.uk/publication/mou/gfin-terms-of-reference.pdf.
20. For further discussion of the GFIN's focus on private sector innovation, *see* Hilary J. Allen, *Sandbox Boundaries*, 22 Vand. J. Ent. & Tech. L. 299, 317 (2020).
21. *See*, for example, the following publications from the Financial Stability Board: Fin. Stability Bd., Financial Stability Implications from Fintech (2017); Fin. Stability Bd., Artificial Intelligence and Machine Learning in Financial Services (2017); Fin. Stability Bd., Fintech and Market Structure in Financial Services: Market Developments and Potential Financial Stability Implications (2019); Fin. Stability Bd., Bigtech in Finance: Market Developments and Potential Financial Stability Implications (2019).
22. Elizabeth Pollman, *Tech, Regulatory Arbitrage, and Limits*, 20 Eur. Bus. Org. L. Rev. 567, 570 (2019).
23. For a discussion of the FDA drug approval regime as precedent for a financial product licensing regime, *see* Saule T. Omarova, *License to Deal: Mandatory Approval of Complex Financial Products*, 90 Wash. U. L. Rev. 64, 90–93 (2012).
24. For further discussion of the ancillary benefits of a licensing regime for financial products, *see* Hilary J. Allen, *A New Philosophy for Financial Stability Regulation*, 45 Loy. U. Chi. L.J. 173, 222–24 (2013).
25. For more arguments in favor of using principles-based approaches to regulate nascent fintech innovation, *see* Chris Brummer & Daniel Gorfine, *Fintech: Building a 21st-Century Regulator's Toolkit*, Center for Financial Markets 7 (Oct. 2014), http://assets1c.milkeninstitute.org/assets/Publication/Viewpoint/PDF/3.14-FinTech-Reg-Toolkit-NEW.pdf.
26. For a discussion of a principles-based approaches to financial regulation, *see* Julia Black et al., *Making a Success of Principles-Based Regulation*, 1 L. & Fin. Mkt. Rev. 191 (2007).
27. For more discussion of the critiques of principles-based regulatory regimes, *see* Hilary J. Allen, *Regulatory Sandboxes*, 87 Geo. Wash. L. Rev. 579, 601–2 (2019).
28. Black et al., *supra* note 26, at 198.
29. "Human-in-the-loop suggests that human oversight is active and involved, with the human retaining full control and the AI only providing recommendations or input. Decisions cannot be exercised without affirmative actions by the human, such as a human command to proceed with a given decision." This requires more human control than "human-over-the-loop,", which the human acts only "in a monitoring or supervisory role, with the ability to take over control when the AI model encounters unexpected or undesirable events." InfoComm Media Development Authority & Personal Data Protection Commission of Singapore, Model Artificial Intelligence Governance Framework 30 (2nd ed. 2020).
30. David Lehr & Paul Ohm, *Playing with the Data: What Legal Scholars Should Learn aAbout Machine Learning*, 51 U.C. Davis L. Rev. 653, 708–09 (2017).

31. *Id.* at 710
32. John Crawford, *Wargaming Financial Crises: The Problem of (In)experience and Regulator Expertise*, 34 Rev. Banking & Fin. L. 111, 111 (2014–15).
33. For more on using wargames in financial regulation, *see id.* at 161 et seq.
34. For more on agent-based modeling, *see* Joshua M. Epstein, Agent Zero: Toward Neurocognitive Foundations for Generative Social Science (2014).
35. For an argument that analyzing digital data is superior to relying on simplified model simulations, *see* Tommaso Venturini et al., *Fill in the Gap. A New Alliance for Social and Natural Sciences*, 18 J. Artificial Societies & Soc. Simulation 11 (2015).
36. For a discussion of financial instability as the result of collective action problems, *see* Robert C. Hockett, *Recursive Collective Action Problems: The Structure of Procyclicality in Financial and Monetary Markets, Macroeconomies and Formally Similar Contexts* 3 J. Fin. Perspectives 1 (2015).
37. Crawford, *supra* note 32, at 166.
38. Andrew G. Haldane & Vasileios Madouros, Speech at the Federal Reserve Bank of Kansas City's 366th Economic Policy Symposium, "The Changing Policy Landscape" titled The Dog and the Frisbee (Aug. 31, 2012).
39. On the matter of internal models leading to lower capital and increased vulnerability for financial institutions, *see* Erik F. Gerding, *Code, Crash, and Open Source: The Outsourcing of Financial Regulation to Risk Models and the Global Financial Crisis*, 84 Wash. L. Rev. 127, 181 (2009).
40. Haldane & Madouros, *supra* note 38. For a discussion of how regulatory capital regulation currently treats VaR models, *see* Deloitte, *In Defence of VaR: Risk Measurement and Backtesting in Times of Crisis*, Deloitte 3 (June 1, 2020), https://www2.deloitte.com/content/dam/Deloitte/uk/Documents/risk/deloitte-uk-risk-in-defence-of-var.pdf.
41. Complexity scientists Alderson and Doyle have observed that complex systems with lots of diverse components and complex interactions between those components are "robust yet fragile,", in the sense that steps taken to make components of those complex systems more robust can inadvertently make the system as a whole more fragile. David L. Alderson & John C. Doyle, *Contrasting Views of Complexity and Their Implications For Network-Centric Infrastructures*, 40 IEEE Transactions on Systems, Man & Cybernetics 839, 839–840 (2010).
42. *Id.*
43. Erin Douglas, *Texas Wwas "Seconds and Minutes" Away From Catastrophic Monthslong Blackouts, Officials Say*, Tex. Trib. (Feb. 18, 2021), https://www.click2houston.com/news/texas/2021/02/18/texas-was-seconds-and-minutes-away-from-catastrophic-monthslong-blackouts-officials-say/.
44. For a discussion of the blackout's death toll and disproportionate impact on vulnerable communities, *see* Shawn Mulcahy, *Many Texans Have Died Because of the Winter Storm. Just How Many Won't Be Known for Weeks or Months*, Tex. Trib. (Feb. 19, 2021), https://www.texastribune.org/2021/02/19/texas-power-outage-winter-storm-deaths/.

45. For further discussion of the United States bank holiday imposed in 1933, *see* Richard Scott Carnell et al., The Law of Financial Institutions 216 (6th ed. 2017).
46. Annie Lowrey, *Alone in the Dark in the Bay Area*, The Atlantic (Oct. 12, 2019), https://www.theatlantic.com/ideas/archive/2019/10/californias-power-outage/599935/.
47. Samuel amuel Arbesman, Overcomplicated: Technology at the Limits of Comprehension 107 (2016).
48. *Id.* at 127.
49. *Fed's Banks Budget Includes Money for Y2K-Related Currency Demands*, Wall St. J. (Jun. 25, 1999), https://www.wsj.com/articles/SB930183857689183884.
50. A policy preserving cash as a means of transacting would also benefit people who don't have access to electronic financial services and are would therefore be shut out of a cashless society. For a report on this issue, *see* Ginia Bellafante, *How the Cashless Economy Shuts Out the Poor*, N.Y. Times (Dec. 6, 2018), https://www.nytimes.com/2018/12/06/nyregion/how-the-cashless-economy-shuts-out-the-poor.html.
51. For a discussion of how the FDA phased in approval requirements for existing drugs, *see* Peter Barton Hutt et al., Food and Drug Law: Cases and Materials 775–86 (4th ed. 2014).
52. For a survey of unfinished FDA safety programs, *see* Peter Barton Hutt, *The State of Science at the Food and Drug Administration*, 60 Admin L. Rev. 431, 447–50 (2008).
53. The relevant proposals are set out in Omarova, *supra* note 23, and Eric A. Posner & E. Glen Weyl, *An FDA for Financial Innovation: Applying the Insurable Interest Doctrine to Twenty-First-Century Markets*, 107 Nw. U. L. Rev. 1307 (2013).
54. Omarova, *supra* note 23 at 124; Posner & Weyl, *supra* note 53, at 1352.
55. Omarova, *supra* note 23, at 67.
56. *Id.* at 121.
57. For more on automated trading and flash crashes, *see supra* Chapter 3.
58. For a discussion of the incentives for regulatory forbearance in another context (deciding whether to shut down an ailing bank), *see* Carnell et al., *supra* note 45, at 270.
59. In the United States, "a 15-minute pause kicks in when the price of the S&P 500 index declines by 7% or more before 3:25 p.m. Another is triggered if it declines by 13% or more. If it crosses 20%, all trading is halted. If there is a 7% or 13% decline at or after 3:25 p.m., trading continues unless it reaches 20%." Bradley Hope & Dan Strumpf, *The Problem with Circuit Breakers*, Wall St. J. (Jan. 7, 2016), https://www.wsj.com/articles/the-problem-with-circuit-breakers-1452205576.
60. Office of Financial Research, Annual Report to Congress: 2017, 11 (2017)
61. For further discussion of the construction of this index from publicly available information sources, *see* Phillip J. Monin, *The OFR Financial Stress Index*, 7 Risks 1, 2 (2019).
62. For further discussion of these types of suptech innovations, *see* Greg Feldberg, *Don't Dismantle the Post-Crisis Early Warning System*, Brookings, 11–12 (Nov. 21, 2018),

https://www.brookings.edu/research/dont-dismantle-the-post-crisis-early-warning-system/.

63. For an analogous discussion of how fear of a different kind of regulatory action (triggering the conversion of contingent convertible bonds into equity) might create market turmoil, *see* Hilary J. Allen, *Cocos Can Drive Markets Cuckoo*, 16 LEWIS & CLARK L. REV. 125, 156 et seq. (2012).

## Chapter 7

1. ANTHONY TROLLOPE, PHINEAS FINN 556 (2011).
2. As Saule Omarova puts it, "an inquiry into the nature and dynamics of the 'fintech revolution' is, and should be, an integral part of the broader inquiry into the nature and dynamics of *finance itself*." Saule T. Omarova, *New Tech v New Deal: Fintech as a Systemic Phenomenon*, 36 YALE J. REG. 735, 739 (2019).
3. MARIANA MAZZUCATO, THE ENTREPRENEURIAL STATE: DEBUNKING PUBLIC VS. PRIVATE SECTOR MYTHS (2015).
4. CRISTIE FORD, INNOVATION AND THE STATE 220 (2017).
5. Ronald Reagan, *President's News Conference* (Aug. 12, 1986), https://www.reaganfoundation.org/media/128648/newsconference2.pdf.
6. "[T]he emergence of 'new public management' theory, which grew out of 'public choice' theory in the 1980s, led civil servants to believe that they should take up as little space as possible, fearing that government failures might be even worse than market failures, and hence abide by a culture of restraint." MAZZUCATO, *supra* note 3, at xxiii.
7. For an introduction to the concept of public goods, and regulation as a response to the public goods problem, *see* Matthew D. Adler, *Regulatory Theory, in* Dennis Patterson (ed.), A COMPANION TO PHILOSOPHY OF LAW AND LEGAL THEORY 598–99 (2d ed. 2010).
8. Luca Enriques, *Financial Supervisors and RegTech: Four Roles and Four Challenges*, REVUE TRIMESTRIELLE DE DROIT FINANCIER 53, 55 (2017).
9. For a discussion of "super wicked" problems that may require types of expertise that have not yet been developed, *see* Peter Conti-Brown & David A. Wishnick, *Technocratic Pragmatism, Bureaucratic Expertise, and the Federal Reserve*,130 YALE L. J. 636, 645 (2021).
10. TOM NICHOLS, THE DEATH OF EXPERTISE: THE CAMPAIGN AGAINST ESTABLISHED KNOWLEDGE AND WHY IT MATTERS 216 (2017).
11. *Id.* at 206–07.
12. *Id.* at 174–76.
13. MAZZUCATO, *supra* note 3, at 29–30.
14. "The concept of "agile" workflow . . . is ubiquitous in the technology world. Agile methodology involves breaking complex projects into smaller ones and bringing together multi-disciplinary teams to do rapid building of solutions. It contrasts with the traditional "waterfall" processes that dominate finance and regulation, in which

initiatives travel through a linear process and sequential reviews." JoAnn Barefoot, *A Regtech Manifesto: Redesigning Financial Regulation for the Digital Age*, Alliance for Innovative Regulation 63 (Jul. 2020), https://www.dcfintechweek.org/wp-content/uploads/2020/10/Barefoot_Jo-Ann_AIR-Regtech-Manifesto-July-2020.pdf.

15. For a discussion of innovation as an example of Knightian uncertainty, *see* Mazzucato, *supra* note 3, at 42.
16. For an argument (made in the context of central banking) that past tendencies toward secrecy must move toward transparency about experimentation with new approaches, *see* Conti-Brown & Wishnick, *supra* note 9, at 640. For an illustration of the perceived importance of confidentiality in banking supervision, *see* the discussion of the legal protections used to keep the work product of bank examiners confidential in Richard Scott Carnell et al., The Law of Financial Institutions 353–54 (6th ed. 2017).
17. For an argument that experimental regulation is more easily justified when it's less coercive, *see* Conti-Brown & Wishnick, *supra* note 9, at 664.
18. Mulligan and Bamberger note that, if left to their own devices, technical personnel may "maximize engineering values such as interoperability, efficiency, elegance, and innovation." Deirdre K. Mulligan & Kenneth A. Bamberger, *Saving Governance-by-Design*, 106 Calif. L. Rev. 697, 755 (2018).
19. This discussion relies heavily on the "rules for engagement" developed by Mulligan and Bamberger for using technology to regulate. *Id.* at 742 et seq.
20. For an early examination of the predatory potential of fintech business models that offer immediate access to earned wages, *see* Nakita Q. Cuttino, *The Rise of "FringeTech": Regulatory Risks in Earned-Wage Access*, 115 Nw. U. L. Rev. 1505 (2021).
21. For in-depth exploration of public actors' potential to create markets and provide capital for socially beneficial activities, *see* Robert C. Hockett & Saule T. Omarova, *Public Actors in Private Markets: Toward a Developmental Finance State*, 93 Wash. U. L. Rev. 103 (2015); Robert C. Hockett & Saule T. Omarova, *The Finance Franchise*, 102 Cornell L. Rev. 1143 (2017); Saule T. Omarova, *The People's Ledger: How to Democratize Money and Finance the Economy*, 75 Vand. L. Rev. (forthcoming).
22. For a discussion of the controversy over central banks buying green bonds, *see* Christina Parajon Skinner, *Central Banks and Climate Change*, 75 Vand. L. Rev. (forthcoming).
23. Jen Wieczner, *Why Dogecoin, the Joke Crypto, Is Forcing People to Take It Seriously*, N.Y. Mag. (Apr. 17, 2021), https://nymag.com/intelligencer/2021/04/why-dogecoin-is-forcing-people-to-take-it-seriously.html.
24. Christina Criddle, *Bitcoin Consumers "More Electricity Than Argentina,"* BBC (Feb. 10, 2021), https://www.bbc.com/news/technology-56012952 (reporting on the University of Cambridge Bitcoin Electricity Consumption Index).
25. For further discussion of proof of work and proof-of-stake methods of verification, see Chapter 3.
26. *See*, for example, Noah Smith, *The Riddle of the Wall Street Brain Drain*, Bloomberg (Aug. 17, 2016), https://www.bloomberg.com/opinion/articles/2016-08-17/the-riddle-of-the-wall-street-brain-drain.

27. For further discussion of the jurisdictional challenges that cyberspace poses for financial regulation, *see* Jason Grant Allen & Rosa Maria Lastra, *Border Problems: Mapping the Third Border*, 83 Mod. L. Rev. 505 (2020).
28. *See* Eric A. Posner & E. Glen Weyl, *An FDA for Financial Innovation: Applying the Insurable Interest Doctrine to Twenty-First-Century Markets*, 107 Nw. U. L. Rev. 1307, 1348 (2013); Saule T. Omarova, *License to Deal: Mandatory Approval of Complex Financial Products*, 90 Wash. U. L. Rev. 64, 134 (2012).
29. For a discussion of the trade-offs involved in targeting regulation at these types of infrastructure providers, *see* Primavera De Filippi & Aaron Wright, Blockchain and the Law: The Rule of Code, 177–78, 189–92 (2018).
30. Yesha Yadav, *Fintech and International Financial Regulation*, 53 Vand. J. Transnat'l L. 1109 (2020).
31. *Id.* at 1136.
32. *Id.* at 1141.
33. For further discussion of the benefits of twin peaks regulation, *see* Hilary J. Allen, *Putting the "Financial Stability" in Financial Stability Oversight Council*, 76 Ohio St. L.J. 1087, 1140 et seq. (2015). In terms of the implementation of twin peaks, there is also a debate about whether it would be better to break the market conduct "peak" into two separate agencies, with one focusing on consumer finance and the other on investor protection, but since that debate is largely separate from questions about financial stability, we won't get into it here.
34. Australia Prudential Regulatory Authority Act 1988 Section 8(2) provides that "In performing and exercising its functions and powers, APRA is to balance the objectives of financial safety and efficiency, competition, contestability and competitive neutrality and, in balancing these objectives, is to promote financial system stability in Australia." In 2012, the UK Financial Services Act added a new Section 2B to the Financial Services and Markets Act, 2000, c.8 (Eng.), to, among other things, establish the Prudential Regulatory Authority and give it a mandate to

    > promote[e] the safety and soundness of PRA-authorised persons . . . That objective is to be advanced primarily by—(a)seeking to ensure that the business of PRA-authorised persons is carried on in a way which avoids any adverse effect on the stability of the UK financial system, and (b)seeking to minimise the adverse effect that the failure of a PRA-authorised person could be expected to have on the stability of the UK financial system. Financial Services Act, 2012, c.21, §2(b) (Eng.).

35. Allen, *supra* note 33, at 1091.
36. *See*, for example, the disagreements over how the SEC should oversee the asset management industry. *Id.* at 1118–19.
37. For further discussion of potential OFR expansion, *see* Hilary J. Allen, *Resurrecting the OFR*, 47 J. Corp. L. (2021).
38. A lot has been written on these issues. For an overview of the goals and ideologies informing the debate, *see* Lina M. Khan, *The Separation of Platforms and Commerce*, 119 Colum. L. Rev. 973 (2019).

39. Jay Peters, *Prolonged AWS Outage Takes Down a Big Chunk of the Internet*, The Verge (Nov. 25, 2020), https://www.theverge.com/2020/11/25/21719396/amazon-web-services-aws-outage-down-internet.
40. Press Release, Velázquez, Porter Urge FSOC to Oversee Tech Giants (Aug. 23, 2019), https://velazquez.house.gov/media-center/press-releases/velazquez-porter-urge-fsoc-oversee-tech-giants.
41. *About Financial Innovation Now*, http://financialinnovationnow.org (last visited May 28, 2021).
42. For a definition of network externalities, *see* BIS, Annual Economic Report 62 (Jun. 30, 2019), https://www.bis.org/publ/arpdf/ar2019e.pdf.
43. *See id.* for a discussion of the "data-network-activities" loop as an incentive for the largest tech companies to get involved in finance.
44. For a discussion of the contours of the separation of banking and commerce in the United States, *see* Saule T. Omarova & Margaret E. Tahyar, *That Which We Call a Bank: Revisiting the History of Bank Holding Company Regulations in the United States*, 31 Rev. Banking & Fin. L. 113 (2011–12).
45. For more background on the problems associated with "too big to fail" financial institutions, *see* Carnell et al., *supra* note 16, at 38–39.
46. H. Subcomm. on Antitrust, Commercial and Administrative Law of the H. Comm. on the Judiciary, Investigation of Competition in Digital Markets: Majority Staff Report and Recommendations (2020) (available at https://judiciary.house.gov/issues/issue/?IssueID=14921). "Facebook has monopoly power in the market for social networking." *Id.* at 12. "Google has a monopoly in the markets for general online search and search advertising." *Id.* at 14. "Amazon has significant and durable market power in the U.S. online retail market." *Id.* at 15. "Apple has significant and durable market power in the mobile operating system market." *Id.* at 16.
47. For a discussion of the "too big to save" issue, *see* Asli Demirgüç-Kunt & Harry Huizinga, *Are Banks Too Big to Fail or Too Big to Save? International Evidence from Equity Prices and CDS Spreads*, World Bank Policy Research, Working Paper 5360, 2010, https://openknowledge.worldbank.org/handle/10986/3844.
48. *See* Lina M. Khan, *Sources of Tech Platform Power*, 2 Geo. L. Tech. Rev. 325 (2018).
49. This would require a legal determination of whether electronic wallets "count" as deposits.
50. For a discussion of FSOC designation as a looming threat that discourages risky behavior, *see* Daniel Schwarcz & David Zaring, *Regulation by Threat: Dodd-Frank and the Non-bank Problem*, 84 U. Chi. L. Rev. 1813 (2017).
51. For an analysis of the complex trade-offs between competition and financial stability, *see* Franklin Allen & Douglas Gale, *Competition and Financial Stability*, 36 J. Money, Credit & Banking 453 (2004).
52. The seminal Supreme Court case on this issue is Camp v. Pitts, 411 US 138 (1973) (deferring to regulators' decision not to grant a bank charter in a market they considered oversaturated).

53. Rory Van Loo, *Making Innovation More Competitive: The Case of Fintech*, 65 UCLA L. Rev. 232, 250–51 (2018).
54. For a discussion of current trends in fintechs seeking banking charters, *see* Troutman Pepper, *Trend of Fintech Companies Seeking US Banking Licenses Continues*, JD Supra (Mar. 20, 2021), https://www.jdsupra.com/legalnews/trend-of-fintech-companies-seeking-u-s-2001550/.
55. Senator Klobuchar's office summarized the relevant parts of the bill as follows:

> Certain categories of mergers pose significant risks to competition, but are still difficult and costly for the government to challenge in court. For those types of mergers, the bill shifts the legal burden from the government to the merging companies, which would have to prove that their mergers do not create an appreciable risk of materially lessening competition or tend to create a monopoly or monopsony. These categories include . . . Acquisitions of competitors or nascent competitors by a dominant firm (defined a 50% market share or possession of significant market power).

Press Release, Senator Klobuchar Introduces Sweeping Bill to Promote Competition and Improve Antitrust Enforcement (Feb. 4, 2021), https://www.klobuchar.senate.gov/public/index.cfm/2021/2/senator-klobuchar-introduces-sweeping-bill-to-promote-competition-and-improve-antitrust-enforcement.

56. Van Loo, *supra* note 53, at 242–43.
57. These kinds of issues are explored in depth in Frank Pasquale, The Black Box Society: The Secret Algorithms That Control Money and Information (2015).
58. "[T]he FBI, the U.S. Treasury, and the Securities and Exchange Commission (SEC) rely on financial algorithms to track unusual or structured cash deposits, international transfers, or stock manipulation. These pattern-matching investigative techniques look for suspicious movements in the flow of money and are expanding in sophistication alongside improved technologies" Andrew Guthrie Ferguson, The Rise of Big Data Policing: Surveillance, Race, and the Future of Law Enforcement, 116 (2017).
59. Jo Ann S. Barefoot, *Disrupting FinTech Law*, 18 Fintech Law Report 1, 5 (Mar./Apr. 2015), https://static1.squarespace.com/static/535edb77e4b0cd207fff9e6e/t/554ff231e4b0261b84be36e4/1431302705880/Fintech1802_AA_Barefoot.pdf.
60. Shoshana Zuboff, The Age of Surveillance Capitalism: The Fight for a Human Future at the New Frontier of Power 19 (2019).
61. Financial Crisis Inquiry Report: Final Report of the National Commission on the Causes of the Financial and Economic Crisis in the United States, xxiii (2011).
62. For a discussion of how predatory practices can translate into systemic risks and broader economic harm, *see* Patricia A. McCoy et al., *Systemic Risk through Securitization: The Result of Deregulation and Regulatory Failure*, 41 Conn. L. Rev. 493 (2009).
63. These kinds of consumer abuses may already be a feature of some fintech business models (although the scale is not yet clear), as law professor Chris Odinet found in

a review of complaints made to the Consumer Financial Protection Bureau about fintech lenders. Christopher K. Odinet, *Consumer Bitcredit and Fintech Lending*, 69 ALA. L. REV. 781 (2018). Many of these complaints focused on the fact that after receiving an initial attractive offer, the loan application process provided consumers with confusing and inconsistent information about their eligibility and cost of credit. Others complained of changes to interest rates and fees once the loan was in place. One complaint stated "[t]hey are outrageous with regard to how many problems they create to prevent you from paying your monthly installment. Clearly, they are trying to get consumers to default, so they can jab you with excessive late (and other) fees." *Id.* at 836.

64. *See* Articles 16 and 22 of the European Union's General Data Protection Regulation. Council Regulation 2016/679, 2016 O.J. (L 119) 1. For further discussion of these rights, *see* Margot E. Kaminski & Jennifer M. Urban, *The Right to Contest AI*, COLUM. L. REV. (forthcoming).
65. For a discussion of the impact of data breaches on confidence, *see* Nizan Geslevich Packin, *Too-Big-To-Fail 2.0? Digital Service Providers*, 93 IND. L.J. 1211, 1235 (2018).
66. Barefoot, *supra* note 14 at 48–49.
67. For an overview of cyberthreats and cybersecurity measures, *see* Chris Jaikaran, CONG. RSCH. SERV., R45127, CYBERSECURITY: SELECT ISSUES FOR THE 115TH CONGRESS (2018).
68. For example, the G20 Communique issued in 2017 recognized that "The malicious use of Information and Communication Technologies (ICT) could disrupt financial services crucial to both national and international financial systems, undermine security and confidence and endanger financial stability." G20 Finance Ministers and Central Bank Governors Meeting, Baden-Baden, Ger. Mar. 17–18, 2017, ¶ 7 *Communiqué*, available at http://www.g20.utoronto.ca/2017/170318-finance-en.html.
69. For a discussion of central bank digital currencies and cyberthreats, *see* BIS, Central Bank Digital Currencies: Foundational Principles and Core Features 5 (2020), https://www.bis.org/publ/othp33.htm.
70. V. Gerard Comizio, *The Cyber Threat Looming over Virtual Currencies*, AM. BANKER (May 6, 2021).
71. DE FILIPPI & WRIGHT, *supra* note 29, at 32.
72. Ram Shankar Siva Kumar & Frank Nagle, *The Case for AI Insurance*, HARVARD BUS. REV. (Apr. 29, 2020), https://hbr.org/2020/04/the-case-for-ai-insurance.
73. Ben Dickson, *Machine Learning Adversarial Attacks Are a Ticking Time Bomb*, TECHTALKS (Dec. 16, 2020), https://bdtechtalks.com/2020/12/16/machine-learning-adversarial-attacks-against-machine-learning-time-bomb/.
74. THOMAS M. EISENBACH ET AL., FEDERAL RESERVE BANK OF NEW YORK STAFF REPORTS, NO. 909: CYBER RISK AND THE US FINANCIAL SYSTEM: A PRE-MORTEM ANALYSIS 43 (2020), https://www.newyorkfed.org/research/staff_reports/sr909.

## Conclusion

1. For further discussion of this "Kaldor-Hicksian" version of efficiency, *see* Yoon-Ho Alex Lee, *The Efficiency Criterion for Securities Regulation: Investor Welfare or Total Surplus?*, 57 Ariz. L. Rev. 85, 87 (2015).
2. Carmen M. Reinhart & Kenneth S. Rogoff, This Time Is Different: Eight Centuries of Financial Folly (2011).
3. The Emperor's New Clothes analogy has also been used to highlight problems in the traditional banking system. See Anat Admati & Martin Hellwig, The Bankers' New Clothes: What's Wrong with Banking and What To Do About It (2013).
4. Olaf Storbeck, *Wirecard: The Frantic Final Months of a Fraudulent Operation*, Fin. Times (Aug. 25, 2020), https://www.ft.com/content/6a660a5f-4e8c-41d5-b129-ad5bf9782256
5. Paul Tucker, *Time to Look Again at the Financial System's Dangerous Faultlines*, Fin. Times (Jan. 20, 2021), https://www.ft.com/content/0d848d03-7d66-4a76-a4f2-8f09980747fa.

# Index

*For the benefit of digital users, indexed terms that span two pages (e.g., 52–53) may, on occasion, appear on only one of those pages.*

Printed in the USA
CPSIA information can be obtained
at www.ICGtesting.com
CBHW051408200724
11475CB00001B/1

9 780197 62680